DIRECT OBSERVATION AND MEASUREMENT OF BEHAVIOR

Publication Number 763

AMERICAN LECTURE SERIES®

A Monograph in

The BANNERSTONE DIVISION *of*
AMERICAN LECTURES IN RADIATION THERAPY

Edited by

I. NEWTON KUGELMASS, M.D., Ph.D., Sc.D.
Consultant to the Departments of Health and Hospitals
New York City

Second Printing

DIRECT OBSERVATION AND MEASUREMENT OF BEHAVIOR

By

S. J. HUTT

*Research Psychologist, Human Development Research Unit, Park Hospital for Children
Fellow of St. Catherine's College
Oxford, England*

and

CORINNE HUTT

*Research Psychologist, Human Development Research Unit, Park Hospital for Children
Research Fellow, Lady Margaret Hall
Oxford, England*

CHARLES C THOMAS · PUBLISHER
Springfield · Illinois · U.S.A.

Published and Distributed Throughout the World by

CHARLES C THOMAS • PUBLISHER

Bannerstone House

301-327 East Lawrence Avenue, Springfield, Illinois, U.S.A.

© *1970 by* CHARLES C THOMAS • PUBLISHER

ISBN 0-398-00892-2

Library of Congress Catalog Card Number: 78-91850

First Printing, 1970
Second Printing, 1974

Printed in the United States of America

N-1

To KIT

FOREWORD

OUR Living Chemistry Series was conceived by Editor and Publisher to advance the newer knowledge of chemical medicine in the cause of clinical practice. The interdependence of chemistry and medicine is so great that physicians are turning to chemistry, and chemists to medicine in order to understand the underlying basis of life processes in health and disease. Once chemical truths, proofs and convictions become sound foundations for clinical phenomena, key hybrid investigators clarify the bewildering panorama of biochemical progress for application in everyday practice, stimulation of experimental research, and extension of postgraduate instruction. Each of our monographs thus unravels the chemical mechanisms and clinical management of many diseases that have remained relatively static in the minds of medical men for three thousand years. Our new Series is charged with the *nisus élan* of chemical wisdom, supreme in choice of international authors, optimal in standards of chemical scholarship, provocative in imagination for experimental research, comprehensive in discussions of scientific medicine, and authoritative in chemical perspective of human disorders.

Dr. S. J. Hutt and Dr. C. Hutt of Oxford present a fascinating ethologic and/or psychologic approach to the exploration of attention, learning, and behavior in young children. It is correlated with experimental inquiry, drawing on a wide range of species with due regard to the uniqueness of man, since behavior is elementary in the animal kingdom. Ethology emphasizes direct observation of free behavior, social activity in living Nature, organized patterns of adaptive behavior, and species diversification in the study of innate or instinctive behavior. The methodology of direct observation by tape-recording, check-lists, video records, etc., and the measurement of behavior of normal, brain-damaged and autistic children for meaningful interpretation involve delineation of the phenomenon under study, generation of law-like propositions relating these measurements to other selected variables, and development of interrelationships of these propositions into theories. Such intensive research into human nature is gradually changing the meaning we attach to such words as explanation or understanding. Originally they signified a representation of the strange in terms of the commonplace; nowadays, scientific explanation tends more to be a description of the relatively familiar in terms of the unfamiliar. Yet in our search for understanding, we still consider it important to get the physical picture of the process behind the treatment of the theory for behavior has a structure with a finite number of vital elements that can be displayed with a temporal restriction for intensive observation.

Behavior has every appearance of being the macroscopic result of microscopic processes in the behaving organism, and no scientific research can restrict itself to any set phenomena having causal connections with some other set, yet leave that other set alone. So the term behavior, while purporting to supply an objective correlate for the mental phenomena, which are the original material of psychology but stand condemned as subjective, really creates methodological difficulties of its own. Normal behavior is characterized by an alternation between an attitude involving abstract and one involving concrete behavior, and this alternation is appropriate to the situation and individuality, to the task for which the organism is set. If either attitude becomes independent and governs the behavior of a normal individual too completely, then we are faced with anomalous behavior. Systematic observation of such a complex situation is extremely difficult, involving unsuspected errors. There is no lack of data but an excess of them, hence the need for some model in order to filter facts before their quantity is overwhelming. The acute observer observes minutely without being observed, noticing something and giving it significance and relating it to something else related or already known, embodying an element of sense perception and an element of mentality. It is impossible to observe everything and so the observer has to give most of his attention to a selected field but watches out for other things, especially anything odd. There is no such thing as holding Nature still and looking at it for while we crystallize some fleeting moment, it passes on. In this lies the poignancy of all life, the moment that cannot be immortalized.

Psychology complements ethology, the one largely restricted to laboratory experimentation of behavior; the other, to direct observation of behavior in the natural habitat. Behavior measurement embodies many areas—sensory capacities, perceptual abilities, intellectual abilities, learning and remembering, motor skills, coordination, motivation, emotion, temperament, social behavior, attitudes, interest and values by quantitative application of basic scientific concepts. It uses what we do know, acknowledges what we do not know, and encourages expansion of the former to shrink the latter. But scientific concepts of human behavior always have associated values, however implicit. The observer changes everything he touches again and again in never-ending responses with the inevitability of change as the only constant. We see only what we look for, and we look for only what we know, for we are creatures that look before and after and occasionally around to really see what is passing under our very eyes. The empiricist thinks he believes only what he sees, but he is much better at believing than at seeing, hence the clinical value of this research contribution. It is like a loom on which certain threads are woven into a particular fabric; the loom is the theoretical framework; the threads, empirical facts about behavior; the process of weaving, the scientific method; and the emerging fabric, human behavior.

> "For only in the process of Becoming
> does the form of life complete itself
> And the eidos of the person become realized."
> I. Newton Kugelmass, M.D., Ph.D., Sc.D., *Editor*

PREFACE

SOME five or six years ago when initiating a series of studies of attention and learning in young children, the problem in hand seemed daunting and depressing. To record, measure and meaningfully interpret the behavior of brain-damaged and autistic children in particular seemed an invincible task. It was largely the encouragement and support we received from Professor Niko Tinbergen at this time that emboldened us to feel our efforts might not be entirely futile and that some knowledge might result from our inchoate attempts. He has continued to encourage and reassure and we owe him an immeasurable debt of gratitude. At a later, but no less critical stage, Professor and Mrs. Konrad Lorenz most generously and hospitably gave us the invaluable opportunity of many days of refreshing education and stimulating discussion at Seewiesen. We cannot adequately thank them for their kindness.

The aim of this book is to set down some of our own experience in attempting to record and to measure behavior and to discuss some studies which are illustrative of the techniques or of the methodology we are proposing. It will be clear from our preliminary remarks that our interests are primarily in children and in animals and that our biasses are ethological. We have allowed ourselves the licence of following both our interests and our biasses. We have drawn extensively from studies of children both because we now know a little about them and because the approach we are advocating seems especially suitable for their study. We shall draw equally upon studies of animals because it is here that the greatest amount of work on the behaviour of unrestrained organisms has been done and where the appropriate methodology has been most fully elaborated. The fact that we have concentrated on studies of animals and children does not mean that the approach is not a valid one for studying adults.

In the preparation of this text, we have to acknowledge the help of many kind people and institutions: Dr. J. M. Cullen for introducing us to many animal studies using film techniques and which we might otherwise have overlooked; Drs. John Marshall, Sheila Zinkin and W. C. McGrew for allowing us to quote extensively from their unpublished work; Mrs. Jennifer Morcom for the illustrations from film; the librarian and staff of the Radcliffe Science Library of the University of Oxford, who have dealt with our numerous requests benevolently, efficiently and promptly; and the many publishers who have permitted us to quote their copyright material. We owe a very special debt of gratitude to Miss Jacqueline Potter, who prepared the manuscript and figures with painstaking thoroughness and who has dealt with our outrageous demands with equanimity and patience.

We are most grateful to the Nuffield Foundation and Oxford Regional Hospital Board, who have very generously supported much of the work, and to our respective Colleges for enabling us to spend time in writing this book.

Finally, it is with much pleasure that we acknowledge our great indebtedness to Dr. Christopher Ounsted. Our work owes its origins, its development and its continuation to his serendipidity and perspicacity. It is with gratitude and affection that we dedicate this book to him.

SJH
CH

Oxford

CONTENTS

DIRECT OBSERVATION AND MEASUREMENT OF BEHAVIOR

Chapter 1

WHY MEASURE BEHAVIOR?

T HIS book has two aims: one practical, the other methodological. The first aim is to reexplore the use of methods of direct observation in the study of psychological problems. The second aim is to show how recent thinking in ethology, the biological study of animal behavior, may contribute significantly to an objective, quantitative and descriptive science of behavior. The conjunction of *descriptive* and *science* will be an anathema to many experimental psychologists, but we maintain that for certain problems (and for the study of certain subjects) direct observation of the free behavior of the organism is the method par excellence. Some workers, notably clinicians, have correctly identified some of the problems for which observational methods are the appropriate tool, but they have been careless in their application. What is required in observational studies, but is seldom applied, is a degree of rigor in measurement commensurate with that expected of experimental studies.

Techniques of systematic observation are not themselves new: they have been used scientifically, at least since the time of Darwin (1872), in studying the behavior of men and of other animals. The heyday of observational studies of behavior was the 1920's and early 1930's. Zoologists and psychologists each concerned themselves with the "systematic recording in objective terms of behaviour in the process of occurring, in a manner that [would] yield quantitative individual scores" (Jersild, and Meigs, 1939). Zoology, while giving increasing prominence to controlled experiments, has continued to be sustained by a core of field studies; coherent and comprehensive principles of animal behavior (see, for example, Hinde, 1966; and Marler, and Hamilton, 1966) have been induced as much from observational as from experimental studies. Psychology on the other hand has witnessed a gradual decline of observational studies. Very little is now heard of the early observational work on humans; even in child development, where such studies have always been more popular than in other areas of investigation, estimates of recent studies employing exclusively observational techniques have been as low as 8 percent (Wright, 1960).

Several reasons have been given for this decline of interest in direct observation: "Experimentally-oriented workers soon decreased their interest because of the degree to which the method (that is, observation) permitted and perhaps even encouraged absence of manipulative control over the situation in which the behaviour occurred" (Nowlis, 1960). Systematic observation "also lacks the clean, decisive flavour of an experiment" (Gellert, 1955). Probably the overwhelming reason for this decline of interest in direct observation was the psychologist's need for scientific respectability. Tinbergen (1963) puts the case thus: "It has been said that, in its haste to step into the twentieth century and to become a respectable science, Psychology skipped the preliminary descriptive stage that other natural sciences had gone through, and so was soon losing touch with the natural phenomena." Hence by 1960 in a review of studies of child development, Mussen was able to comment that "There are proportionately fewer purely descriptive, normative studies, and more studies geared to the "whys" of children's behavior." Mussen's preceding sentence shows clearly that he regards this as one of the "signs of scientific maturating." A decrease in descriptive, normative studies however is not evidence *eo ipso* of scientific maturation. Astronomy, which ranks as an important scientific discipline in its own right, is based entirely upon observation. In this book we wish to restate the case for using observational techniques as an essential part of behavioral studies. We shall first consider some of the areas in which such techniques may be applied.

BEHAVIORAL REPERTOIRE

Many psychologists might wish to take issue with the statement quoted above from Tinbergen (1963); we regard the statement as essentially true. Present-day psychology is essentially an analytic science, concerned with the whys of behavior, and as such its method is experimental. It is often forgotten that an animal in an experimental procedure already has a well- established behavioral repertoire and that knowledge of this repertoire may be essential to understanding the results of an experiment. In other words, before attempting to modify behavior, we need to know what behavior there is to modify. A detailed knowledge of the natural history of behavior is necessary from several points of view.

The animal under study may have an endogenous cycle of activity whose periodic waxing and waning could be erroneously attributed to the experimental conditions. Such periodicities have been described in the behavior of a wide variety of animals from lizards (Hoffman, 1960), through rodents (Richter, 1965) to Man (Thomae, 1957; and Aschoff, 1965). The sleep states are an obvious manifestation of periodicity in human activities. Since responsiveness to stimuli is a function of the state of the organism, we might expect that a stimulus repeatedly presented would elicit periodic responses. If the underlying endogenous periodicites are not adequately documented, it may be tempting to interpret the changes in responsiveness as evidence of (say) habituation and dishabituation. A study where such an interpretation was made and where at least part of the results may have been due to endogenous periodicites is discussed in Chapter 2.

A detailed analysis of the motor patterns recruited by an animal may give a much more precise indication of what motivational changes may be taking place within the animal's central nervous system than a single measure, such as bar pressing, chosen on the basis of its ease of intrumentation.

An almost allegorical example of the importance of detailed behavioral observation is provided by a recent study of memory-interference effects in rats (S. Zinkin, personal communication). If a rat is placed on a stand above the floor of a cage, its normal response is to step down fairly rapidly to the floor. If the floor is electrified so that the rat receives a shock as it steps down, it is likely to do so less rapidly the next time it is placed in the apparatus. This situation has been used to test the effect of ECS (electroconvulsive shock) on memory. It has generally been thought (e.g. Chorover and Schiller, 1965) that ECS, if administered soon enough after a learning trial, will disrupt the consolidation process believed to be necessary to establish a long term memory trace. In the step-down situation, this effect appears to be demonstrated if animals who have received the treatment after a shock to the feet show no retention of the learning trial when tested 24 hours later. However, retention is always assessed in terms of the animal's step-down latency, no other aspect of its behavior being studied. Zinkin suspected that other components of the animal's behavior might indicate retention. She therefore carried out an experiment in which not only was the step-down latency measured before and after various treatments, but also several other aspects of the animal's behavior were recorded after stepping down. The results were somewhat surprising. There were many animals who, after treatment, stepped down from the platform just as rapidly as before treatment (often in less than one second). However, their behavior after they had stepped down changed dramatically compared with that before treatment. Animals who previously had stepped down and then spent the next thirty seconds exploring the apparatus, were now likely to freeze on the grid floor for the whole thirty second observation period. Others, after a delay of perhaps ten seconds, attempted to jump out of the apparatus. This type of behavioral change was found as frequently in the animals who had received ECS one-half second after the learning trial as in those who had received only the punishing foot-shock. These changes were not seen in animals who had had no treatment.

If only latency had been recorded (and this could have been done automatically without even looking at the animal) the interpretation would have been that foot-shocked animals had remembered the learning trial but the others had not. By studying what the animal was actually doing, it was apparent that at least some retention was present in both experimental groups. The theoretical importance of this and of sub-

sequent studies by Zinkin is considerable. The fact that, as a result of observation of the animals rather than the timing device, studies with an accepted interpretation over two decades should have been thrown into theoretical disarray is a salutary lesson.

Lack of knowledge of the behavioral repertoire of experimental animals
can often lead to experiments which are quite unsuitable to answer the
question for which they were conceived. Riess's experiment (1954) to test
the innateness of nest building in rats is such a case. From shortly after birth
female rats were reared in isolation in wire mesh cages which did not provide them with any opportunity to handle objects. Later, they were allowed
to mate and were then placed with their young in a test box containing only
strips of paper. The mother rats neither built nests nor retrieved their
young. Instead they scattered both the paper and their young around the
cage with the result that many of the nestlings died from lack of care. Riess
concluded that during ontogeny the rat learns to build nests and retrieve
young through experience in handling objects.

Eibl-Eibesfeldt (1961) carried out an experiment which was identical
with that of Riess except that he used virgin females who were experienced
in nest building. When placed in the test box, none of them began building,
and only three out of ten animals had built within five hours. The explanation for Riess's results was, according to Eibl-Eibesfeldt, that when placed in
a novel environment, rats first freeze and then show escape and exploratory
behavior. These behaviors inhibit all others, and it does not require much
biological sophistication to recognize that such a hierarchy of behavior patterns would have survival value. It is only when the environment has become fully familiar that nest building begins. If, on the other hand, isolation-reared rats were tested in their home cage, eight out of thirty-seven animals began building immediately, and all had built within five hours. In
contrast with Riess, Eibl-Eibesfeldt also made detailed observations of the
motor patterns used by the animals in nest building. The behavioral sequence could be subdivided into eleven discrete elements, e.g. collecting,
grasping, and depositing. The morphology of these elements was identical in
the experienced and isolation-reared animals; only the sequence was different. Inexperienced animals would often employ an element too early or too
late in the sequence for it to be optimally useful.

Clearly Eibl-Eibesfeldt's results did not support Riess's interpretation that
rats learn to build nests through experience in handling objects. The behavior patterns of nest building are available, given an appropriate material, as
tools ready to be used. Only the optimal ordering of the elements has to be
learned.

Eibl-Eibesfeldt's study has many interesting implications which are am-
plified by a number of complementary studies not mentioned here. For our
purposes the lesson to be drawn is clear. Without a detailed knowledge of

the behavior patterns normally exhibited by animals, inept experiments may be set up which in turn lead to misleading conclusions. In Riess' investigation the main independent variable, rearing in isolation, was of little relevance in understanding the ensuing behavior of failing to build nests, since a crucial fact about the normal everyday behavior of rats was not known to the experimenter.

It may be hazardous to treat any behavior as biologically irrelevant. Some activities are derived, that is they contain elements from sequences of behavior which occur in other situations. So-called displacement activities are of this kind. Displacement activities are behavior patterns which appear to be inappropriate in the environmental context: They may appear as an unexpected discontinuity with respect to antecedent behaviors, they may have components of motivationally contrary behavior patterns (e.g. approach and avoidance), or they may occur in the absence of their usual causal antecedents. Fidgeting, nailbiting, nose picking in humans, rocking in higher primates, twirling in dogs, and staring down in gulls are all of this kind. In recent years evidence has accrued suggesting that displacement activities may have an arousal-reducing function (Stone, 1964; Delius, 1967; and Hutt, and Hutt, 1968). It is difficult to see how the notion of displacement activity could have arisen without the 'displaced' activity having been seen in its original functional context.

Again in some animals, and indeed in some humans (as we shall see below), certain behavior patterns seen in the laboratory may have no counterpart in the animal's natural habitat, and vice versa. Thus Lehrman (1962) warns: "Analyses of behavior based solely on the behavior of captive animals may represent important distortions of the actual ways in which the animals relate to their natural environment." This leads us to the second main area in which direct observation is required.

ADJUSTMENT TO PHYSICAL AND SOCIAL ENVIRONMENT

There are certain major areas of human and animal behavior the very concern of which is how the subject relates to his natural environment, both physical and social. Adjustment to the physical environment comprises the group of behaviors of particular importance in the development of the young of the species: exploration and play. Exploration has been described as that behavior which "brings the organism into contact with certain selected parts of the environment rather than others . . . any behavior, motor or perceptual, which has as its end-state contact between organism and selected portions of its environment" (Dember, and Earl, 1957). It has been pointed out that most early learning in children comes about through exploration of their environment:

> To a great extent learning comes about through the motility, exploratory behaviour, or curiosity of the child. It occurs in response to environmental changes produced

by the manipulations of the individual himself or of other persons. In his "search for novelty" as Piaget terms it, the child explores the actions of doors, drawers, stairs and light switches, learns to produce the effects which intrigue him and learns to avoid the hazards they impose (Strauss and Kephart, 1955, p. 166).

There is little possibility of obtaining real-life records of the development of exploration and learning in this sense except where the life history of individual children are completely known (see Hutt, 1967b). The monumental work of Piaget has been very largely the result of intensive behavioral observations of a limited number of children; *The Origins of Intelligence in the Child* is a model of painstaking observations made on his own children.

Exploratory behavior can be studied by simulation of a real-life situation to which children are first familiarized and in which they are then introduced to standard novel objects. Since part of the interest of such studies is in the range of behaviors displayed by the child, only direct observation by an observer is both sufficiently flexible and sensitive to record the nuances which ultimately may prove important.

The social environment of an animal comprises the contacts between individuals we might call communication, cooperation, aggression and territoriality. In animals and young children, such transactions are largely carried on by means of nonverbal signals, and it is only by virtue of detailed observational analysis that the morphological vocabulary can be ascertained. A recent spate of books on aggression (Carthy, and Ebling, 1964; Lorenz, 1966; Morris, 1967; Storr, 1968; and Russell, and Russell, 1968), which have freely homologized from subhuman to human mechanisms has served to emphasize the need for an adequate analysis of the components and organization of human aggressive behavior.

Even where a relatively sophisticated level of verbal analysis of a problem is possible, it is doubtful whether a questionnaire study of how subjects *say* they behave is a suitable substitute for a real-life situational analysis of how they actually behave. The kind of discrepancy which may arise between report and fact is shown by the classic series of studies by Hartshorne *et al.* (1928, 1929).

The aim of these studies was to "apply the objective methods of the laboratory to the measurement of conduct under controlled conditions" (Hartshorne, and May, 1928). Children were given written ethical judgment tests and were then observed in real-life situations involving ethical behaviors, such as cooperation and honesty. Cooperation was studied by observing the children in real-life situations offering the child the opportunity of doing work for, or giving away things to, other children or of taking and retaining things for himself. To test honesty, party games, athletic contests, classroom and everyday situations were arranged with inherent opportunities for cheating and (apparently) little likelihood of detection. In fact, the tests were devised so that the observer not merely could detect cheating but could measure its magnitude. For example, the children were sent on standard errands with excess change, so that the amount appropriated could be measured. The correlations between ethical judgment scores and scores on the tests of actual ethical behavior were around +.25. (It is of interest that the correlation between the scores on the ethical judgment tests and intelligence was +.70, suggesting that good intelligence confers some fluency in telling lies.) As Rosensweig (1948) comments: "what the subject says about his behavior and personality is a very unsafe guide for prediction about his actual performance in real-life situations." This brings to mind Gellert's complaint of the time-consuming and cumbersome nature of direct observation studies (see Ch. 4). Regrettably, if we are to find out how people actually behave when they are not being tested by psychologists, there seems to be no substitute for detailed and painstaking observation. Ethologists apparently have never felt the need to spare themselves this drudgery, in the knowledge that there are no shortcuts to scientific postulates. In the following sections we shall consider a number of areas in which research workers have been particularly determined to find such shortcuts.

UNCOOPERATIVE SUBJECTS

Professional psychologists have become so used to finding a constant supply of eager volunteers, ready to play almost any game, that psychology, the scientific study of human behavior, has become virtually synonymous with performing mental tests and working laboratory gadgets. Indeed, it probably would be no exaggeration to say that over 95 percent of our total information about how human beings behave is based upon studies in which the subject's total behavior repertoire is reduced to one or two responses to a carefully regulated stimulus constellation.

When faced with the problem of finding out how a hitherto neglected subgroup of *Homo sapiens* behaves, the natural tendency of the psychologist is to reach for his handbook of psychometric tests or manual of laboratory methods. It therefore comes as a shock to find that the subjects under study are neither willing nor able to answer conundrums, to fill up questionnaires or to work laboratory models. There are two main subgroups of *Homo sapiens* who are particularly perverse in these respects: preschool children and psychiatric patients. In general, the younger the child, the less likely he is to cooperate in investigations involving traditional psychological paraphenalia; should he be both young and psychiatrically disabled, he ceases to be a viable object of scientific psychological inquiry.

One of the aims of direct observation studies is to bring within the purview of objective analysis the behavior of subjects who might otherwise be excluded by virtue of their unsuitability for psychometric or laboratory study. The main reason for looking towards ethology for guidance is that its subjects of inquiry too have been free ranging and hence relatively uncooperative. The ethologist learns to work with the behavioral data the animal provides in his natural habitat. While fundamentally more complex, the behavior of *Homo sapiens* can in principle be treated in the same way as that of any other animal studied in his natural habitat.

CLINICAL ADJUSTMENT

While interesting questions can be, and have been asked about the perceptual and learning abilities of schizophrenics in laboratory situations, the questions usually asked about a patient by doctors and medical ancillaries are ones about his aggressive and impulsive behavior, his eating habits and personal hygiene, his working and social relations. These behaviors are usually subsumed under the umbrella term of *adjustment*. Since important (and expensive) decisions depend upon the correct evaluation of this ill-defined concept, it is not surprising that those entrusted with such decisions are impatient if all the psychologist has to offer are measurements of reaction time, susceptibility to illusions, and so on. Granted that such measurements are relevant—and we are not arguing for or against—their validity must still be established against criteria of adjustment derived from real-life situations outside the laboratory or testing room.

Whatever meaning we attach to the term adjustment, which consists of an amalgam of behaviors, all of which are necessary but none sufficient to define it, it has to be assessed in the patient's own habitat. Most of the behaviors which would have to be included in an estimate of personal adjustment are directly observable; they are therefore in principle quantifiable. Here however, a curious phenomenon is encountered. While almost all the physical and physiological data about a patient are measured to at least one decimal point on parametric scales, the behaviors of the patient, with the exception of the small proportion measurable on psychometric tests, are given only ordinal ratings. The rating may be as rudimentary as good—poor, better—worse, or it may contain odd numbers of items up to seven arranged on an ordinal scale. Often the midpoint of such a scale is treated as an optimal or neutral condition from which the variable in question may deviate in either direction.

In general, ratings of adaptive behavior have been of three kinds: (1) A single, easily observed variable is chosen as representative of behavior as a whole. For example, an assessment of locomotion may serve as an indicator of the overall behavior of a hyperkinetic child or of a catatonic schizophrenic patient, since aberrant motor behavior is such an obvious feature of each disorder. This we shall call the *representative* model. (2) Assessments are made, again on ordinal scales, of several different areas of behavior, the scores from each assessment being added to give an overall measurement of behavior adjustment (the *additive* model). (3) A single gross assessment is made which purports to characterize behavior as a whole (the *global* model). It seems to us that each of these approaches has an inherent weakness.

The representative model comes to grief because it ignores the fact that behavior has a structure. The word structure is used about behavior in much the same sense as it is used in building. If a building has to fill a certain space we have a restriction upon the total amount of material which can be used in its construction. If we assume that the building will be comprised of certain elements, say mortar, bricks, wood, glass, nails, we may juggle with the amounts of each which will be used; but for every increase in one element, there will have to be a corresponding decrease in one or more of the others. In behavior, we again have a finite number of elements which can be displayed with a temporal restriction, not all behaviors can be manifested in unit time. If one element of behavior increases, it must be at the expense of others. Thus if we restrict our attention to one variable, we must not assume that other variables bear a monotonic relationship to it. As we shall see later in the book (Ch. 7), a drug administered to reduce or increase the prevalence of one behavior may have no effect upon, or even an adverse effect upon, an equally undesirable behavior. For example, a drug such as Ospolot, which produces the greatest reduction in the aggressive behavior of an hyperkinetic child (Hutt *et al.*, 1966) may actually increase his locomotion. Changes may therefore be best assessed in terms of shifts in the structure of behavior.

A particularly unfortunate example of the practice of adding ordinal assessments of several behavioral variables is provided by a study of the effects of changes of occupational regime upon the behavior of chronic psychotic patients (Hutt, *et al.*, 1964). Assessments were made on five -point scales of the patient's locomotory, eating and toilet behaviors, speech retardation, delusional utterances. The scores on each five-point scale were then added to provide an overall measure of adjustment. This practice is to be deplored on at least three grounds. In the first place, most of the twenty variables could have been measured objectively without resort to the crudity of ordinal guesswork. Degree of speech retardation can easily be assessed by recording speech samples and counting their rate of generation (Hutt, and Coxon, 1965); number of delusional utterances per unit time can be counted (Rickard, *et al.*, 1960); and amount of food eaten, frequency of spilling can all be counted (Ayllon, and Michael, 1959). Where a variable actually can be measured, there is no justification for ordinal assessment. In the second place, it is manifestly absurd to add ordinal scores for delusions, for cleanliness and for cooperativeness to obtain a gross score for adjustment. Qualitatively, these are different subsystems with their own appropriate units of measurement. To add them is as indefensible as adding together watts, decibels and centimeters to give a measure of bigness. In the third place, the practice is indefensible on statistical grounds. Each scale is highly correlated with the others, since all are a function of the underlying physiological process illness called schizophrenia or depression. To add measures which are themselves intercorrelated is to produce spuriously large changes in scaled scores for minimal changes in the underlying physiological process.

Whether a single global measure can legitimately be used to characterize behavior as a whole is a matter of considerable doubt. The intelligence quotient is probably the only measure which even approaches such a role. However, just as the contributions of the subitems of an intelligence test to the global IQ measure are unequal, so are the weightings given to different behaviors in assessing (say) social adjustment. This is seen clearly in the study already referred to (Hutt *et al.*, 1966) of the effects of drugs upon hyperkinetic behavior in an epileptic child. When nurses and other medical staff were asked to say which drug regime improved her behavior most, they unanimously selected the one which had increased attention span most even though it was less effective than other drugs in reducing destructive activity. It is thus clear that the global assessments attached greater weight to attention span than to other variables. The nurses themselves were quite unaware of this bias. We might thus argue that the notion of a global assessment is illusory.

CORRELATIONS OF BEHAVIORAL AND PHYSIOLOGICAL MEASURES

Even if an assessment were truly global, it would be open to one conceptual criticism which it shares with both the representative approach and the additive approach above. Behavior may be treated as either the dependent or as the independent variable of an investigation. In the first case, changes in behavior are measured in response to specific stimuli, to prevailing environmental conditions, or to alterations in the subject's internal milieu effected by drugs, brain disease, epileptogenic lesions, etc. In the second case, changes in the subject's behavior are observed while records are collected of electrocerebral activity, of metabolic changes, skin temperature, and so on. In almost every case behavior is being correlated with variables which can be specified with great precision on a parametric scale. A sound stimulus can be quantified in terms of its frequency, band width, sound pressure level, rise time and other characteristics; a drug may be specified in terms of its concentration, its dosage, its blood plasma level. The concentration of sodium and potassium ions in a blood sample may be precisely estimated: the power-density spectrum of an electroencephalogram epoch may be measured, and so on. To correlate behavioral measurements of the crudity of better—worse, more—less with physiological variables measured to two decimal places in micrograms is, to say the least, faintly ridiculous. In physics such a situation would be treated with derision. Yet this is the situation which obtains in psychology.

Let us take for a typical example a recent correlative study of the 'behavior' of psychiatric patients and catecholamine metabolite excretion (Nelson, *et al.,* 1966). Six psychotic patients (2 schizophrenic, 1 manic-depressive and 3 depressed) were studied over periods varying from twenty to seventy-four days. At the same time each day the patients were observed and interviewed, following which a sample of urine was taken. The trouble taken over the biochemical analysis of the urine and of the analysis of behavior contrast markedly:

> The urine was refrigerated; after collection, aliquots of all samples were frozen until processed. The samples were analyzed for creatinine, metadrenaline (MA), and normetadrenaline (NMA). The analysis for MA and NMA involved ion exchange resin purification, bidimensional paper chromatographic separation, and photometric quantitation. All samples were tested in duplicate. The coefficient of variation of duplicate measures was 8% for MA and 11% for NMA. Mean recoveries of NMA and MA were 71% ($\pm$9) and 84% ($\pm$9), respectively (p. 217).

The presence of metadrenaline and normetadrenaline was determined in nanograms per milligram creatinine. An attempt was then made to correlate the metabolite excretion with behavior during the previous twenty-four hours.

> When possible, direct quotations of the patient regarding expressions of emotional states and attitudes were recorded. In addition, the notes of continuous observation by the ward staff were obtained from the hospital record. Both sets of behavioural observations were organized and recorded before the urinary levels of catecholamines were determined and were presented to two psychiatrists, neither of whom was acquainted with the patients involved. These judges were asked to evaluate independently the patient's course and to identify periods of relatively homogeneous behaviour. Gross changes in physical activity, eating and sleeping patterns, social interaction, and emotional content of speech were used as major indicators of behavior (p. 217).

While three references are given to technical papers showing precisely how the biochemical assays are made, no information is given as to the circumstances and form in which the behavioral information was recorded or for how long. Except by later inference from the diagrams in the paper, we have no idea what kind of information was given to the two judges whose task it was to provide a perfunctory quantification of the material. What, for example, are periods of homogeneous behavior? It was found that the course of each patient's illness could be divided into three stages: an initial period of "psychotic turmoil," a period of "relative equilibrium," and finally a period of "anticipation and mild anxiety during the terminal part of hospitalization as a patient began to prepare for adjustment outside the hospital." The judges' task was to decide whether the notes on the patient's behavior suggested primarily a state of psychotic turmoil (given a numerical value of 3), a state of relative equilibrium (value of 1) or a state of mild anxiety and anticipation (value of 2).

It is not surprising perhaps that the results of the study are somewhat equivocal. In some subjects there appears to be a positive relationship between phase of illness and metabolite excretion, and in others, a negative relationship. The overall trend is slightly positive. Had a detailed quantitative analysis been made of the behavior, it would have been possible to apply a powerful parametric statistical test to the data. As it is, we are left with at least one doubt: the role of increased motor activity in determining the metabolic excretion. We are told categorically that the results could not have been explained on these grounds: "The changes observed are greater than those produced by mild exertion and none of the patients engaged in more than moderate amounts of activity." What meaning are we to attach to the terms mild and moderate? In the preceding two sentences we are told: "Exercise even in moderate amounts, increases the secretion of NA and A. The increase in these hormones is roughly parallel to the amount of *physical* activity, so that mild exericse, as in everyday experience, is sufficient only to produce moderate elevations in NA and A." Are we to assume that psychotic excitement and agitation are not in quantity sufficient to account for the elevated metabolite excretion at behavioral rating 3?

One of the main features of so-called psychotic excitement is increased physical activity. It is interesting therefore that the only significant differences found in the study were between rating 3 and the others for the total creatinine and normetadrenaline determinations. We presumably have to accept the authors' contention that physical activity was not the operative factor, but the point could have been settled beyond dispute had they made time-samping observations each day of what in practice is quite the simplest behavioral variable to quantify locomotion. Moreover, had a more systematic quantification of behavior been undertaken, we would have been in a much stronger position to evaluate whether we were dealing with a statistically reliable association, a suggestive trend, or a procedural artefact.

If we appear to have been overbelligerent to this study, it is because the study illustrates a general feature to which we take exception in the correlation of physiological and behavioral findings: the hidden assumption that either it is too difficult or too much trouble to quantify behavior with anything like the precision of the physiological data.

We hope that this book will go some way in modifying this attitude. Because this is an attitude not shared by students of animal behavior and since the greater part of the work upon the quantification of free-ranging behavior has been carried out by ethologists, we shall draw freely from their studies. Moreover, since our thinking about this problem has been greatly influenced by ethology, it seems appropriate to devote the next chapter to a consideration of the ethological approach in contrast with some of the approaches adopted by psychologists.

Chapter 2

OBSERVATIONAL APPROACHES TO THE STUDY OF BEHAVIOR

THE approach to direct observation taken in this book owes more to ethology, the biological study of animal behavior, than to psychology. We shall therefore devote this chapter to a discussion of the special features of ethology, comparing and contrasting ethological thinking with two approaches prevalent in psychology, described as the experimental and the ecological, respectively. In experimental pscyhology, observation is either completely replaced by some form of automatic recording or, if used, is subordinated to methodological considerations. The most noteworthy characteristic of the ecological approach is its novelese flavour: impressionism, inferentialism and imprecision.

THE ETHOLOGICAL APPROACH

Ethology is characterised both by a method—direct observation—and a particular type of biological approach. To illustrate the special method of ethology we can do no better than quote a well-known ethologist, Carthy (1966):

> The first aim of the study of the behaviour of a particular animal is to record it in all its detail, correlating it with the stimuli which evoke the different sections of it. Such a complete catalogue of behaviour is called an ethogram. It is vitally important that such an ethogram should be recorded quite impartially. That is, the observer must not be influenced by his own evaluation of what is going on but must seek to record everything no matter how unimportant it may seem at the time. Even details of weather conditions may later prove necessary in analysing the causation of the behaviour. At least in the first place when confronted with the behaviour of an animal with which the observer is not familiar, no anthropomorphism must be allowed to creep in (although it is often a useful form of shorthand!). The report must not be in terms of human thoughts and desires but must be plain recording. Later putting one's self into the position of the animal may give insight into the problems which the behaviour throws up and suggest hypotheses which can form the basis of experiment and analysis. But this should always be done with the greatest care and the approach quickly discarded after it has given the indication necessary to organise future research (p. 1-2).

One way in which the ethological approach differs from other observational approaches (e.g. Anthony, 1968) is immediately clear: The report should not be in terms of human thoughts and desires but in terms of observables and activity statements. It may be argued that to eschew anthropomorphism when recording the behavior of anthropomorphs is an artificial exercise. The problem remains however, that we simply are not adept at inferring the motivations, intentions and emotions even of other adults. We constantly misunderstand each other's motives, we make social blunders, we misinterpret the other's expressions. In view of this, a close analysis of the components of actions and expressions seems a primary requirement so that the critical features of the various behaviors may be elucidated. If our perception of adults' signals is likely to be faulty, it will be even more so with respect to young children and psychiatric patients. Children are not miniature adults, and extrapolation from adults seldom yields valid statements about children's behavior. Again, since the maladjustment of psychiatric patients may, in many cases, be an aberration of motivation, long-term analysis of these aberrations may be better served by detailed and painstaking observation—records of which can be scrutinized over and over again—than by premature inferences about underlying states.

The ethological approach differs from that of experimental psychology and other branches of behavioral sciences in that it insists upon an *ethogram* as the legitimate point of departure of any experimental study. Before attempting to modify behavior, the ethologist demands to know what behavior there is to modify. Before reaching conclusions about the effects of external physical stimuli, he seeks to know the endogenously generated patterns of behavior shown by an organism. Psychologists seem constrained to stimulate their subjects of study. Ethologists generally prefer to leave them alone. Until we know what an animal will do in the absence of a particular stimulus, we are in no position to make assertions regarding the effect of the stimulus.

The way in which interpretation of a behavior pattern may change once the repertoire of the unstimulated organism is known, is illustrated by a recent study of habituation in human neonates. Bartoshuk (1962) had shown that the cardiac acceleration observed on presentation of an auditory stimulus showed a progressive decrement with repeated stimulation. Forty stimuli were applied at intervals of fifteen, thirty, or sixty seconds, the experiment thus lasting ten, twenty or forty minutes. It has been demonstrated that babies show very clear recurrent patterns of behavior which have been termed *states* (Wolff, 1959; Prechtl and Beintema, 1964). Within minutes of being brought to an examination room after feeding, they usually show a downward change of state: if they are awake and restless, they tend to quieten; if alert and quiet, they fall asleep; and if they are in rapid-eye-movement (REM) sleep, within twenty minutes they fall into regular (nonrapid eye movement (NREM)) sleep. By the end of twenty minutes, some babies will have shown two downward steps, and by forty minutes most will be in regular sleep. It has been shown, however, that the behavioral and automatic reactions of infants to sound are directly related to state, NREM sleep being associated with less responsiveness than REM sleep (Hutt, *et al.*, 1968). The habituation demonstrated by Bartoshuk and attributed by him to the influence of stimulus repetition, may in fact be simply a reflection of endogenous state changes. Bartoshuk counters this suggestion by saying that in both the ten- and forty-minute experiments the levels of activation of the infants, measured by their terminal unstimulated heart rates, was higher than their preexperimental levels. This however does not settle the argument. Studies of unstimulated babies (Prechtl, 1968) have shown that heart rate increases for some thirty minutes after feeding despite the downward changes of state which have ensued. Thus, an increase in heart rate through the experiment does not conflict with the interpretation that the so-called habituation may have been primarily a function of change of state.

It can be seen that the manner in which we interpret the effects of a stimulus may be quite different according to whether or not we are fully acquainted with the behavior of the unstimulated organism. This concern with endogenously generated behavior and with making as detailed a behavioral inventory as possible contrasts with the approach of a large proportion of experimental psychological studies.

THE EXPERIMENTAL PSYCHOLOGICAL APPROACH
Nonsocial Behaviors

The experimental psychological studies of behaviors other than social ones generally has been concerned with single, easily measured responses to carefully restricted stimulus constellations. The merit of an experimental study might be judged in part from the extent to which the experimenter had succeeded in limiting the possible range of irrelevant stimuli likely to distract the animal. Only in recent years has the importance of stimulus selection as a class of behaviors been recognized, resulting in the study of exploratory behavior. Exploration however may be seen to have two aspects: the selection of that part of the environment to which behavior is to be directed, and the selection of a response from the pool of possible responses potentially available to that stimulus. Studies of exploratory behavior have usually limited consideration to the former aspect, namely, the types of stimuli most selected. The importance of response selection, or the variability of response morphology towards the same stimulus, has been little recognized. Psychologists with a Skinnerian bias are especially reluctant to consider response variability as a relevant issue. Results are generally given in terms of responses, meaning presses of a bar in a Skinner box, and this in turn is measured by number of clicks on a cumulative recorder. It is not clear from most texts whether the animal consistently pressed the bar with one forepaw, used both forepaws, hindlegs, snout or head, or whether perhaps he sat on the lever. Authors like Russell, and Ochs (1963) who report such facts seem exceptional in their temerity or in their recognition of the possible importance of these.

It may be argued that it is of no possible relevance how the animal makes his response, if by 'response' is meant 'presses lever.' If consistent regularities in the shapes of cumulative frequency curves relating responses to time can be obtained, with different response-reinforcement contingencies, then clearly response is a sensitive behavioral measure. That this is not always the case, however, is shown by two recent studies, one involving monkeys, the other, three- to five-year-old children.

In a study by Butler and Harlow (1954) it was reported that monkeys would continue opening the door of their cage for periods of nine hours or more with visual exploration of the laboratory as the only reward. Repeating the experiment a few years later, Symmes (1959) made the following interesting observations:

> Ss were not exploring visually during all the response time. They appeared to spend more than half the response time manipulating the door, chewing on the sill, and exploring tactually what they could not see through the open door. Very commonly they sat near the door holding it open with one hand and moving it against the spring resistance, only occasionally turning to look through the opening. These informal observations suggested that this sort of activity increased through the period of testing and probably accounted for most of the rise in total response time (p. 186).

Moreover, it was found that the animals persisted in activities directed towards the door even in darkness. It is thus clear that during the course of these experiments a marked morphological change occurred in the behavior. Taking the number of door openings as the sole measure of behavior, it appears that investigative exploration was maintained at a high level for hours on end. By taking cognizance of the kinds of behaviors which occurred, a rather different picture emerges. It would appear that there was a gradual waning of investigation of the laboratory which was replaced by more 'diversive' activities (Berlyne, 1960). Since it is likely that the two types of activities are not merely morphologically different, but have different underlying mechanisms, a count of the number of door openings is a misleading measure unless it is accompanied by detailed behavioral observations.

In a recent study of exploratory behavior in young children (Hutt, 1966), a novel object was presented under different conditions of visual and auditory feedback. Counters in the object registered each manipulatory movement so that a reading of them would give a measure of how much a child had responded to the object. Figures 1 and 2 show relative amounts of this responsiveness under various incentive conditions, and inspection of these will suggest that when auditory feedback was contingent upon manipulation, exploration increased with successive exposures, whereas an accelerated decrease was observed in the absence of such feedback.

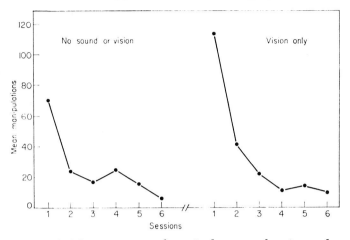

FIGURE 1. Mean amounts of manipulatory exploration under (1) no sound or vision, (2) vision only, conditions. n = no. of subjects (from Hutt, 1966).

As will be demonstrated in Chapter 6, close observation of the children's behavior showed that under the sound conditions there was a marked change in the type of response directed towards the object. During the first few exposures the children primarily investigated the object; after some transitional phases of exploratory activity, investigation ceased and by the

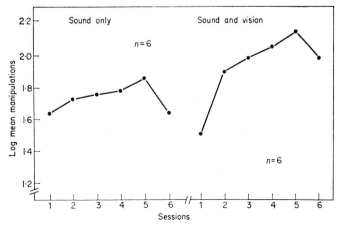

FIGURE 2. Manipulatory exploration of the novel object on successive trials under (3) sound only, and (4) sound and vision, conditions. n = no. of subjects (from Hutt, 1966).

fifth or sixth exposures 'play' activities were the most prominent responses, i.e. the object was now serving as a bridge or seat, or being ridden as a horse. The distinction between the two behaviors is quite clear, as can be seen in photographs (Hutt, 1966) or motion picture (Hutt, 1967) film. Such play responses were not observed in the absence of the auditory incentive. Thus to use an overall response measure as the counter readings would have been grossly misleading, since they masked two disparate behaviors having different determinants, being differently motivated, and very probably having different functions.

Far from being gratuitous, detailed observations of behavior in a psychological experiment may throw light directly on the mechanisms activated by a particular set of environmental variables.

Social Behaviors

Ethologists proceed from naturalistic observations; they are interested in questions of *why* and *how* animals do what they do. Methods serve these ends and therefore are not of primary consideration. Psychologists are much more concerned with methodology, usually dictated by theoretical tenets or the requirements of statistical propriety. Consequently, what ethologists find out is interesting and significant even if methodologically circumspect, whereas what psychologists find is technically exemplary even if its validity and significance are sometimes obscure.

Differences between the two approaches are exemplified by two studies concerned more or less with the same problem: mother-infant interactions in monkeys (Hinde, *et al.*, 1964; Hinde, and Spencer-Booth, 1967; and Bobbitt, *et al.*, 1964). The introductory remarks of the two groups of workers are illuminating:

> It is thus necessary also to study development in a more natural setting, and recent field studies have greatly enriched our knowledge. In the field, however, recognition of individuals is often difficult and precise quantification impossible. The present study aims at a compromise, the animals being kept in small groups so that they live in a moderately complex environment under conditions which permit a moderate degree of experimental control and moderately precise recording, (Hinde, and Spencer-Booth, 1967, p. 169).

> The development of practical, reliable, and objective methods for securing detailed observations of ongoing and (particularly) of social behaviour—and the related process of recording and analyzing such events in relation to each other— have long been basic problems in a large number of research approaches. A number of investigators have attempted to develop observational techniques more adequate to their needs. The problems are far from solved, but many believe that if more refined observational techniques can be developed such techniques will provide an important avenue to investigation of the processes involved in social development and interaction (Bobbitt, *et al.*, 1964, p. 257).

The findings of the two sets of studies are essentially similar, but of course the points of emphases differ:

It will be apparent from the preceding sections that mother-infant relations undergo profound changes during the first 6 months. During the first few weeks, the infants often set out to explore the environment in an apparently intrepid manner. During this time the mothers often restrain them, either by holding them on to their bodies, or by holding on to a leg or tail when they are off. They also watch over them closely, may intervene in their infants' encounters with other monkeys, and are likely to go after their infants if they move far away. During this period the infants leave their mothers more than they approach them.

Restraining behaviour decreases after the first 2 months, and at the same time hitting and rejection of infants increases. From this time the infant comes to play an increasing role in the maintenance of proximity with its mother (Hinde, and Spencer-Booth, 1967, p. 178).

Summarizing briefly, the foregoing and similar analyses of other dimensions indicate the following principal developments in the elaboration of behavior: (a) The infant shows increasing general activity, including that during periods of physical contact with the mother. (b) Physically and visually, the infant contacts the mother relatively less often. (c) The mother tends to respond to the infant's increasingly active contact behavior with a great proportion of rejecting behavior. (d) More of the mother's locomotion involves departing from the infant. And (e) Less of the mother's locomotion involves carrying the infant around with her (Bobbitt, *et al.*, 1964, p. 269).

Despite the greater attention paid to the method of recording by the latter workers, the findings of Hinde and Spencer-Booth are more informative.

THE ECOLOGICAL APPROACH

The ecological approach is best exemplified by the work of the Midwest Psychological Field Station at the University of Kansas (Wright, and Barker, 1950; Barker, and Wright, 1951, 1955; Barker, *et al.*, 1961; Barker, 1963; and Barker, and Gump, 1964). A recent reissue of part of an earlier work (Barker, and Wright, 1955) provides a useful introduction to the thinking of the Kansas Group (Wright, 1967).

The aims of the Midwest team are similar to those outlined in our own first chapter: "to describe the life situations of individuals" . . . in order (i) to study behaviours not easily reproduced in the laboratory (e.g. extreme aggression, affection); (ii) to show the sequential dependencies amongst different items of behaviour, and (iii) to corroborate laboratory findings (e.g. pessonality studies) by direct observation of particular critical incidents (Wright, 1967, pp. 1, 64-65).

The children are observed in "their natural habitats" which are typical everyday situations, such as the school, the home, the swimming pool. As in our own and other descriptive recording systems, detailed commentaries are made of all activities and stimuli with which the child comes into contact. A retrospective report is dictated after thirty minutes observation, aided by handwritten notes made at the time. The typescript of this report is revised and any ambiguities smoothed out after examining and questioning by a colleague who did not himself witness the events. While the order of differ-

ent activities may be recorded correctly, no precise measurement of duration is possible.

In Wright's system the units of behavior, which he calls actions, are long
sequences of behavior lasting several minutes (some as long as 210 minutes)
having the same direction. "Molar behavior is goal-directed and it generally
occurs within the cognitive field of the person. . . . An action is always 'getting to' or 'getting from' a part of the environment." Actions, according to
Wright's scheme are therefore *molar* events such as going to school; walking
with friend; or playing catch. The *Molecular* events—gestures, postures and
visual fixations—which make up such a pattern, are called *actones*. Actones
are not performed by people but by muscle groups: Actones are "not organ-
ised by cognitive processes into meaningful things and events. . . . Molar
units are molar in the sense that they occur in the context of the person as a
whole and a molar environment." The first difference of approach between
the ecological and ethological approaches is immediately apparent. The
scale of the units which would be called an action is different; ethological
units are those which Wright calls actones.

It is our contention that facial expressions, gestures, postures and visual
fixations are the essential raw material of behavior. They play subtle and
vital roles in all social interaction; their distribution in time provides basic
information about the effects of the environment upon behavior and of underlying functional mechanisms. Moreover, they are of the appropriate degree of mensuration for correlating with physiological changes. Heart rate
for example may show dramatic changes over but a few beats; the possible
significance of such changes can be appreciated only if behavioral changes
are measured over the same kind of time continuum.

The second important difference between the ethological and ecological
approaches concerns the matter of goals and end points. In order to break
up the behavior protocol into episodes, it is necessary to infer "the goal or
end point the actor intends to achieve. . . . Continual rediagnosis of the terminal intended position . . . is essential in episoding." In our own work, diagnosis of goals is not crucial since units of behavior are determined by the
motor patterns employed by the subject. Moreover many of the behaviors in
which we have been interested and are extant in both children and psychiatric patients belong to the class of displacement activities or stereotypies.
Such behaviors are striking largely on account of the apparent absence of
any goal achievement. They may nevertheless subserve important functional
mechanisms.

A more important issue pertaining to end points is that identifying the
goals of action involves not merely retrospective inferences from the behavior protocols, but also a description of the "psychological habitat," i.e. a re-
structuring of the environment from the point of view of the actor. This involves "some form of the question: what does the person see and how does

he see it?" This involves identifying "how others look at, feel about, or 'take' things, recognising often that the viewpoint of another differs from our own." It is precisely because we agree with this statement of Wright's that we regard the exercise of putting ourselves in the place of the actor to see things from his point of view, as well beyond the scope of scientific description.

This leads to the third and most crucial way in which the ethological and ecological approaches differ. Whereas Carthy (1966) demands that behavioral reports should not be in terms of human thoughts and desires but must be plain recording, the ecologists allow themselves much greater licence to make inferences of attitudes, motives and intention. Wright asks frankly whether perhaps inferential description should be left out. He argues:

> the record could never make available for study what it is meant to preserve. . . . A motion picture can show John throwing a ball to Jim. But it cannot show whether John is trying to hurt Jim or to engage him in a game of catch. . . Only observation involving implicit or explicit inference can enable one to say what John is really doing (p. 40).

A fourth and related point of difference between the ethological and ecological approaches revolves around the use of descriptive labels. In giving basic procedural rules for recording behavior Wright says:

> Give the "how" of everything the subject does. It is assumed that everything a child ever does is done some*how*. No child ever just walked, for example. The first time the subject walked he did so slowly, haltingly, awkwardly, unsteadily. Several years later, on his way to get a tooth pulled, he walked reluctantly (p. 50).

Whereas it might be conceded that slowly, haltingly, awkwardly, unsteadily are second-order descriptive labels, reluctantly is an inference about motivation. But this does not worry Wright: "In the 'how' of the child's behavior, there is its constructiveness, its intensity, its social maturity level, its efficiency, the affect that accompanies it."

It will be informative to give a more extensive sample of the protocols contained in Wright's book. These, much more adequately than our summary, give the flavor of the ecological approach.

> Looking wise and kind, Olivia pretended to read from the letter (p. 170).
>
> Wally's reluctance seemed to make Ben more insistent. (p. 174).
>
> Margaret looked very surprised and annoyed. The expression on her face showed definitely that she wanted to return the blow. (p. 175).
>
> Roy stared after Geoffrey with a hurt and hostile look. (p. 175).
>
> Bradley seemed to expect this. When she came toward him, he know what was coming. He cowered as if it were rather a regular occurrence for her to hit him. (p. 176).
>
> Sarah was unable to speak. She obviously wasn't very enthusiastic about this, but said nothing. (p. 177).
>
> Mary showed no awareness of Sarah's disapproval. She was having a wonderful time. (p. 177).

Mary seemed pleased, but took this as a matter of course. (p. 184).
Celeste smiled companionably. (p. 186).
Ben got the upper hand and sat on top of Morris. (p. 197).
Morris almost began to cry. (p. 197).

Most of the behavioral categories are vague; a whole sequence of complex interaction may be subsumed under a phrase such as "got the upper hand" inferences about feeling and motivation are accorded the same status as behavioral description. It is thus clear by now that the ecologists have abandoned any attempt at objective description. The apparent vividness of the ecologists' protocols stems from the novelese quality of much of their reporting. Both in scale and in precision, the ecologists' approach is unsuitable for the types of problems outlined in these first two chapters.

THE BIOLOGICAL STUDY OF BEHAVIOR

In addition to a particular method, ethology may be characterized by its concern with four interlocking biological problems: those of causation, function, evolution and ontogeny. The problem of ontogeny is not unique to ethology; it is a primary concern of developmental psychologists. Concern with any behavior pattern ultimately leads to the question, How did it begin? In Aristotle's words, "He who sees things grow from their beginning will have the finest view of them."

The problem of causation is treated somewhat differently mainly because the phenomena being studied by the two sciences are different. Psychology is primarily concerned with responses to stimuli presented by the experimenter. In consequence, these are seen as causally related to the stimulus. Ethologists, in their initial inquiries, often apply no stimuli at all, merely recording behavioral elements as they occur in sequence. The cause of a particular element may then be regarded as the antecedent element or elements in the sequence. In practice relationships between more than two behavioral elements are seldom considered, i.e. the interactions between elements are essentially dyadic. While some patterns of behavior may be regarded as endogenously motivated, others are clearly initiated by events occurring in the animal's habitat. A special case of this is where the events are themselves behavioral items produced by another animal. Here the elements of behavior of both animals are written down in the order in which they occur; each behavioral element of one animal may then be treated as either stimulus or response to the adjacent elements of the other. We shall return to this problem in Chapter 8. One method which is specifically ethological is that of identifying releasing stimuli. A typical example of the method is provided by the study of Tinbergen and Perdeck (1950). These authors were interested in the behavior of newly hatched herring gulls, who obtain regurgitated food from the parent by pecking at its bill. By presenting the chicks with models resembling the parent's bill and by varying their shape, color, size and pattern, the authors were able to show that there were certain critical features of the bill (it had to be yellow with a super imposed red spot) which determined the chick's pecking response. In humans, models have been used to identify the essential characteristics of the face which release smiling in four- to six-week-old babies (Ahrens, 1954). Hutt and Ounsted (1966) used models in a study of the facial constellations which produce approach and avoidance in human autistic children.

Problems of function in its biological sense are seldom studied by psychologists. This is due primarily to the fact that psychologists study relatively circumscribed behaviors which are abstracted from their biological context for reasons of experimental expediency. Even when studying a lower mammal such as the rat, the behavior pattern chosen may be selected because it can be easily 'shaped' rather than because it is an important aspect of the life of the rat. It is therefore difficult to ask: "what is the function of this behavior?" if it is never seen in a context conducive to its deployment. In humans a second restraint is added to the first. The term function in ethology is used interchangeably with survival value, survival value itself being defined as conferring fitness, and the latter term meaning facilitating procreation of the species. Even though we may be interested in the organism's self-generated activities, in humans the extent of the human behavioral repertoire, plus the specialization of intellectual activity, makes the narrow definition of function untenable.

There is however a second, more interesting manner in which the term function may be used. Behavior has effects, and the human ethologist tries to find out what effects performance of an action has upon the actor's own physiological condition and upon the environment, including the actor's conspecifics. Some actions may subserve clear biological functions, such as eating, mating, caring for offspring, and so on; others may have the effect of removing noxious stimulation, exposing new properties or relations in the environment, bringing certain people into greater or less proximity, and increasing or decreasing the morale of a group. Such activities may aid survival by increasing the individual and/or the group's pool of knowledge by increasing the cohesiveness of the social group, diversifying its labour, and so on. Some behaviors may make little sense as part of a human repertoire until the question of function is asked.

A good example is that of persistent gaze aversion, which is mentioned later (see Ch. 7). One of the most striking and puzzling features of children suffering from Kanner's syndrome—and very probably its most important defining characteristic—is the failure of these children to make eye to eye contact with conspecifics. Physiological evidence suggested that these children were highly activated (Hutt, *et al.*, 1964). Since gaze aversion apparently has the effect of avoiding visual stimulation from conspecifics, especially from their faces, it was postulated that gaze aversion has the effect of limiting further sensory input and might therefore have the function of regulating level of arousal in these children. Similar functions have been suggested for stereotyped behaviors in these children (see Ch. 10).

Apart from the Freudians, few psychiatric research workers until recently have suggested that behavioral abnormalities may subserve essential biological functions in psychiatric patients. Such behaviors have merely been described as present or absent in particular diagnostic groups. The value of asking questions about function is admirably illustrated however by recent advances in behavior therapy, where patterns of apparently irrational behavior have been shown to subserve anxiety-reducing mechanisms.

Closely related to questions of survival value are those connected with phylogeny. Biological characters have survival value when they confer upon the members of a species advantages in coping with a hostile environment. Sometimes when the environment changes, the characters are gradually selected out. An obvious example is sickle cell anemia. Certain characters however which have once conferred advantage upon members of a species possessing that character, may remain present in the species even though they no longer subserve an important biological function, because their continued presence is not harmful. It is sometimes helpful therefore in attempting to understand the function of a particular pattern of behavior to ask not merely, What is the function of this pattern now? but also, What function might this behavior pattern have subserved in the history of the species?

To show that this is neither an impossibly difficult, nor a fatuous question, we will describe a study of Prechtl (1965) of the so-called Moro reflex of babies. What possible function can this behavior pattern have or have had for the human organism? In 1918 the German pediatrician Moro described what happened if he hit the pillow on either side of the baby with his hands. The baby's arms flew out symmetrically and came together again in an arc. The necessary conditions for eliciting this response in the supine baby seemed to be a sudden jolt, shake or blow. On the other hand, if the baby is carried or suspended, rapid retroflexion of the head (or head drop) is a very effective way of eliciting the same response.

This reflex is actually a very complex pattern consisting of several components: an abduction of the upper limbs at the shoulder, extension of the forearms at the elbow, and extension of the fingers. Electromyographically too there is a very consistent pattern of activity. In the typical Moro response the prominent activity occurs in the deltoid, triceps and extensor carpi muscles. Subsequently there is adduction of the arm at the shoulder, bringing the hands again near the chest. If however the baby is held by its wrists or hands resulting in a palmar grasp reflex, and mild traction is exerted on its upper limbs, a dramatic change takes place in the pattern of the response when the baby is stimulated in exactly the same way. It is no longer the extensor muscles of the arms that contract strongly, but the biceps and flexor carpi muscles. In other words, upon traction the extensor reflex is replaced by a flexor reflex, thereby strengthening the clinging considerably.

Prechtl argues that the response elicited by the blow plus the grasp is the real Moro reflex and that the reflex elicited when the baby's arms are free is a strange pattern obtained in a biologically inadequate condition. The head drop is very effective in the awake and active baby but fails when the baby is asleep, whereas the blow against the substrate is effective when the baby is asleep but very much less so when the baby is awake.

Prechtl sees this as fairly conclusive evidence for regarding the primarily flexor Moro response as a phylogentically old behavior pattern present in all primates, its biological function being manifest in the awake and actively clinging infant primate, but not in the sleeping one which is supported by its mother.

Other phylogenetic comparisons provide alternative explanations. Dr. R. Martin* has described a posture of the tree shrew (*tupaia*) very similar in form to the Moro response. This pattern occurs when the tree shrew's nest is disturbed and has the effect of eliciting withdrawal or flight by the predator. We ourselves have seen a similar phenomenon in an encounter between a newborn baby and an older child. The older child smacked the surface on which the baby was lying producing a Moro response. The older child then ran away crying. It is therefore possible that the incomplete Moro still has the function of driving away predators even though the complete behavior pattern no longer is necessary in relation to the mother-child interaction. The clinging response when traction is placed on the baby's arms is probably one of many behaviors which no longer have any important function but are harmless and are therefore not selected against. It can thus be seen that questions of phylogeny or evolution may lead to explanations and even to experiments which make sense of hiterto puzzling or neglected behaviors.

To summarize, the ethological approach presumes a certain way of looking at behavior: it demands that we drop our preconceptions and assumptions of special inside knowledge about human behavior. It also suggests certain questions about behavior which are biological rather than psychological. While it is frequently interested in prolonged sequences of behavior, it is concerned with analyzing these sequences into their components. Its approach is therefore both molar and molecular.

The approach of this book owes most to this latter ethological approach and offers a groping start to what we hope will become a fully fledged ethology of human action. While much of the book will be concerned with practical hints and wrinkles, the underlying philosophy of the book will be that observation and analysis of naturally occurring behavior should be undertaken from a comparative standpoint. The examples will be chosen primarily from studies of children, mainly because the writers have worked very largely with young children, but also because the young child is a particularly suitable subject for the comparative approach we are advocating. While we would not happily accept Haeckel's law that ontogeny recapitu-

---

* Personal communication.

lates phylogeny, it is clear that the inhibitory processes associated with the massive cortical development of man take a prolonged time to develop in the individual's life history. Thus despite the development of language, the biological kinship of the human animal to other primates is much more evident in the young, preschool child than it is in the adult human. Nevertheless, much of the behavior of adults is not exposed to careful, introspective, rational analysis and control, and the considerations which apply to the behavior of the young child also apply to much adult behavior, gestures, postures, facial expressions and nonverbal utterances as they occur in all situations and particularly in social interactions. The problems of how such behaviors are recognized as morphological units, measured and analyzed, form the subject matter of this book.

The behavior of psychiatric patients has been mentioned at many points. The behavior of such patients generally defeats attempts to measure it by indirect (psychometric) means and to subject it to experimental analysis and control. Because of the very unexpectedness of many behaviors and the low probability of occurrence of particular sequences, inferences about the meaning of behavior, based upon the pool of social expertise assumed by Wright (1967), are doomed to failure. This is accentuated by the unreliability of verbal report, when it exists, in psychiatric patients. It would appear therefore that an objective method of quantifying the behavior of psychiatric patients, which does not depend upon either psychometric or experimental techniques, is of some value. The ethological approach outlined above has distinct advantages over its two rivals. Compared with the psychological approach, it endeavors to take into account the patient's total repertoire of behavior. This is clearly of great importance where it is overall adjustment which is under consideration. Moreover, because the approach is molecular, it is moving towards a mensuration of behavior which is compatible with the degree of analysis employed in those fields with which it is to be correlated. We have already discussed the methodological difficulties of correlations between fine cardinal and gross ordinal measurements in Chapter 1. Suffice it to say here that it may be more informative to show that particular stereotyped behaviors increase or decrease in duration or frequency by a given amount in relation to particular dosages of a drug than to evaluate the patient's behavior as worse or better. The point becomes even more important when the problem concerns contemporaneous correlation between behavior and events in the patient's nervous system. This is becoming increasingly feasible with improved telemetric techniques. It is clearly important that the resolution with which we can read off changes in behavior from film or videotape can keep pace with changes in accompanying physiological events.

Assuming therefore that we are aiming at a molecularization of behavior, how may the units of behavior be recognized and quantified? We shall deal with these problems in the following chapter.

Chapter 3

IDENTIFICATION OF BEHAVIOR ELEMENTS

IN HIS book on the behavior of red deer in Scotland, Fraser Darling (1937) depicts the attitudes of mind the successful naturalist must acquire:

> It takes time for the eye to become accustomed to recognise differences, and once that has occurred the nature of the differences has to be defined in the mind by careful self-interrogation if the matter is to be set down on paper . . . The fact remains that an observer has to go through a period of conditioning of a most subtle kind. . . . The observer must empty his mind and be receptive only of the deer and the signs of the country. This is quite severe discipline, calling for time and practice. . . . It is necessary intellectually to soak in the environmental complex of the animal to be studied until you have a facility with it which keeps you as it were one move ahead. You must become *intimate* with the animal. . . . In this state the observer learns more than he realizes (pp. 24-26).

These extracts which are quoted in the present form by Marler and Hamilton (1966) might well be regarded as canons of ethological discipline. Before we can study how behavior is modified by changes in environment or physiological milieu, we must know what behavior there is to be modified, and this can only be discovered by intimate and sustained contact with the animal. It is only by repeated sampling of a child's behavior in many different situations that the consistencies in behavior emerge. Whereas on initial contact the child's behavior appears to be infinitely variable, with repeated observation it becomes clear that certain *patterns* tend to recur in similar circumstances, that patterns bear a temporal relationship to each other, and that some patterns occur frequently, others, infrequently. Most important of all, we begin to realize that far from being infinitely variable, the child's repertoire of behaviors is finite.

If we appear to labor this point, it is because in a large proportion of behavioral investigations this part of the study is treated most superficially. Too often the investigator has preconceptions of what behavior *ought* to occur, rather than knowledge of what *actually* occurs, and imposes a spurious orderliness upon his data, either by juxtaposing classes of behavior which are morphologically distinct, or by ignoring large segments of the animal's behavioral repertoire.

29

MORPHOLOGY AND FUNCTION AS DEFINING CRITERIA OF BEHAVIORAL ELEMENTS

The notion that certain behaviors appear to us as patterns which are easily remembered and recognized when they recur has been treated by Lorenz (1960) who called them behavioral *Gestalten*. That behaviors are seen as Gestalten may be incontrovertable to the seasoned ethologist, but it is of little practical value to the beginner in behavioral observation, who may feel little certainty that his Gestalten correspond with anyone else's. Indeed, he may feel that his behavioral Gestalten are more like the perception of a Necker cube: He sees them first in one way, then in another. Since the notion of behavioral Gestalten is tied up with the whole question of defining behavior elements, it may be profitable to examine this problem in some detail.

We may identify a behavior element in either of two ways: in terms of its morphology or of its effects. Attneave (1954) has pointed out that much of the stimulation received by the visual system is highly redundant, that is, it is highly predictable, homogenous, and regular. So-called good Gestalten are figures with high degrees of redundancy in the sense that if we wished to code them for transmission as a television picture, we would require very few items in our code. If, for example, we look at a black cross on a white ground, we would not require items to transmit each pinprick of the black surface. It would be sufficient to have symbols for black and white, for example *1* and *0*, and to specify the places where there was an abrupt change from white to black and from black to white again. These changes we refer to as contours. Moreover, it is not necessary to denote every conceivable point on a contour in order to obtain an accurate representation of the cross when our code has been received and decoded. Information about the position of twelve critical points, the corners of the cross, will be sufficient. Thus, we could specify our cross very economically in terms of contours, and these in turn could be reduced to a series of items about abrupt changes in the direction of contours, it being otherwise assumed that the contour continued in the same direction. In Attneave's terms, information is concentrated along contours and where contours change direction. Recent physiological work (e.g. Hubel, 1962) would suggest that the visual system is organized in such a way as to make use of the redundancies found in the visual world. So long as the receptors are exposed to homogeneous stimulation, neural activity in the visual pathways and cortex is low, but when exposed to contours and discontinuities the rate of firing is increased.

A similar kind of analysis may be applied to *temporal* observation of contour. Where an edge is moving in a constant direction with uniform velocity, it is essentially predictable, its motion regular. We see its motion not as a series of discrete positions but as a smooth whole, until it changes direction or speed by some critical amount, whereafter we see it as a new movement until a new change in direction occurs. It can be seen that here again, if we are coding movement of a shape in space for transmission over a communication system, we need only specify the position at beginnning and end and the direction and speed of movement in order for it to be correctly interpreted after decoding by the receiver. It sometimes happens that after a discontinuity, the direction of movement is simply reversed and then is again reversed to produce the original movement, and so on several times. It will be appreciated that here again redundancy is involved. If the sequence recurs several times, we simply need a code item for the first movement, the same item with the sign reversed for the second, and a number to say how often the pair is repeated. We only need a new code item when a new direction of movement or of orientation of contour occur.

If we consider the body as a series of contours in three-dimensional space and activity as changes in the orientation and direction of these contours, it can be seen that what the visual system sees as Gestalten are the regularities which occur when the body is moving with a uniform velocity in a constant direction. The points at which we would need to recode our communication system (and the points at which the visual system may itself show a burst of information coding) are the points where direction of movement changes and where the orientation of the contours of the body change. These are the end points of movements, the changes of posture which we treat as behavioral elements. Where redundancy occurs, in the sense of the same movement being repeated again and again, we need not record every occurrence as a separate element, but simply record one behavioral element with an attached frequency or time label.

Interestingly, the everyday language we use for describing behavior recognizes both the discontinuities and the redundancies. There are many thousands of words which describe motor activities, such as running, jumping, butting, crying. Discontinuity, or the fact that the transition from one activity to the next is perceived as a step function, is shown by phrases, such as "He broke into a run," "He began to cry." Where we do not perceive changes from one behavior to another as step functions, but as slow transitions, we generally have another word to describe the transition itself. Redundancy is recognized by the use of words like 'running,' where we have only one word for what may be several hundred discrete paces; but it is only when the rate changes or the contours of the body change during the activity that we abandon the word 'running' and substitute 'galloping' or 'jogging.'

A complementary way of dissecting behavior into natural units is by definition of their functional regularities. Certain behavior patterns result in a particular effect upon the environment, an end result which is clear and decisive. One might say therefore that the goal of the behavior was the achievement of the particular end result, and a single pattern of behavior has ended when this result has been achieved. For example, one might delineate a particular pattern of behavior directed towards building bricks by reference to what structure is achieved with the blocks: 'builds tower,' 'joins two blocks,' 'places in circle,' and so on. This type of analysis tells however, only *what* was achieved, not *how* it was achieved. The everyday observation that similar ends may be achieved by very dissimilar means, should alert us to an appreciation that many data of possible significance are lost in this way. We have found for example that children with gross brain damage and normal children differ significantly from each other in terms of the number of different motor patterns exhibited in unit time, even when these motor patterns result in similar environmental effects (Hutt, *et al.*, 1965a).

The effects of a pattern of behavior need not be limited to the physical environment. Some behaviors are primarily socially directed, for example the 'displays' of animals to mates, enemies and young. Their goal appears to be to effect a change in the other animal observing the behavior. We might therefore take as our cutoff point for the end of a behavior sequence in animal one a subsequent change in the behavior of animal two, e.g. fleeing, attacking, or vocalizing.

This type of analysis in terms of functional units has been used to great effect by Altmann (1965) in a field study of social communication in rhesus monkeys:

> The first step in the study of rhesus communication was to draw up a catalogue of socially significant behaviour patterns of the members of the society. Such a catalogue is essentially what has been referred to in the literature as an 'ethogram,' except that we will specify two desiderata. First, the catalogue should completely and exclusively specify the behavioural repertoire of the species; that is, one and only one of the behaviour patterns should occur at each trial in every social interaction. Second, all the behaviour patterns that are included in the catalogue should be communicative; that is, their occurrence should affect the behaviour of other members of the social group. . . . Like other problems in classification, categorising the units of social behaviour involves two major problems: when to split and when to lump. If one's goal is to draw up an exclusive and exhaustive classification of the animal's repertoire of socially significant behaviour patterns, then these units of behaviour are not arbitrarily chosen. To the contrary, they can be empirically determined. One divides up the continuum of action whenever the animals do. If the resulting recombination units are themselves communicative, that is, if they affect the behaviour of other members of the social group, then they are social messages. Thus, the splitting and lumping that one does is, ideally, a reflection of the splitting and lumping that the animals do. In this sense, then, there are natural units of social behaviour (p.492).

It can be seen therefore that there are natural units of behavior whether these are specified in terms of morphological characteristics or in terms of functional characteristics. The former describe the patterns of behavior recruited by the animal, the latter what effects the behaviors have upon the environment. There are no insurmountable difficulties in recording both morphological and functional units simultaneously. In practice, both are necessary for a full analysis of behavior. Moreover, some behavioral abnormalities are manifested primarily in the morphological characteristics of behavior, and others by the specificity of the changes wrought upon the environment.

QUANTIFICATION OF BEHAVIORAL ELEMENTS

The problems of definition and measurement of behavioral elements are inextricably fused. It is obvious that we cannot measure what we cannot define. It is equally true that the way we define and record behavioral elements will be affected by the types of measurement we wish subsequently to apply to them. It is therefore appropriate briefly to digress at this juncture in order to consider the problem of measurement.

The division of behavioral elements in terms of morphology and function provides a useful framework for a classification of behavioral measurement. Behavior may be measured with respect to one or more of four parameters: frequency of occurrence, total duration, mean bout length, and rate. If we focus primarily upon the morphology of the behavior, we may count the frequency with which different motor patterns are recruited, measure the total amount of time spent in particular postures or in making particular movements, compute the mean duration of such movements, and calculate their velocity. If we focus upon the functional aspect of behavior, (i.e. what are its effects upon the environment), we may count the number of different stimuli sampled, measure the total amount of time spent in contact with a

TABLE I

SUMMARY OF MEASURES USED IN BEHAVIOR STUDIES
(FROM HUTT, *et al.*, 1965)

Measure	*Organismal Variables*	*Environmental Variables*
(1) Frequency	Number of different behavior patterns recruited in unit time = DEPLOYMENT	Number of stimuli engaged in unit time = SCOPE
(2) Mean Duration (span)	Duration of activity, e.g. running jumping hitting looking at = ACTIVITY SPAN	Duration of continuous engagement with same stimulus, e.g. blocks light switch sink radiator = ATTENTION SPAN
(3) Total time	Spent in each activity per session	Spent upon each stimulus per session
(4) Brilliance	Velocity of activity	Rate of change effected in stimulus

particular stimulus, compute the mean duration of contacts with each stimulus, and calculate the rate of change effected in a particular stimulus. A summary of the different measures is given in Table I. In practice a complete analysis of behavior will consist of a conjunction of the two classes of measurement, a particular action being related to its environmental consequences.

THE CONSTRUCTION OF A BEHAVIORAL REPERTOIRE

It is probably clear that the most likely source of difficulty lies in providing an accurate description of the behavior. Everyday language consists of many thousands of words which describe motor activities. Some of these will be transitive verbs, such as hitting, pulling, joining, and patting, and these clearly demand a stimulus object; others are intransitive verbs, such as running, jumping, crying, talking, and waving. These words will generally be used with remarkable consistency by two or more observers describing the behavior of the same person. Unfortunately, the words are injunctive concepts, learned by usage rather than by definition. Nevertheless, in principle they are amenable to definition and indeed the *Oxford English Dictionary* affords an excellent starting point for simple descriptive statements. Other useful sources of definitions may be found in the primate literature (Schaller, 1963; and de Vore, 1965, are useful source books). The most comprehensive dictionary of motor patterns in human children is that of W. C. McGrew, which at present consists of 111 items. We are privileged to be able to reproduce this in full in the Appendix of this book.

In general, the first order terminology of behavior consists of descriptive terms from everyday language. Where several, roughly synonymous terms exist, the one with fewest phonemes is taken. Terms for five main categories of movement are required:

1. Visual fixations, i.e. direction of fixations which last 1½ seconds or more;
2. Postures, i.e. orientation of the trunk and limbs while static relative to the horizon.
3. Locomotion, i.e. manner and direction of changing locus relative to fixed points on the ground.
4. Manipulation, i.e. what objects are manipulated and how; this includes moving objects with the hands or the feet.
5. Gestures, i.e. bodily movements which do *not* bring the child into contact with selected parts of the environment.

While watching a bout of activity or immediately afterwards, a list of brief activity words is written down. This is added to each time a further bout is observed. In practice it is found useful to write each activity word at the top of a filing card. An attempt is then made to write a brief but terse definition of the activity word. As more bouts are observed, it is frequently found that some definitions are overinclusive in that they cover patterns of behavior for which ordinary language has two or more terms.

The fact that we have, in ordinary language, words for two actions which are similar, usually means that there are components present in one which are absent in the other, and it is in principle possible to specify these differences. Two sharper and mutually exclusive definitions are then framed, headed by their appropriate descriptive term. On the other hand, it is legitimate to use one term to describe two or more slightly variant forms of infrequently occurring behavior, such as head scratching, provided that the head scratching card contains both definitions. Referring to the same problem within a social context, Altmann (1965) remarks:

> One sometimes observes two or more variations of what was initially thought to be a single pattern. . . . The rule of thumb, then, is to split when in doubt. Later, if the differences between the categories do not appear to be significant, the categories can be lumped. But if during observation one has lumped what are, in fact, distinct patterns, then nothing can be done to recover the lost data.

At this stage, reliability checks of the activity vocabulary are undertaken. If a permanent record of some behavioral sequences is available, intraobserver reliability checks may be carried out. The film or video recording is played back several times. Each time a separate protocol is constructed consisting of sequences of activity words, each with an identificatory time label corresponding with the appropriate part of the permanent record (in the case of film records, the frame numbers; in the case of video records, the time-counter readings). By comparing the protocols, it is possible to check that on each occasion the permanent record was analyzed, the same cutoff points between behavior items was made and the same activity words were used to describe the behavior.

Without permanent visual records of behavior, the problem of checking the behavioral vocabulary becomes more difficult. This is especially so for the investigator who works alone, using either tape recordings, or written records. Such a person we can only refer again to the passage by Darling (1937), quoted at the beginning of this chapter. Only by intimate and sustained contact with his subjects can the lone investigator hope to evolve a consistent and reliable activity vocabulary. Where two or more investigators are involved in a joint study, the checking of vocabularly is much easier, even without permanent records. Two investigators observing the same subject together can quickly ascertain for what behaviors they use the same or different words and where disagreement occurs can set about analyzing the nature of the disagreement. This may be simply the result of forgetting a term or a definition; or may be the result of differential observing. One observer sees certain components in a behavioral sequence more readily than the other. In such a case it is fairly easy to agree about the components one observer is seeing and which the other is missing. This may in turn lead to a

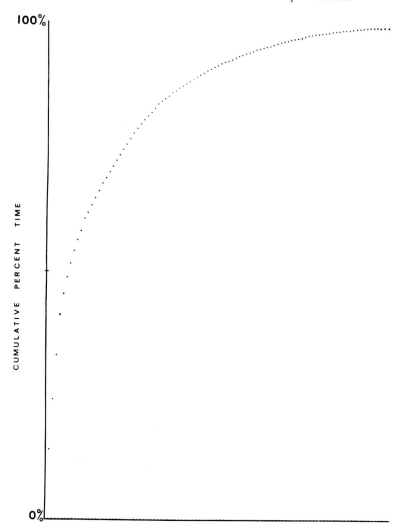

RANK ORDER OF OCCURRENCE OF BEHAVIOUR PATTERNS

FIGURE 3. Cumulative percent time spent in different behavior patterns relative to their rank order by frequency of occurrence.

modification in the activity vocabulary; either a new word is coined or an extra definition is added to an already existing activity word. These problems are closely connected with that of interobserver reliability, which is treated in the next chapter.

The problem of whether a catalogue of behavior elements is or is not exhaustive has been discussed by Altmann (1965). "The obvious solution here is to have an open catalogue, that is, one to which new categories can be added *ad libitum.*" Altmann points out that his own initial catalogue of the behavior elements of the rhesus monkey contained only thirty-six items. "As patterns were seen that were not in the catalogue, yet which seemed to be communicative, they were recorded and added to the catalogue. By the end of our study, some 123 patterns had been observed." It will be remembered that McGrew's catalogue consists of 111 morphologically distinct items. The catalogue was constructed on the assumption that every identifiably different element of behavior was equally important. If, however, we plot a cumulative percentage curve of total time (Y) against number of elements in the catalogue (X) an interesting relationship emerges (Fig. 3); approximately 60 percent of the total time is accounted for by only ten movements; 75 percent by twenty movements and 95 percent by sixty movements, or less than half the behavioral repertoire. Thus while the catalogue of motor elements is in principle infinitely expandable, in practice effectively the whole of a child's motor activity could be subsumed under sixty categories.

It clearly would be unwise to assume that items of behavior with a low frequency of occurrence are unimportant. In terms of their social effects such items contain considerably more information than more frequently occurring items: so-called Protean displays (Chance, and Russell, 1959) are of this kind and have dramatic effects upon predators and conspecifics. Nevertheless, for many purposes, e.g. examination of the effects of drugs, that part of the behavioral repertoire which most commonly is displayed by most subjects is of greater utility than more idiosyncratic behaviors. A cumulative percent time curve enables a decision to be made as to when a behavioral repertoire shall be declared closed on the basis of how much of the total time is accounted for. In this way, a catalogue can be kept within manageable limits.

Chapter 4

METHODS AND TECHNIQUES I:
TAPE RECORDING

THE behavioral scientist, beginning his studies of any species, requires a preparatory period of acquaintance with his animal of study. This should be true equally of the observer of cockroaches and of children. The process of interpretation from behavioral recording and analysis is essentially the same whatever the species, and no amount of special pleading should make it more legitimate for the observer to dispense with these training procedures in studying members of his own species. Furthermore, it is necessary to develop or use a method of recording which is systematic and reliable; this is particularly so when the object of study is a member of the primate class, since variability and not stereotypy is one of its very characteristics.

When initiating such studies, the use of motion pictures would be both premature and uneconomical. The use both of check lists and of event recorders presupposes the formulation of well-defined and clearly delineated behavior categories, which in turn presupposes more than a superficial acquaintance with the data. A verbal, contemporaneous description of events recorded on magnetic tape avoids any such presuppositions; moreover, in the very act of using this technique, one can additionally familiarize oneself with the behavioral data.

The method of recording a spoken commentary on magnetic tape has much to recommend it. We have all at some time or other described another person's actions; the amount of detail supplied by different individuals may vary, but the process is familiar and comes naturally to most of us. Furthermore, the broadcasting media have demonstrated that even intricately complex and rapidly occurring events can be simultaneously and accurately covered by an able commentator. A great deal of experience may be required before a performance as accomplished as those of these commentators is achieved, but the process has been shown to be feasible. The nature and degree of selectivity imposed upon the recording depends upon the scope of the study. In general, tape-recording seems the most suitable means of recording behavior in a free-field situation.

Essentially the method consists of uttering an abbreviated commentary as contemporaneously as possible with the occurrence of the respective acts.

The abbreviation can simply be achieved by omission of the words and phrases which are unnecessary. Predicates and objects are the definitive utterances; additional description is optional.

For purposes of analysis the tape is transcribed since it is useful to have a written record when timing the various acts, postures or sequences. Since the tape is replayed at the original recording speed, it is a reasonable assumption that the time lapsed from the beginning of the utterance denoting act A and the beginning of the following utterance denoting act B is the duration of A.

It is not always necessary however to transcribe the entire record, particularly if there is a plentiful supply of tapes. In such cases the tape may be analyzed in the same manner as a motion picture, a specific category being extracted on each playback. The relative proportions of time spent in different forms of locomotion (i.e. running, walking, or crawling), and the average duration of any of these individual locomotor acts, or the total time spent in locomotion, can all be obtained on a single playback of the tape by noting down the type of each locomotor act and its duration. Quite often it may be economical of time and effort to carry out an analysis in this manner, particularly if not much qualitative detail is required.

ILLUSTRATIVE RESULTS

Animal Studies

Many animal studies which have utilized direct observation in accumulating their behavior data nevertheless omit to specify details of the recording techniques. Most often we are told *where* or *when* observations were made (e.g. Rowell, 1967; Brown, *et al.*, 1967) but not *how*. The authors may refer to entries in notebooks, diary records or written observations, but details of criteria for selection of the populations, of sampling methods, or of form of record are lacking. Such omissions are presumably due to the fact that the behavior of many animals is relatively stereotyped, hence easily recognizable and identifiable. Problems of reliability are therefore reduced, although many workers, particularly in the primate field, are very much concerned with these questions.

When such details of recording and analysis are available, the studies invariably turn out to be investigations of social behavior. Although social behavior is specifically dealt with in a later chapter, two related studies will be referred to in this chapter, since one is concerned with methodological issues germane to the study of human behavior, and the other deals with some interesting postures and expressive movements.

The Behavior of Macaques

Kaufman and Rosenblum (1966) were concerned with drawing up a catalogue of behavioral elements or ethogram for two species of monkeys (namely, pigtails, *Macaca nemestrina* and bonnets, *Macaca radiata*).

Rightly, they wished to have such an inventory of normative behavior in naturalistic surroundings before attempting to evaluate the effects of experimental manipulation upon behavioral categories.

Much the same reasoning as our own apparently determined their method of observation:

> Inasmuch as behavioral events occur with a certain repetitiveness, last for varying intervals at each occurrence, seem to be sequentially ordered, and are directed at the self or other objects of the physical or social environment, and since our experimental procedures might produce effects reflected in any one or more of these measures, we selected a system which could provide the frequency, duration and object of each behavior, as well as the sequence of behaviors for a given animal and, to a limited extent, the interaction between animals (p. 207).

The system consisted of direct observation with a continuous commentary dictated on to tape. These authors were considerably aided by the taxonomic systems already developed for other related species, and wherever appropriate they retained already existing terminology and descriptions. Otherwise they attempted to provide an "exact description of each behavior and a title that would embody the description." Beginning, end, nature, and object of a behavior were dictated. The units of the observational system were discrete patterns such as bite, stare, and autogrooming. Each animal had a number and each behavior a code name; thus 2-1 socex = animal 2 performs social exploration to animal 1. The tape ran in parallel with an electric clock, so that when the tape was replayed, exact durations of activities could be obtained.

The individual behavior units were classed together with other behaviors achieving similar ends, e.g. threat, stare, and brow movement were part of the category *intimidation*. In turn, Intimidation together with Attack and Pursuit formed the larger category of Hierarchical Behaviors, i.e. behaviors which are directed towards establishing or maintaining the individual's position in the social hierarchy by intimidating or submitting to other individuals. These generic categories were defined by different criteria: in the case of Hierarchical Behaviors, it is by functional characteristics, whereas in the case of maternal behaviors, it would be by the identity of the actor. Heuristically this seems a legitimate procedure so long as the heterogeneity of the classificatory criteria is made explicit. These authors, moreover, are well aware of the desirability of comparable taxonomic groups, each based, for example, on a single motivational system. An admirable attempt has been made to give operational definitions for most of the behaviors, e.g. attack = "any act which causes physical insult to another animal"; brow movement = "slow or rapid retraction of scalp and brow, often with accompanying ear movements." In cases where there are differences in degrees of expression of a behavior, however, the definitive distinctions are less adequate.

For instance Threat is defined thus:

A varied communicative pattern which may include opening of the mouth with exposure of the teeth, thrusting the head forward, flattening the ears against the head and retracting the brow; the body is generally held stiff and upright and is thrust forward.

The authors however omit to state which of these elements is (are) necessary and sufficient for the recognition of this display. Furthermore, as the illustrations (Figs. 4 and 5) show, threat can be of high or of low intensity, one clearly differentiated from the other. Here the authors could perhaps have specified the extremes of this expression in greater detail: in terms of

FIGURE 4. A threat of relatively high intensity by a bonnet male monkey (after Kaufman, and Rosenblum, 1966).

extent of mouth opening, degree of retraction of ears and upper lip, position of tail, etc. But this is a small deficiency in comparison with their informative attempts.

This taxonomy was utilized by the authors (Rosenblum, *et al.*, 1966) in a quantitative and comparative study of grooming in the same two species. Grooming is an important social behavior, but it can also be directed at the animal's own body. Two groups of bonnet and two groups of pigtail monkeys were studied, each group comprising one adult male and four adult females. The observational technique was as described, each animal being the focus of observation for two 90-second periods on any one day. The grooming activities were defined as follows:

Social grooming: Careful picking through and/or slow brushing aside of the fur of a partner with one or both forepaws. The material that is picked out, if any, such as small hairs and flakes of skin, may be placed into the mouth.

Autogrooming: The same behavior as above except directed at the subject's own body (p. 440).

The results were in terms of mean daily durations of grooming in each group. The differences between the groups of a species were too great to allow clear differences between species to be demonstrated, suggesting that group composition and structure is more important than species differences in determining the incidence of these behaviors.

FIGURE 5. A low level, hesitant threat by the same animal
(after Kaufman, and Rosenblum, 1966)

Bouts of social grooming were found to be much longer than bouts of autogrooming (mean durations of 36.4 seconds and 16.7 seconds respectively). Female animals, irrespective of species, showed considerably more social grooming than males. The authors were unable to find a clear relationship between the initiation or receipt of social grooming and dominance or subordinance of the participants. This is rather surprising in view of the traditional assumption of a correlation between low dominance rank and initiation of grooming in most primate species.

Many other studies, notably those by Brockway (1964) on the ethology of the budgerigar, Grant (1963) and Grant and Mackintosh (1963) on the laboratory rat, Rosenblum, *et al.* (1964) on monkeys, which have utilized tape recordings for their observations, have largely or exclusively concentrated upon social behaviors. Some of these will be referred to subsequently in Chapter 7.

Human Studies

Advances in methods are largely determined by technological innovations. The advent of sound tape recorders being such an innovation, it should have revolutionized the field of behavior study. On the contrary, it seems to have had relatively little impact in this respect, largely due perhaps to the lingering disillusion over the observational studies of the early developmental psychologists. The methods and techniques of direct observation were pioneered by workers such as Olson (1929), Thomas (1929), and Arrington (1932). Many early studies of children's behavior used some form of written commentary or record of activities as they occurred. Unfortunately, conceptually these workers operated at a molar level, their behavior data were often subjective, inferential and interpretative. Escalona, *et al.*, (1952) went so far as to make a virtue of this subjective element and even used a particular observer's predilections as part of the data; in her study clearly inferential statements, e.g. "baby focussed upon mother's face in his usual impassive way," had the same status as an objective fact, e.g. "baby sucks bottle."

It seems too that an unfair dividend was expected of this method. In her review Gellert (1955) supposes that the popularity of the system declined because it was time consuming and did not lend itself to measurement of "some of the more elusive but often more interesting aspects of human personality such as presence of guilt feelings"; at the same time she complained that "systematic observation also lacks the clean, decisive flavor of an experiment." In consequence, and contrary to expectation, the advent of magnetic tapes did not result in an increase in the number and variety of observational studies; the very methods they would have facilitated had already fallen into disrepute.

These seriatim observational studies of the 1930's therefore are of some historic interest, and although the technical problems of the spoken and written commentary are by no means the same, the general orientation, as well as the conceptual and content analyses have a great deal of affinity. For this reason two studies using written observations are included in this chapter.

Measuring Emotionality in Infants

Bridges (1934) used the method of systematic observation in studying the emotionality of infants in their natural surroundings. During ten 1-hour observation periods, distributed over a month, she made descriptive records of the nature, duration and frequency of the infant's emotional reactions and of the situations that provoked them. Timing was done with the aid of a stop watch. "Short cries or fleeting smiles too rapid to time accurately were arbitrarily counted as of 2 secs duration. Many cries and smiles satisfactorily measured lasted about so long."

The responses were recorded in two columns, one for all forms of distress and the other for all forms of delight or enjoyment. The distress responses consisted of tearful crying, rigid tension and arrested activity, fretful whining or grunting, and furious banging. The frequency and total duration of the distressful and joyous reactions were calculated separately for each child and compared with the medians for the group.

Bridges made a distinction between directly and indirectly expressed emotions: for distress these were respectively (1) tearful crying with puckered face and (2) arrested movement, body stiffness, pouting, grunting, frowning; for delight they were (1) smiles and laughter, and (2) shouting, thumb sucking, jumping up and down, patting, etc.

The results primarily showed up individual quantitative differences in emotional expression; a very few infants showed very little emotion of either kind, whereas others showed either brief and frequent outbursts or prolonged excitement.

Although one might contest the validity of the categorization (e.g. is thumb sucking unequivocally associated with delight, and may it not frequently occur as a displacement activity?), the author herself was well aware of the arbitrariness of this classification. In view of this it would seem more legitimate to consider the frequency and duration of the individual response. Nevertheless, the concern with a problem of this kind, as well as the attempt at a systematic execution of such a study as long as twenty-five years ago, is remarkable.

Play of Preschool Children

Cockrell (1935) too was limited to written seriatim observations, but her emphases in recording and analysis were very similar to our own.

The investigation was concerned with questions of what effects changes in the children's play environment had upon their behavior, and what their reactions were to different play materials. Six children between the ages of two and one-half and three years were observed, each with every other child as well as individually, in six play settings, in each of which the following different materials were provided:

1. Bare room with only table and two chairs.
2. House-keeping materials: two baby dolls with blankets and carriages for each, crockery and chest containing dolls' clothes.
3. Blocks: three kinds of blocks available.
4. Story books and pictures cut from magazines.
5. Two lumps of clay, two boards, two boxes of crayons and two blocks of paper.
6. All material above combined.

The children were free to terminate the sessions themselves.

Preliminary diary-type records were later replaced by slightly more formalized records. The observations were made from behind a one-way screen and recorded in parallel columns for two children at a time. Some selectivity was imposed upon the recording, special emphasis being given to: (1) material approached or attended to, (2) time of approach, (3) shifts in activity while with material, and (4) time of shift in activity. For example, the activities and their durations of two children playing together were recorded as follows:

Andrew		Barbara	
Andrew continues with his clay		Holds a piece toward Andrew	2.25
Pats clay flat	2.45		
Rolls it between his		"I make a rabbit"	
hand	2.50		
Continues rolling clay			
Still rolling	3.10	Also pats	2.50
Presses it on to his		Pats her clay again	3.00
lump			
"I'm through"	3.30		
		Holds a piece toward Andrew	3.20
		"I'm not"	(p. 405)

After computation, the results were given in a graph showing how the child had allocated his time in successive minutes over the environmental static fixtures as well as the individual play objects. Cockrell's definitions of interest span and activity are very similar to our own definitions of attention span and activity span (given later in this chapter): "a child was considered to have shifted his interest when he turned from one toy to another," and activity is clearly defined in terms of motor patterns, although this is not explicitly stated.

... the observation made for Andrew between 1.50 and 3.30 is tabulated as:

Clay
2 pieces together
pinches
moulds
pats
rolls
presses

In the record it will be seen that "rolls" is recorded three times, but it is called only one 'activity' under 'clay' in the chart, for though it continued long enough to be mentioned three times, there was no change in the activity (p. 415).

Thus the author counted pats as one activity, rolls as another, presses as another, and so on.

A number of interesting findings emerged from this study. In terms of activities the greatest variety (i.e. number of different activities) was seen in the clay-and-crayons situation and the least in the bare room. Clay-and-crayons also elicited the longest average interest or attention span, while the shortest attention span was observed in the bare room (see also Hutt, *et al.*, 1965). The time spent with extraneous objects was lowest with clay-and-crayons and highest in the bare room. In terms of interest or holding power, housekeeping materials did only slightly better than the bare room. This is a particularly salient finding, not least for its unexpectedness.

Considering that this study must have been carried out about thirty-five years ago, the agreement between many of its findings and our own, as well as the methodological affinity, seems quite remarkable.

Analysis of Play Patterns

In sharp contrast to the objectivity and succinctness of the previous study is one which appears to be characterized by obscurity and equivocality. This study by Loomis, *et al.* (1957) is informative in that, from our viewpoint of behavior studies, it illustrates in a negative manner many of the points we have hitherto attempted to emphasize.

These workers were concerned with obtaining "verifiable methods of recording non-verbal behavior which make it susceptible to comparison from period to period, child to child, observer to observer." Their hypothesis was that certain defects and distortions in play were associated with behavior disorders in childhood. They thus observed three groups of children at play: psychotics, defectives, and normals. An adult examiner adopting a fairly passive role remained with the children in the playroom while observations were made from behind a one-way mirror. The room contained a table, two chairs and a box of toys. (Later on the toys were grouped in three corners of the room). A running account of the child's behavior was dictated (presumably into a tape recorder) and the records were subsequently transcribed. Three methods of scoring were used. In the first, data from the typewritten protocols were transferred to tabular charts. "the vertical of this page listed arbitrarily selected concrete examples of behavior predicted to demonstrate each of the following ego functions: perception, motility control, memory, communication, reality testing and contact, and the executive function of the ego." The second method of scoring apparently consisted of condensing the seven pages of the previous system to one page, "to make possible the cross-scoring of interactions and relationships." It is not clear how the scoring was done, but categories were added or subtracted depending upon their discriminative power. The third method consists of using a five-point rating scale to rate ten aspects of behavior, or in the somewhat pretentious language of the authors, "adds verifiable holistic and judgmental elements" to the first two methods. Some of the ten scales are given below:

I. The scales related to the inanimate
   A. *Construction-Transportation.* On this scale we rate activities of the child in which he demonstrates

1) constructing, combining, and containing; and/or

2) transporting and positioning.

B. *Nurture-Body Representation.* B behavior is humanizing or personifying the inanimate, giving human shape, form or function to the nonhuman.

C. *Disruption-Deanimation.* This scale measures the extent to which the child is involved in fragmentation, disruption, and using equipment with an obvious animation potential as if unaware of or actively avoiding the latter.

II. The scales related to the animate

E. *Proximity to Examiner's Body.* This scale is primarily rated on a topographical basis; i.e. lessening of distance between child's and examiner's body increases the score.

S. *Autoerotic or Body Involvement.* This scale measures the extent to which evident body pleasure and body stimulation are self-induced by the child.

RS. *Social Relationship with Examiner.* This scale seeks to identify attempts by the child to involve himself with, communicate with and/or become overtly aware of the examiner as an animate, personalized being capable of responding physically and/or verbally to the child's overtures in the here-and-now setting. (p. 696/697)

A score on each scale was assigned per three-minute period and plotted on a graph (time on abscissa and rating on ordinate), animate interactions being plotted below and inanimate interactions above the zero line. Illustrative profiles characteristic of each type of subject are provided by the authors. But since the criteria by which the scales are rated are not expounded, it is difficult to interpret the profiles. One thing that seems clear however is that the psychotic child shows more frequent, more intense, longer lasting autoerotic behaviors. In the absence of more specific information, any interpretation is equally likely and equally permissible. The authors conclude that "this method of study will lead to a new and effective discriminator between schizophrenia and mental deficiency in perhaps otherwise untestable children," but it is difficult to share their optimism.

This study was hardly distinguished by its perspicuity. The authors' conceptual confusion was regrettable. Strictly separate levels of discourse were treated as a uniform system, and the critical distinction between observable and demonstrable phenomena on the one hand, and abstract categorizations, hypothetical constructs or inferences on the other seemed to have been overlooked. The discriminant power of their recording techniques was disproportionate to the heterogeneous and interpretative categories used in analysis. Moreover, the preconceptions of the authors constrained them to the extent of finding certain kinds of differences between the groups, thereby precluding the emergence of significant data extrinsic to their conceptual system. It is difficult to concur with, even if they could be comprehended, such statements as: "Through play, reality can be met obliquely instead of head-on, and thereby the child can shift from past reality to future reality to fantasy and unreality and back to present setting without harsh clashing of gears."

Studies of Children's Free Field Behavior

RECORDING

In our studies the child was observed from an adjoining room through a one-way mirror and a behavior commentary made on to a two-channel tape recorder. The aim was to make the activity commentary as coincident as possible with the occurrence of the behavior. An activity was defined in terms of the motor patterns involved. Thus wrist rotation with fingers grasping an object was defined as turning, whether this was done in a horizontal plane as with a block, or in the vertical plane (with door knob); alternate semiextension and palmar flexion of the fingers against a surface was defined as scratching, whether this was against the head, leg, floor or block. After some weeks of recording, it was possible to stylize the dictation, omitting all redundant words, so that the commentary consisted primarily of activity words, such as running, scratching, throwing. Other qualifying and specifying terms included names of limbs, left/right, stimulus objects (e.g. door, tap, block), and locational numbers.

It was also possible to use certain shorthand terms, which further helped to abbreviate the commentary. This was particularly so with respect to postures. For example, a frequently recurring posture was one initially described as sitting left leg tucked under body, right leg outstretched, supporting trunk on left arm outstretched; this was subsequently abbreviated to sitting side position left. Many preparatory observation sessions were necessary before such abbreviations were evolved.

Only directly observable behavior was recorded, without resort to statements about the presumed feelings or motivations of the child. Terms, such as anxious, happy, angry, were never used, as they imply inferences rather than observables about the child's emotions; nor were intentional concepts as withdrawal or avoidance. In some cases it is easier and perhaps more natural to use such terms, but the observer must simply state the observed behavior, e.g. stands still, face whitens, lips tremble, fists clenched, shoulders hunched. Although this may seem a somewhat pedantic procedure, to do otherwise would be to beg the question, since one of the questions under investigation is whether in fact all these elements do occur together when we think the child is fearful or is in a specific situational context.

CONVENTIONS

In the development of such a stylized commentary, the purpose of the investigations is critical in determining the conventions to be applied. In studies of free-field behavior in general, amount and speed of movement, length of attention spans, and nature and duration of specific activities are usually more informative than more static aspects, like postures. Thus when the behavior becomes too complex or occurs too rapidly, as is invariably the case with young children, some selection has to be made. Since this selectivity is not arbitrary but based upon certain conventions, it need not detract from the validity of the recording. In our studies we decided to concentrate primarily upon those categories enumerated in Chapter 3. In the event of several movements or activities occurring concurrently, postures were given the lowest priority. Clearly the nature of the selectivity will be determined by the purpose of the study. In a study of expressive behavior for example, eye, brow, and mouth movements, postures and head movements would have had priority over locomotion.

Since it was essential to record activity synchronously with the occurrence of the behavior, it was necessary to omit all dispensable terminology. Thus direction of visual fixation was assumed to be synchronous with the object of manipulation and hence would only be recorded if different from it. For example, 'opens door' or 'taps radiator' would have a fixation statement attached only if the direction of fixation were other than at the door or the radiator.

RELIABILITY AND VALIDITY

It is important that such a method should be easily and reliably used by an observer. With a two-channel tape recorder, two observers can independently but simultaneously record a child's behavior and the degree of concordance can be subsequently assessed from transcripts. The level of agreement achieved by two observers is illustrated from the following analysis of a typical protocol:

No. of observations identical in content made within 1 second of each other.	78 (86%)
No. of observations different in content made within 1 second of each other.	2 (2%)
No. of observations identical in content but separated by more than 1 second.	9 (10%)
No. of observations recorded by one observer but not the other.	2 (2%)

It will be seen that there was remarkably good agreement regarding content, i.e. the nature of the behavior. For the study as a whole, this agreement was 95 percent. Discrepancies arose chiefly over the timing, but as these were of the order of two seconds, they were minimized with practice.

ANALYSIS

A written transcript was made of the tape recording. Termination of activities (as defined in Ch. 3) was indicated by double vertical strokes on the transcript; termination of attention spans was indicated by a red stroke.

What has been briefly outlined in Chapter 3 perhaps needs some expansion here. An activity was defined in terms of its morphology: its appear-

Direct Observation and Measurement of Behavior

TABLE II

TRANSCRIPT OF THE TAPE-RECORDED COMMENTARY MADE DURING A 3-MIN
SESSION (STROKES INDICATE TERMINATION OF ACTIVITY SPANS,
THE DURATIONS OF WHICH ARE NOTED BY EACH STROKE)

Standing 4 looking bricks, holding wire $9\frac{1}{2}$ // walks 7/8 twirling $2\frac{1}{2}$ // looking bricks $2\frac{1}{2}$ // walks to screen 15
4 // turns to O's call, walks 10/11 $3\frac{1}{2}$ // twirling, looking bricks twirling 11 7 // walks 10/11 to 2 2 // bangs
wall 2 // looking bricks, twirling 5/6 4 // walks 7 picks brick 2 // runs screen 15, puts brick in mouth and
bangs on screen 6 // rubbing screen walks 13 to 9 3 // puts brick window $2\frac{1}{2}$ // standing 5 bangs brick on
window 2 // turns throws brick 15 and goes after it 4 // picks up brick 15 throws at 0 4 // walks 8, climbs
on chair 6 // sitting chair, looks screen to 0 to window $3\frac{1}{2}$ // looks at brick $5\frac{1}{2}$ // gets off chair walks 7 $2\frac{1}{2}$ // picks
up brick throws at screen $4\frac{1}{2}$ // banging screen walks 13/14 3 // throws brick at 0 2 // turns, runs 8, climbs
chair $4\frac{1}{2}$ // stands arm of chair holding door frame 8 // jumps on seat, turns $3\frac{1}{2}$ // bangs window holding on
to chair 9 // turns to O's signal, reaches for O's brick $3\frac{1}{2}$ // sits chair looking over side at floor 13 // looks
window 2 // looks ceiling, leaning over back of chair, hand in mouth 5 // looks door 8 // gets off chair looking 12 4 // walks 13 3 // stands 13 biting jumper looking corner 8 // turns, walks 13 to 9 to 5, biting jumper
while walking to 6 to 7 10 // throws brick to 16 3 // twirls $3\frac{1}{2}$ // walks 16 to 15 $4\frac{1}{2}$ // picks brick throws it to 1
$2\frac{1}{2}$ // walks to 8 climbs on to chair 5 //

ance or outward characteristics, and its intensity and/or amplitude. An attention span on the other hand was delineated entirely by the stimulus involved. The distinction is best illustrated by an example. A child might throw a block across the room, look at the other blocks for some seconds and then build a tower by placing the blocks on top of each other. In this case throwing, looking, and building were three different activities, but since they were all directed to the same stimulus, namely blocks, they all formed one attention span.

After the transcript had been marked, the tape was replayed, and the duration of each activity timed with a stop watch. The times were indicated alongside the appropriate stroke; the relevant activity spans could then be summed to give the attention span. Such a timed transcript protocol of an entire session is given in Table II.

In practice it was found that any activities or visual fixations shorter than 1.5 seconds could not be reliably timed; they were thus incorporated in the subsequent activity. Such activities consisted of fleeting glances, perhaps while some other activity was in progress, or transitory movements, such as turning, which were often a prelude to the subsequent activities. In addition when a child looked away from the task in hand for a period of 2 seconds or more (e.g. looking at observer or light), he was judged to have switched his attention, even if he returned to the original activity. Such an operational definition of attention switching is in accordance with the conventions used by workers in the vigilance field and in such experiments as that on mind wandering by Cohen, *et al.* (1956).

3{ The data were then transferred to an analysis sheet (Table III): visual fixations (in terms of object fixated and its duration) were entered in the left hand column; manipulations (nature, duration and object), were entered in the central column; locomotion occupied the column on the right. (A separate column could register attention spans or could be read off directly from the transcript.) All entries on the same horizontal line occurred simultaneously. Locomotion or mobility could also be plotted on a scale floor plan of the room; the lines of movements could then be measured to give a rate of movement (Fig. 6).

TABLE III

ANALYSIS SHEET OF THE TRANSCRIPT SHOWN IN TABLE II

Visual	*Time*	*Manipulation*	*Time*	*Mobility*	*Time*
bricks	$9\frac{1}{2}$	holding wire	$9\frac{1}{2}$		
nonspecific	$2\frac{1}{2}$	twirling	$2\frac{1}{2}$		
bricks	$2\frac{1}{2}$				
screen	4			walking	4
O	$3\frac{1}{2}$			walks	$3\frac{1}{2}$
bricks	7	twirling	7		
nonspecific	2			walks	2
wall	2	banging wall	2		
bricks	4 ⎫ 6			twirling	4
bricks	2 ⎬	picks b	2		
screen	6 ⎭ 9	b in mouth,	2	runs	4
	3	bangs screen			
		rubbing screen	3		
brick	$2\frac{1}{2}$ ⎫	b on window	$2\frac{1}{2}$		
brick	2 ⎬ $8\frac{1}{2}$	bangs b on window	2	runs	2
brick	4 ⎭	throws b	2		
chair	6			walks and climbs	6
scanning	$3\frac{1}{2}$				
brick	$5\frac{1}{2}$ ⎫ 8			walks	$2\frac{1}{2}$
brick	$2\frac{1}{2}$ ⎬				
screen	$4\frac{1}{2}$ ⎬	throws b at screen	$4\frac{1}{2}$	walks	3
screen	3 ⎭ $7\frac{1}{2}$	banging screen	3		
O	2	throws b at O	2		
chair	$4\frac{1}{2}$			runs and climbs	4
door	8 ⎫ $11\frac{1}{2}$			climbs	8
door	$3\frac{1}{2}$ ⎭			jumps on chair	$3\frac{1}{2}$
window	9	banging window	9		
O	$3\frac{1}{2}$	b from O	$3\frac{1}{2}$		
floor	13			(sitting)	
window	2				
ceiling	5	hand in mouth	5	(leaning back)	
door	2 ⎫ 6				
door	4 ⎭			climbing down	4
13	3			walking	3
corner	8	biting jersey	8 ⎫ 18		
nonspecific	10	biting jersey	10 ⎭	walks	10
brick	3	throws b	3		
nonspecific	$3\frac{1}{2}$ ⎫ 8			twirling	$3\frac{1}{2}$
nonspecific	$4\frac{1}{2}$ ⎭			walks	$4\frac{1}{2}$
brick	$2\frac{1}{2}$	throws b	$2\frac{1}{2}$		
chair	5			walks and climbs	5

N. B. b = brick;
O = observer

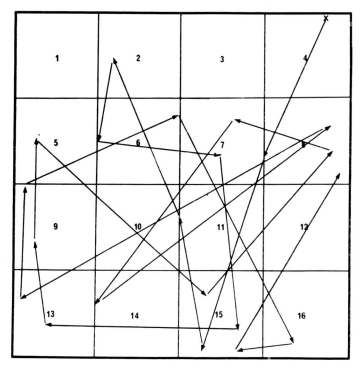

Figure 6. Mobility plot of a five-year-old hyperkinetic girl during three minute period in a room empty except for the fixtures and a box of playing blocks.

Situation and Procedure

We decided to first simplify as much as possible the environment in which the children were studied and then to see what effects increasing complexity would have on behavior. Four environmental conditions, A, B, C and D, were used. A was a well-illuminated waiting room from which the furniture had been removed but which still retained a number of fixtures, as seen in Figure 7. The floor had a squared covering, each square (1 yard by 1 yard) having a reference number. In B a box of coloured blocks was present. In C, in addition to the blocks, an observer who was already known to the children sat in square 8 but remained passive and relatively unresponsive throughout the session. In D the observer attempted to engage the child in building a standard design with the blocks. Each child was studied individually and in all four conditions, though the order of these was systematically varied over all the subjects. Each condition lasted three minutes; this duration was empirically determined, being a reasonable period for which to leave a child on his own without provoking anxiety. The instructions given to the children were: "Would you wait here a few minutes while I fetch some blocks?" (in A if A was first condition); "Would you like to stay here for me while I put these (blocks) away?" (In other A's); "Would you

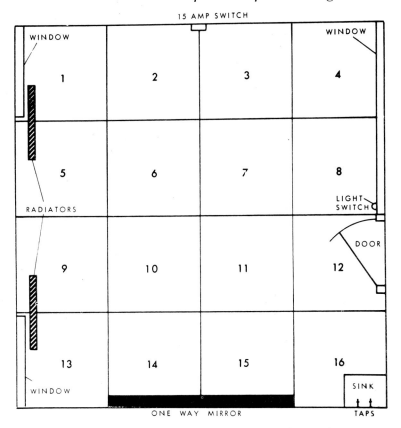

FIGURE 7. Plan of room (from Hutt, *et al.*, 1965).

like to play with these (blocks) while I put some things away?" (in B). Except in D the child was free to wander around the room and the door was left unlocked so that he could leave the room if he wished.

RESULTS

The behavior of children with and without upper central nervous system lesions. This method of recording and analysis was found to be particularly appropriate to the study of children with generalized brain damage, usually resulting from birth trauma, measles, encephalitis, meningitis, etc. (Hutt, *et al.*, 1965). In practice children were diagnosed as brain damaged only when at least two of the following three criteria were satisfied:

1. Classical neurological signs.
2. History of gross cerebral insult.
3. Specific electroencephalographic abnormalities.

Many of these children had already been found untestable by traditional psychometric methods.

Twelve brain-damaged children between the ages of three and eight years were compared with twelve children with no cerebral pathology (hereafter called normal for convenience) matched for age and sex. Each group was further divided into older and younger subgroups, with a cutoff point of five and one-half years. The results of two behavior categories will be presented here; similar results of other categories will be presented later in the chapter.

GESTURES. Gestures were defined as bodily movements which did not bring the child into contact with selected parts of the physical environment, e.g. rocking, picking the nose, and waving. When gestures were examined in detail, they were seen to be of three kinds: (1) manipulation of parts of the body, (2) complex patterns of movement involving coordination of several muscle groups, e.g. shadow-boxing, and dancing, and (3) single movements, such as flexing a leg or nodding the head. Only in situation A did gestures appear to any appreciable extent in the normal children. The relative frequencies with which the three kinds of gestures were manifested by the different children is shown in Figure 8. In the older, normal children body manipulations and complex patterns occurred far more often and for longer pe-

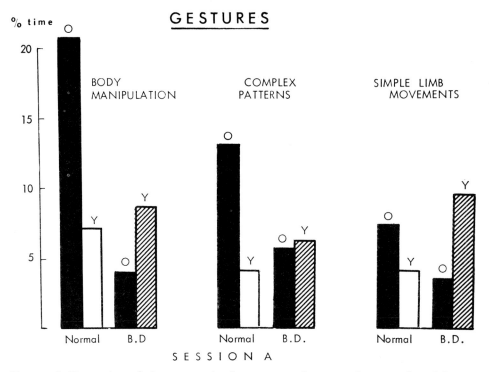

FIGURE 8. Proportion of time spent in three types of gesture by normal and brain-damaged children during a three minute session in an empty room. (O = older; Y = younger) (from Hutt, *et al.*, 1965).

riods than in the other groups; the differences between the older and younger normals were significant for both these categories. The younger normals were not found to differ from the brain-damaged group. There was no significant difference between any of the four subgroups with respect to simple movements.

Some normal children showed long complicated rituals consisting of body manipulation, separated by staring at the limbs, and prolonged repetitive movements of limbs. One little boy spent most of A systematically exploring his body part by part: first the feet, which were picked up by the hands, crossed over, moved to and fro and stared at; then the buttocks, on which he swivelled round several times; then the trunk which was rocked from side to side. Parts of the ritual were repeated with the trunk in several different positions.

It is of some pertinence that the kinds of gestural patterns most frequently shown by the older normal children have in some instances been suggested as being diagnostic of childhood psychosis, "abnormal behavior toward himself such as . . . exploration and scrutiny of parts of his body" is one of the nine points listed for the schizophrenic syndrome of childhood (Creak, *et al.*, 1961). The behavior of our children in the bare room compels comparison more with that of adults subjected to conditions of sensory deprivation (Solomon, *et al.*, 1961); these adults resorted to various subterfuges for increasing sensory input, such as talking to themselves, whistling, and gesturing. Similarly in situation A, where the fixtures held little interest or novelty for them, the older children were endeavoring to increase their sensory input by exploring their bodies in various ways. Thus so-called psychotic behavior appears to be in the repertoire of quite normal children, but the selective influence of maturation results in it eventually becoming a function of the situation. Furthermore, the wider repertoire and greater resourcefulness of the older normals is reflected in the increased complexity of their gestures, while the younger normals and brain-damaged subjects engaged in fairly simple limb movements or a rather primitive kind of body manipulation.

BLOCK PLAY. The brain-damaged children manipulated the environmental fixtures more but played with the blocks less than the normal children. Figure 9 shows the total proportions of time spent with the blocks by the four subgroups, and how this time was apportioned between three activities: looking at the blocks, constructive play, and unconstructive play. The behavior pattern called constructive play had to satisfy an operational criterion of resulting in a design or structure; this occurred for the longest periods in the older normal children. The older brain-damaged children showed little constructive play except in response to the active social stimulus in D. The behavior pattern called unconstructive play consisted of just placing blocks singly, banging or throwing them, and so on. The older brain-dam-

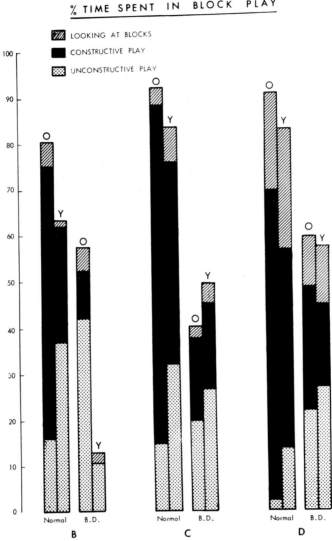

FIGURE 9. Proportion of time spent in different activities involving block play by normal and brain-damaged children in situation B, C and D, see text (from Hutt, *et al.*, 1965).

aged children tended to do the former. The younger brain-damaged children were observed predominantly to hit the blocks, scrub them on the ground, or throw them, and they showed hardly any constructive play. In B these children attended only very briefly to the blocks. In D the relatively longer periods of time spent by the normals in looking at the blocks was a manifestation of their cooperative play, as they were content to watch when the observer constructed. The amount of unconstructive block play was sensitive to *age* differences as well as *group* differences in every situation, whereas visual inspection was not. On the other hand, visual inspection was the category which most reflected *situational* differences, being greatest in the active social situation. Clearly therefore different aspects of the category termed block play were selectively modified by the several variables operating.

The behavior of hyperkinetic and nonhyperkinetic brain-damaged children. The subjects of this study were sixteen brain-damaged children, half of whom had been diagnosed as showing a classical hyperkinetic syndrome. The term hyperkinetic was used by Ounsted (1955) to indicate a syndrome characterised by global and consant overactivity, by distractability, short attention span, mood fluctuations, aggression, lack of affectionate behavior, lack of shyness, lack of fear, and wide scatter on intellectual tests when these could be applied; sleep was characteristically profound. Similar definitions have been given by Ingram (1956), Laufer *et al.* (1957), and Knobel *et al.* (1959).

The comparisons in this study were between eight children who had evidence of generalized brain damage and who also manifested the hyperkinetic syndrome and eight children of comparable age and similar evidence of brain damage but without the hyperkinesis. Where appropriate, comparable figures are shown for the group of twelve normal children (of similar age) described above.

SAMPLING TIME. In part, the amount of information gained by the child from its environment will be a function of what we call sampling time, i.e. the length of time during which a specific stimulus is engaged by a receptor system. In the particular environments in which the children were studied, the main receptor systems for obtaining information were vision and touch.

Duration of visual fixation: We have observed that children's visual behavior may be classified in at least two ways: as visual fixations, and scanning. In scanning, the child's eyes and/or head move over approximately 45 degrees of the visual field in a second. In a visual fixation, the head is stationary and the eyes are focussed on the stimulus for at least two seconds. Figure 10 shows the mean duration of such fixations.

In A all children spent approximately ten seconds in looking at any part of the environment before passing on to the next. The effect of introducing the blocks in B was greatly to increase the duration of visual fixation in the normal children, vision now being primarily upon the blocks.

In C, the normal children divided their visual fixations between the blocks and the passive social stimulus. In D, with the social stimulus now active, visual fixation was again primarily upon the blocks. The variability in the duration of visual fixation shown by the normal children was thus appropriate to the prevailing environmental conditions. Both brain-damaged groups were less variable than the normals, and had short visual fixations, the hyperkinetic group particularly so, hardly varying in any environment from a mean fixation time of ten seconds.

Duration of manipulatory activities: The mean duration of contacts made with the several features of the environment by manipulating in different ways the social stimulus, the blocks or the various fixtures of the room, is shown in Figure 11.

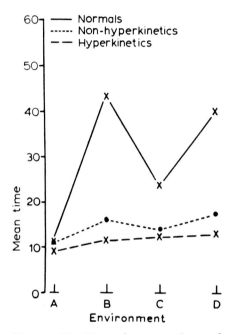

FIGURE 10. Mean duration of visual fixation in the different situations (from Hutt, and Hutt, 1964).

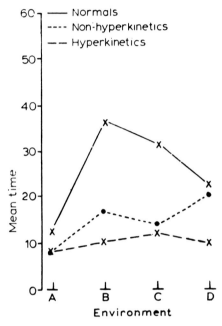

FIGURE 11. Mean duration of manipulatory activities in the different situations (from Hutt, and Hutt, 1964).

In A, B, and C the duration of manipulatory activity in the normal children mirrored their visual behavior. In D the shorter duration of manipulatory activity was due to the intervention of the social stimulus. Instead of working continuously, the child would share the construction of the design with the adult and would also continue visually fixating upon the blocks while she carried out her part of the design. The brain-damaged children as a whole showed shorter manipulatory activities than the normals in all situations. While the nonhyperkinetics showed some variability of response, the inflexibility of the hyperkinetics was remarkable, again hardly varying from a mean of ten seconds.

Attention span: As might be expected from the two previous results, the clinically hyperkinetic children showed very little variability in the duration of their responses, engaging in continuous contact with any objects of their environment for only brief periods of ten to fifteen seconds at a time (Fig. 12). All three groups were similar to each other in the empty room. As the en-

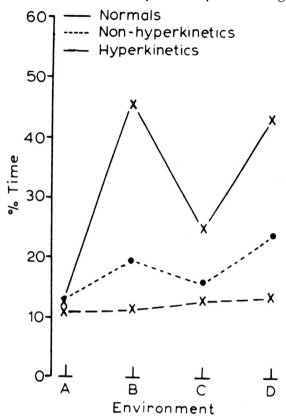

FIGURE 12. Mean attention spans in normal, non-hyperkinetic and hyperkinetic children (from Hutt, and Hutt, 1964).

vironment became more complex, the normal children exhibited corresponding variability in their attentive behavior, and so to a less extent, did the nonhyperkinetics. The behavior of the hyperkinetics on the other hand was minimally modified.

In an attempt to see if age had any effect in increasing the attention spans of the hyperkinetics, Spearman's rank order correlations were calculated between age and attention span for the three groups (Table IV). The correlation between age and attention span was significant in the hyperkinetic

TABLE IV

SPEARMAN'S RANK ORDER CORRELATIONS BETWEEN AGE AND ATTENTION SPAN IN THE THREE GROUPS (FROM HUTT, AND HUTT, 1964)

Subjects	Environment		
	B	*C*	*D*
Normals	0.46	0.43	0.17
Non-hyperkinetics	0.26	0.20	0.50
Hyperkinetics	0.71*	0.76*	0.63*

* $p < 0.05$

group in all situations. In C for example, the mean attention span was 10.0 seconds for the youngest hyperkinetic and 36.0 seconds for the oldest.

ALLOCATION OF TIME TO ACTIVITIES. Locomotion: It would be expected that increased motility would be a feature distinguishing hyperkinetic children from others, since it is a symptom often utilized, albeit in an imprecise and somewhat subjective manner, in formulating the diagnosis. Our concern was to measure just how much more and how much faster than other children the hyperkinetics moved around. We thus calculated the amount of time each group spent in each situation in moving about the room (Fig. 13). The three groups did not differ significantly from each other in the empty room, A. Once environment was structured, especially by the presence of the social stimulus in C and D, locomotion dropped almost completely out of the normal children's repertoire. The same effect, though less pronounced, was observed in the nonhyperkinetic brain-damaged children. The hyperkinetics on the other hand spent the same amount of time moving about in each situation; even the presence of the social stimulus did not significantly reduce their locomotion. Again it seems necessary to emphasise the aspect of invariance, i.e. locomotion occurs to the same extent and at the same intensity in all situation. Alternatively one might comment that normal children are hyperkinetic in a particular environmental situation!

Rate of movement, i.e. ratio of distance covered to time spent in movement, was also calculated for the three groups (Table V). As only one normal and two nonhyperkinetics moved about in D and two normals in C, speed measures were not calculated for the respective cells. The nonhyperkinetics did not differ from the normals in their rate of locomotions. The hy-

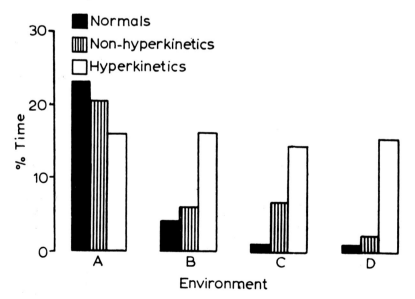

FIGURE 13. Proportion of time spent in locomotion in different environmental situations (from Hutt, and Hutt, 1964)

TABLE V

RATE OF MOVEMENT IN THE THREE GROUPS STUDIED
(FROM HUTT, AND HUTT, 1964)

Subjects	Distance/time-ratio (m/sec) in			
	A	B	C	D
Normals	0.77	0.68		
Non-hyperkinetics	0.73	0.62	0.46	
Hyperkinetics	1.02	0.87	0.85	0.96

perkinetics not only moved significantly faster than the others (P = 0.05 in A), but consistently maintained this high rate in each environment.

Manipulation: The time spent manipulating the fixtures (switch, taps, door, etc.) was considerably reduced when the social stimulus was present, in both the normal and the nonhyperkinetic group (Fig. 14). The hyperkinetics spent more time in fixture manipulation than the other children in all situations, and the decrease with environmental changes was more gradual. Only one normal and one nonhyperkinetic showed any fixture manipulation at all in C or D. The amount of time spent in block play increased from B to D in all groups (Fig. 15), this increase being reciprocal to the decrease in fixture manipulation.

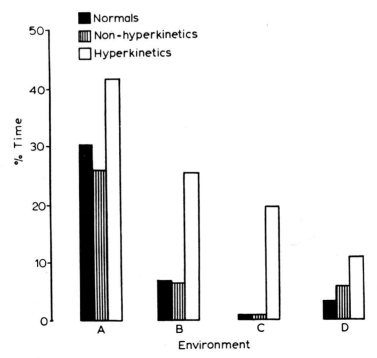

FIGURE 14. Proportion of time spent in manipulation of the fixtures in different environmental situations (from Hutt, and Hutt, 1964).

SAMPLING STRATEGIES. Both brain-damaged groups showed far less flexibility of sampling time than the normal group, best reflected in the attention span measure. The surprising fact to emerge, therefore, was how nearly the nonhyperkinetic brain-damaged children approximated the normals in terms of the total time spent upon fixture manipulation and block play.

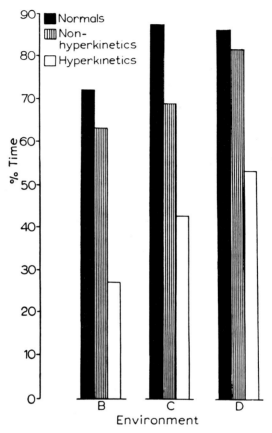

FIGURE 15. Proportion of time spent in block play (from Hutt, and Hutt, 1964).

Clearly the amount of time spent upon block play could not be a function simply of sample time, since the nonhyperkinetics' sampling time was only a little greater than that of the hyperkinetic's. Yet the two groups differed markedly on the total time measures. These differences can be seen in terms of the different strategies whereby the two brain-damaged groups sampled their environments.

Figure 16 shows the number of samples or encounters made with any stimulus by the hyperkinetic and nonhyperkinetic children in each environment. In A the number of samples of fixtures was high in both groups; in the hyperkinetics it remained high in all situations. The hyperkinetics also showed marked preferences for the unmovable stimuli. In C and D, the

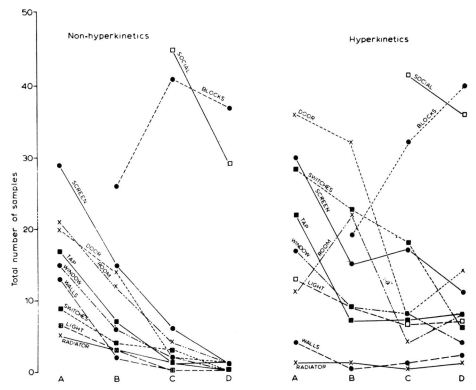

FIGURE 16. Frequency of sampling different stimuli by hyperkinetic and nonhyperkinetic children in four different situations (from Hutt, and Hutt, 1964).

number of samples of the fixtures dropped almost to zero in the nonhyperkinetics, whereas the frequency of sampling blocks and the social stimulus was significantly increased. While the frequency of sampling these latter two stimuli rose in the hyperkinetics as well, the increase was not nearly as marked; conversely, the fall in the frequency of sampling fixtures was also much less striking. The figure shows too that the range of stimuli to which the nonhyperkinetics were responsive was greatly reduced in the social environments. This was not so in the case of the hyperkinetics who continued to sample the same stimuli in the social situations as when they were alone. Once again the hyperkinetic children's behavior was less subject to modification than that of the other children.

Sequential analysis of the order in which stimuli were engaged confirmed that the sampling strategies employed were characteristically different in the three groups of children. These can be represented in simple diagrammatic form and identified as *serial sampling* and *repetitive sampling* (Fig. 17). In the former, stimuli tended to be engaged one after the other in order, but some stimuli might be missed out during the circuit; all children employed this strategy in situation A. In repetitive sampling two stimuli, the blocks and social stimulus, were sampled alternately, but as in the brain-damaged children, excursions were made from one of the two critical stimuli to other stimuli. Thus the general effect of the presence of the adult was to cause a shift from serial sampling of many stimuli towards repetitive sampling of two critical stimuli. In the nonhyperkinetics, the stimulus preference order, or stimulus hierarchy, apparent in A, was maintained in B, C and D (Fig. 16). In the hyperkinetics the stimulus hierarchy was much less clearly defined. Moreover in the nonhyperkinetics the range of stimuli engaged progressively narrowed with increasing environmental complexity, whereas in the hyperkinetics the range was as great in D as in A.

In summary we might say that the attentional modality of the normal children was vision (since the curves for attention span and visual fixation were very similar, manipulations being of shorter duration and following a different pattern). In the nonhyperkinetic brain-damaged children it was tactile (since the similarity was between attention span and duration of manipulation, the latter having higher values than visual fixation). In the case of the hyperkinetics there was no dominant modality (since visual fixation, manipulation and attention span were almost identical). Or, in cybernetic terms, there was no dominant channel.

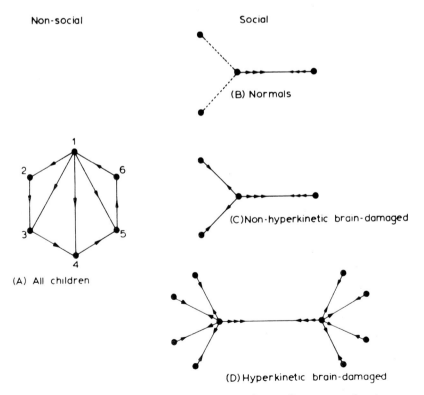

FIGURE 17. Diagrammatic representation of sampling strategies in non-social and social environments (from Hutt, and Hutt, 1964).

The resistance to modification by environmental changes was perhaps the characteristic feature of the hyperkinetics' behavior. To some extent this invariability was also shared by the nonhyperkinetic brain-damaged children. The range of stimuli engaged by the hyperkinetics, even with the active adult present, was as great as if they were alone in B. We may thus conclude that frequent attention switching was a feature of all the brain-damaged children, but in the hyperkinetics there was impairment of some other function or functions affecting their ability to inhibit response to some signals but not others.

The use of tape recordings in these studies yielded more information than we had originally expected. Twelve minutes of detailed observation, recording and analysis provided sufficient qualitative and quantitative data to enable the formulation of hypotheses concerning the processes of learning and the attentive impairments in brain-damaged children as well as providing some information about the behavioral repertoire of young children.

Chapter 5

METHODS AND TECHNIQUES II:
CHECK LISTS AND EVENT RECORDERS

D IRECT observational techniques have a long and respectable history.
They were developed and used by workers who had a keen and gen-
uine interest in the manner in which children and adults behaved and interacted in their normal surroundings, or at least, in slightly modified versions
thereof. They were also concerned with the continued refinement of the
techniques used in obtaining their data and with maximizing the reliability
and validity of their methods, in the words of a pioneer in the field "to apply
the general principles of scientific measurement as evolved in biometric
work to observations of behavior" (Olson, and Cunningham, 1934). These
principles required first the definition of a unit, second, the delimitation of a
field of observation, and third, repeated samples.

Arrington (1939, 1943) has written two admirable reviews of the rationale, construction and use of time-sampling techniques in behavior studies.
Her definition of the term cannot be bettered:

> Time sampling, as here discussed, is a method of observing the behavior of
> individuals or groups under the ordinary conditions of everyday life in which
> observations are made in a series of short time periods so distributed as to afford
> a representative sampling of the behaviour under observation. It is, in other
> words, a method of sampling, the validity of which is primarily a function of
> the amount and distribution of the time spent in observation or of the number,
> length and distribution of the separate observations or time samples. As con-
> trasted with the experimental method, it is a form of controlled observation in
> which the behaviour, the method of recording, and the manner of selecting the
> behaviour to be observed are subject to control rather than the situation in which
> observations are made. Finally, it is a method whose essential function is accurate
> measurement of the incidence of specific behaviour acts or patterns under speci-
> fied conditions (p. 82).

Olson too was one of the originators of time-sampling techniques. In their
review of the subject Olson and Cunningham stated:

> An examination of the various studies reported suggests that a formal time-sampl-
> ing technique will include the following features:
>
> (1) Observation by an eye witness.
> (2) Behavior to be observed defined in terms of overt action.
> (3) Behavior of an individual or group observed for a stated time unit, usually
>   short.

(4) A stated number of repetitions of the time unit employed.
(5) An individual score based upon the number of time units in which the defined behavior occurs, or the total frequency of occurrence of the defined behavior in the total observational time, or the average frequency of defined behavior per unit of time.

Items 3, 4 and 5 are the characteristics which, in combination, suffice to differentiate time-sampling studies from observational studies in general (p. 43).

In view of this fairly clear exposition of what time-samping techniques involve, it seems surprising to find these latter authors including in a section on method of recording one called continuous recording, the characteristic of which is that "the observer makes an entry every time the defined behavior occurs." This however is clearly event sampling. Perhaps because the latter technique had not been developed at that time, the need for a distinction to be drawn between the two was not evident. However, since the emphases of the two methods of sampling behavior data are clearly different, it seems necessary to make the distinction and we might formalize it in the following way: Those methods which sample preselected categories of behavior at regular (and usually brief) time intervals for a specified observational period are collectively called *time-sampling* procedures; in such procedures all behavior categories occurring in any one time interval are recorded and measures of frequency and duration are approximate and relative. Those methods which record every occurrence of preselected response categories over a specific observational period are called *event-sampling* procedures; in such procedures measures of frequency and duration are precise and absolute. Check lists and event recorders are the respective instruments of these methods. Each of these procedures will now be discussed in further detail.

CHECK LISTS

The rationale of time-sampling techniques is most clearly expressed by Arrington (1939):

The major assumption underlying the use of time-sampling procedures in these studies of normal child behavior in natural situations is that reliable quantitative measures of the frequency with which an individual normally displays a given behavior in a given situation can be obtained from records of the occurrence of the behavior in a series of randomly distributed short-time intervals of uniform length, and that similar measures descriptive of the normal incidence of a given behavior in a group of individuals can be derived by combining such records for the individual members of the group (p. 28).

In an earlier publication Arrington (1932) traces, in a most interesting and illuminating manner, the evolution of a time-sampling technique, starting from the diary-type records of Barker (1930). The problems and priorities set by the classificatory criteria used are well illustrated. The final check list that was developed is described later in this chapter.

A decision is made in advance that behavior will be sampled at regular and constant intervals irrespective of how frequently the activities actually occur. In part, how often the sampling is done will depend upon how rapidly changes occur in the behavior under investigation; in her later review Arrington (1943) emphasises that it is imperative that the observer should have some estimate of the frequency of the action in question in order to decide upon an appropriate time interval. Recounting the developmental history of the technique, Arrington (1939) shows how the pioneers, starting with large time intervals, progressively decreased them as the objects of their studies required. Olson (1929) for instance used admirably specified categories in the measurement of the incidence of nervous habits or tics in young children and recorded their incidence in several samples each of five minutes duration. Since any one behavior was only scored once in any five-minute period, irrespective of the frequency of its occurrence, it is not surprising that the method did not reveal any individual differences. A few years later Parten (1932) used 1-minute intervals in a study of social play in nursery school children. About the same time Goodenough (1930) split 1-minute observations into fifteen-second time intervals when studying six specific aspects of behavior in three- to five-year-old children. As Arrington (1939) comments:

> Occurrence within a 1-min. sample, the measure of frequency used by Parten, was more discriminative of individual differences than occurrence within a five minute period. Goodenough increased the discriminative value of the technique still further by subdividing the minute sample into fifteen-second intervals and by differentiating degrees of manifestation of each behavior trait.

Although the time interval to be used has to be largely empirically determined, as a rule the smaller the time interval, the more representative the sampling. In principle, the more frequent the sampling, the more comprehensive and reliable the record, just as a motion picture shot at twenty-four frames per second will give a smoother, more complete record than one shot at eight frames per second. A large number of categories however would reduce the frequency of sampling.

In general check lists utilize time intervals between ten seconds and one minute. Although some studies have used time intervals of five seconds, it is really not very feasible to record observations so frequently when more than three categories are under surveillance. For computational ease those intervals which are common fractions of a minute (10, 15, 20 or 30 seconds) are preferable. The larger the temporal interval between successive entries, the longer the total observation period needs to be, since the rationale of time sampling calls for at least adequate, if not frequent, sampling of the behavior to be made before it can be statistically evaluated. "The number of samples needed for representative measures of individual behavior will vary with the length of the sample, the frequency of the behavior, the variability of the individual and the relative constancy of the environment" (Arrington, 1939).

The use of a check list presupposes that the observer is interested in recording a number of specific behavior categories, whether they occur simultaneously or not. A prerequisite for obtaining reliable and valid data from check lists is a set of clearly defined categories. For this reason a check list would be unsuitable for recording behavior with which the observer was not completely familiar or for recording the complete range of activities in a free-field situation. Although in principle a large number of categories are feasible, in practice an observer is unable to cope reliably with more than fifteen. As the number of categories increase, the problems involved in scanning these and in deciding which to score increase as a positively accelerated function. From a purely practical view it is necessary to have check lists as compact as possible, since they are most commonly used in those situations where the observer is attempting to record unobtrusively and with the minimum of distraction to the subject(s).

Conventions

As in the method of tape-recording, each user of a check list may develop his own conventions. In the first place, it is assumed that the check list has been devised to investigate a fairly well-delineated aspect of behavior and that the response categories are clearly specified. That the criteria for inclusion in any particular category may originally be implicit is of little concern so long as they can be made explicit when necessary.

The most important convention, which must be rigorously applied once a decision about its operation is made, relates to the exact point in time the sampling is done. For example, in using a thirty-second interval, does the entry relate to the behavior that is occurring as the stopwatch hand passes the thirty-second point, or to the behavior that terminated just prior to the end of the thirty-second interval, or to the behavior that has occupied most of the just-lapsed thirty-second interval? The results of the three tactics will in all probability be very different. The use of the first of these can yield overrepresentations of infrequently or rapidly occurring events; suppose a child coughs on two occasions as the watch hand passes a thirty-second point. This would yield a score of 3.3 percent of time spent coughing in a thirty-minute observation session, which is clearly a spurious and grossly disproportionate figure. Similar objections apply to the second tactic. Moreover, as Cockrell (1935) found in her intertester reliability assessments, there were significant discrepancies resulting from the fact that one observer adopted the first and another the second of these tactics.

The third tactic is the one least open to objection, and with ten- or fifteen-second intervals is entirely feasible and should be the accepted convention. Problems arise, however, with the longer time intervals, since with the lapse of time it becomes increasingly difficult to store the items of behavior and even more to make a decision as to which item occupied most of the time interval. The compromise convention in such a case would be to make several entries (assuming different behavior categories occurr) in the same time interval. If this is done, however, there seems to be little advantage in using a large as opposed to a small time interval.

Other conventions are rather similar to those used in tape-recording. For instance it is generally assumed that if an object is being manipulated or moved towards, visual fixation is on that object and need be taken special count of only when it is elsewhere. Or again there are predetermined priorities and certain behaviors are not recorded at the expense of others. It is not possible to give hard and fast rules about these minor conventions, since they are entirely dependent on the problem under investigation and the nature of the observer's hypotheses.

Reliability and Validity

In tests of interobserver reliability with a check list used in a nonsocial situation, there was a 93 percent agreement (Hutt, 1966). The discrepancies were almost wholly related to omissions. The more experienced observer was able to record more comprehensively if more than one activity occurred simultaneously. There were no disagreements regarding the primary activity, although very occasionally one observer might record it as occurring in the immediately preceding ten-second period to the other. However, even in such cases, when the final computation was done, the results were identical. This meant that one observer was sometimes sampling at a slightly different time to the other, but consistently so, so that over all the entries the discrepancies were evened out. Such discrepancies may be accentuated in a procedure involving a large number of behavior categories. As Arrington warns, "Reliability of results tends to vary inversely with the amount of behavior observed, that is, the fewer the number of behavior items observed by one person at a given time, the more reliable the observations" (1939). She also observed:

> one of the most frequent causes of disagreement was the lack of clarity in the definitions of the behavior to be observed, which necessitated frequent judgement, and caused the same observer to be inconsistent with herself at different times, and different observers to be inconsistent with each other (1932).

Regarding validity, Arrington's observation (1943) is again most apposite:

> The validity of the measures derived by time sampling and related techniques is, broadly speaking, a function of three factors: the naturalness of the behavior observed, the accuracy with which it was recorded, and the adequacy with which it was sampled. If the obtained indices are interpreted slowly as measures of the observed frequency of the behavior under the conditions of observation, validity

is synonymous with reliability. If, however, as is usually the case, they are interpreted as representative of the normal behavior of the observed individuals in a particular situation or in all situations of a given type, their validity obviously depends not only upon the accuracy of the records but also upon the representativeness of the sampling (p. 93).

Analysis

The greatest advantage of check lists is the facility and speed with which they can be analyzed and the data computed. The rationale of time sampling, which assumes that if the sampling is done frequently (as in short time intervals) or over a long period (e.g. with larger time intervals), the irregularities will be evened out, permits us to give each time interval a unitary score. Thus the intervals can be summed to yield scores at stated points of the observation session, say every quarter, or to yield a grand total for the whole session. The most usual measure is the percent time spent in any activity, calculated thus:

$$\% \text{ time in activity A} = \frac{\text{no. of samples scoring A}}{\text{total no. of samples}} \times 100$$

Alternatively, the number of A samples could be used as an absolute value. Other measures that might also be easily obtained are as follows:

1. Frequency with which there is a change in activity.
2. Number of *different* activities
3. Number of stimuli encountered
4. Duration of a specific activity.
5. Changes in nature and duration of activities with time (e.g. in successive quarters).

All these measures can be rapidly computed in a few minutes at the end of the session; analysis is thus reduced to a minimum. (It must be pointed out, however, that this very ease in analysis and computation depends upon a careful selection and definition of the categories in advance. The less precise the behavioral categories, the less meaningful the eventual results.)

We may now consider some ways in which check lists have been used by students of both animal and human behavior in collecting their data.

ILLUSTRATIVE RESULTS

Animal Studies

Behavioral Development in Rats

Baenninger (1967) was concerned with obtaining some quantitative data on the development of normal behavior in rats and studied the animals living under normal laboratory conditions as well as others living in social isolation. The subjects were offspring of twenty litters, each of which had been reduced to six male pups by the third day: ten litters of six males each therefore made up the normal group; the other ten litters were reduced by one pup every other day, so that only one was left in each litter by the thirteenth day. Each litter was housed in a separate cage. All animals were weaned at twenty-one days of age.

Behavioral data were obtained by a time-sampling method: recordings were made according to predetermined categories every ten seconds for a daily observation period of five-hundred seconds. The rats were observed from the age of three days to ninty-two days. After the twenty-third day observations were made five days a week. Although both social and nonsocial behaviors were studied, only the latter data will be considered here.

Observations were made according to the categories listed in Table VI. The author states that the main categories "were decided upon only after all data had been collected, in order that knowledge of categories did not influence the experimenter's judgment during the observation." The percentage scores were obtained as follows:

$$\% \text{ of nonsocial category X} = \frac{\text{entries for x of 6 Ss}}{\text{entries for all nonsocial categories}} \times 100$$

The results showed that sleep and rest progressively decreased until weaning and remained low thereafter, the isolated pups tending to sleep less than the others. Although exploration and locomotion increased at one month of age and decreased thereafter, there was an important difference

TABLE VI
NONSOCIAL BEHAVIORS OF THE RAT (FROM BAENNINGER, 1967)

Sleep and rest	*Convulsive behaviors* tremors during sleep and rest awake	sniff {standing still, with head lifted, on hind legs}	*Pawing behaviour*
sleep and rest {on side, on back, with siblings}	jerk head, body up	sniff {with paws on wall, ceiling}	pawing {wall, water nozzle}
changes in position during sleep and rest	convulsions	sniff while climbing wall	*Oral consummatory behaviour* eat pellets
rest with eyes open	lurch forward	sniff {floor, wall, ceiling, nest, material}	drink {alone, with siblings}
Attentive immobility lie still with head raised, sit still/stand still	*Righting behaviours* roll {onto side, back}		*Other oral behaviours* sniff
	righting, *Adult reflexive behaviours*	*Exploratory locomotion* crawl {in circle, in circle using one paw}	push, carry food, sniff water nozzle, sniff/lick/chew bolus
Grooming	stretch and/or yawn		
wash face		crawl with head raised, walk in circle, walk and sniff, sniff wall	chew {floor, wall, nesting material}
lick {paws, toes, leg, genitals, trunk}	shake, sneeze		chewing movements
chew fur, scratch	*Exploration* move {to left, to right} head {back and forth}, stand still with head lifted	turn round while walking, *Run and jump*	
Tail manipulation sniff/lick/chew/chase tail			

between the two groups: isolated pups explored more before weaning, the others after weaning. Pawing appeared earlier and was manifested more frequently in the isolated than in the normal animals. Grooming showed a steady increase with age in both groups. Although tail manipulation originated at the same time in all animals, it showed a greater increase with age in the isolated pups.

In discussing her results, the author says:

> The absence of social stimuli did not prevent the development of any non-social behaviour in any isolated subject. On the contrary, presence of social stimuli prevented the development of two non-social behaviours, pawing behaviour and tail manipulation, in some grouped subjects.

The absence of social stimulation may not actually have prevented the development of any nonsocial behaviors, but it did affect their relative incidence. For example, isolated animals showed more exploration, locomotion, pawing and tail manipulation and less sleep and rest than the normally reared animals. The greater incidence in pawing and tail manipulation in the isolates may be analogous to some stereotyped and repetitive motor patterns seen in humans who are in some way sensorily deprived, e.g. blind children.

This study has succeeded in adequately sampling a very great part of the behavioral repertoire of the young rat. The author has attempted to provide additional definitions where categories may be ambiguous. As her table shows, the individual categories are almost wholly defined in terms of motor patterns, a most desirable achievement. It is difficult to see the necessity for her earlier qualification regarding the main categories, since any observer familiar with the animal would have been aware of the natural groupings of the individual activities. The use of a five-hundred-second observation period is a somewhat curious step in the procedure and, apart from the computational convenience of having fifty entries per session, has little to recommend it. It would have been helpful to know if only one entry was made in any time interval or whether the activities themselves were defined in such a manner as to be mutually exclusive.

Play and Exploration in Chimpanzees

In a series of three related experiments, Welker (1956a, b, c) investigated the effects of different factors upon the play of chimpanzees. In the first study he was concerned with the effects of certain stimulus characteristics that elicit exploration. He used fifteen test situations, most of them consisting of a pair of objects differing in only one modality, such as color, shape, texture, etc. Each situation (a pair of objects on a presentation board) was presented to each of six chimpanzees for six minutes at a time. Each situation was repeated until responsiveness became asymptotic, and then a new pair of objects was introduced. The observer sat outside the cage and recorded the behavior in symbol form on a time-ruled data sheet. Welker was able to use five-second time intervals since he was concerned with only two specific behavior categories directed to the novel objects. His procedure illustrates both the application of conventions, as well as the kinds of measure, that can be obtained with this method of recording:

> Manipulations (M) and head orientations (O) directed towards the stimulus objects were recorded. . . . With the aid of a watch with a sweep secondhand and a time-ruled data sheet, each 5 sec. period during which the animal orientated towards, or manipulated, one or another of the stimulus objects was recorded.
>
> A manipulation was recorded if the animal made contact with an object (i.e. mouthing, biting, smelling, scratching, slapping, rubbing, grasping, etc.) during a 5 sec. period. If S continued to touch the object, all 5 sec. periods of maintained contact were recorded. If manipulation occurred to two objects during the same 5 sec. period, both were recorded.
>
> An orientation was recorded if the animal looked at the stimulus objects during a 5 sec period without manipulating them. . . .
>
> A measure of total responsiveness (ΣR) during a single minute or session was obtained by summing the number of 5 sec. periods during which an animal responded (sum of M & O) to the experimental situation. (1956a, p. 84)

For his computations Welker used the mean number of five-second intervals recorded for any category. The results showed that ΣR declined during repeated exposures to the same stimulus situation; this decline was steeper in the older subjects than in the younger ones. If after satiation a new stimulus situation was presented, ΣR increased appreciably. Satiation was also apparent when minute-by-minute ΣR for any six-minute session was considered. When the situation was presented again however, there was recovery of exploration, indicated by the fact that ΣR of the first minute of the following session was greater than ΣR of the sixth minute of the preceding session.

The second study was concerned with the variability of exploration and play: "How several measures of behavior change over time, and the effect of certain stimulus conditions on such behavior changes." Ten wooden blocks were used in each of three experimental situations: in situation 1 they were homogeneously colored, in 2 they were all of like form; and in 3 they were different in color and/or form. Each situation was presented for three sessions, each session lasting ten minutes; recordings were made as previously. The measures obtained were as follows:

> (a) total responsiveness (ΣR) or the total number of 5-sec. periods during which an animal touched any object in the experimental situation;
>
> (b) contacts (C), or the number of times an animal touched any object for one or more 5-sec. periods. A contact was scored whenever the animal had touched an object after it had been touching either some other experimental object, or some non-experimental stimulus. One "C" was recorded regardless of

how long (in terms of the number of 5-sec. periods) the animal maintained contact with the object;

(c) shifts (S), or the number of shifts of contact from one object to another throughout successive 5-sec. periods;

(d) withdrawals (W), the number of withdrawals of contact from the experimental situation;

(e) objects touched (O), the number of different objects touched; and

(f) length of contact (L), average length of contacts ($\Sigma R/C$) (1956b, p. 181).

The results again showed a decline in ΣR upon repeated exposure to the same situation and an increase in ΣR upon introduction of a new situation. The variability of behavior (C and S) increased with increasing heterogeneity of stimulus objects, but categories W and O remain unchanged.

In the third study Welker investigated the effects of two particular variables—age and experience—upon the exploratory activity of chimpanzees. (Only the first of these will be discussed here.) Ten different stimulus situations were presented to the animals while they were in their cages. Each session was of five minutes duration; records were made in the manner already described.

The subjects were eight chimpanzees between the ages of ten and fifty-seven months; they were divided into the four older animals and four younger ones. The results showed that whereas the older animals manipulated the novel objects more than they oriented to them, the converse was true of the younger animals. However, by manipulation of the experience variable, Welker was able to show that it was not age per se but experience (of which the older animals had more) which reduced the degree of caution shown to novel objects.

Although Welker's definitions of behavior categories are admirably clear and unambiguous, it is a pity that he did not attempt to break them down a little further. What he was really dealing with in these studies was attention span as we described and defined it in the last chapter. In other words, he was considering total responsiveness towards the stimulus objects, irrespective of the nature of the responses. The incidence of the different kinds of manipulation, fingering, rubbing, hitting, etc., might have been more informative. This is of particular importance since Welker simultaneously applies two terms to the behavior he is studying, namely exploration and play. Even in colloquial semantics two words hardly ever have exactly the same meaning. This is even less likely with the terms used by Welker, since often their contextual referents are so different (cf Hutt, 1966; 1967a, b). On the other hand, were he primarily concerned with responses to novelty of whatever sort, then his study was extremely economical and informative, even though it seems important to differentiate between strictly visual responses from those involving some form of manipulation.

Human Studies

Interrelations in the Behavior of Young Children

The time-sampling technique eventually developed by Arrington (1932) and referred to earlier in this chapter, utilized a five-minute observation session, an entry being recorded every five seconds. One hundred and twenty children of different ages were observed, and a different data sheet, depending on the situation and activities of each group, was used for each of the three groups: nursery school, kindergarten, and first grade. Only the nursery school data will be presented here.

These children were observed during their play time between 9 and 11 A.M. The choice of free, rather than experimentally controlled, situations was predetermined by the objectives of the investigation; namely, the study of normal patterns of response to a sociomaterial environment, and the refinement of methods of observing and recording behavior in life situations. Under the informal conditions prevailing in the rooftop playground of the nursery school, intervention on the part of the teacher was minimal, and children were free to engage in whatever materials or social activity they wished.

Two observers recorded different aspects of the children's behavior on two check lists (Fig. 18). Form A was concerned with the amount of time spent in three mutually exclusive categories: use of materials (M), physical activity (P), and no overt activity (No). Form B was concerned with talking (T), physical contact (PC), laughing (L) and crying C). A key to the symbols used, as well as the definitions of the categories, provided by Arrington (1939) are given in Table VII.

> *Materials*—all play apparatus and other nursery school equipment, clothing and parts of the building (walls, posts, iron grating, doors, window ledges, etc.)
>
> *Use of material*—active manipulation of movable objects with hands, feet or other parts of the body, and exploration of, or physical activity evoked by, stationary materials.
>
> *Physical activity* (exclusive of use of materials)—walking, running, jumping, rolling, crawling, moving up and down in position, waving arms, clapping hands, falling down etc., and active physical contacts not involving material.
>
> *No overt activity*—standing, sitting or lying still, making no observable reaction to the environment other than looking around or looking at persons or things.
>
> *Talking to persons*—using a person's name in direct address, or talking while using the same material as other children or different materials in close proximity to others.
>
> *Vocalizing*—making audible sounds that had no meaning for the observer.
>
> *Physical contact*—any direct bodily contact with another person, as in pushing, hitting, striking, embracing, caressing, fighting, or any contact with a person through material, as in confiscation or exchange of toys, having nose wiped or clothes fixed by teacher, taking another child's cap off, etc. No distinction was made between "friendly" and "unfriendly" physical contacts.
>
> It was assumed that the child who pushed and pulled other children at one time

Form A

CHILD __B__   TIME _9⁴² – 9⁴⁷_   DATE _2/25/30_   RECORDER _MSF_

CHILDREN PRESENT: Ⓐ-Ⓐⁿ-Ⓑ-Ⓑⁿ-Ⓓ-Ⓔ-Ⓔⁿ-Ⓖ-Ⓗ-Ⓘ-Ⓙ-Ⓜ-Ⓜ̄ⁿ-Ⓜ̄-Ⓝ-Ⓟ-Ⓟⁿ-Ⓡ- RB -Ⓥ

Time	M	P	NO	Time	M	P	NO	Time	M	P	NO	Time	M	P	NO
0	:Box			15				30				45			
5				20				35				50			
10				25	MMs Hat			40				55	Not		
15				30				45				60			
20				35				50	Not			5			
25				40				55				10			
30				45				60				15	Slides W. Board Train		
35				50				5				20			
40				55				10				25			
45				60	Not			15				30			
50				5				20				35			
55				10				25				40	Box		
60				15				30				45			
5				20				35	Truck			50			
10				25				40				55			

Form B

CHILD __B__   TIME _9⁴² – 9⁴⁷_   DATE _2/25/30_   RECORDER _REA_

CHILDREN PRESENT: Ⓐ-Ⓐⁿ-Ⓑ-Ⓑⁿ-Ⓓ-Ⓔ-Ⓔⁿ-Ⓖ-Ⓗ-Ⓘ-Ⓙ-Ⓜ-Ⓜ̄ⁿ-Ⓜ̄-Ⓝ-Ⓟ-Ⓟⁿ-Ⓡ- RB -Ⓥ

Time	T	PC	L	C	Time	T	PC	L	C	Time	T	PC	L	C	Time	T	PC	L	C
0			✓		15		EB			30			✓		45				
5	✓		✓		20					35			✓		50	✓			
10			✓		25		MM			40			✓		55	Δ			
15					30					45					60				
20	✓		✓		35					50			✓		5				
25					40	ⒺⒷ				55	✓	✓			10	✓			
30					45	EB				60	✓				15			✓	
35	✓		✓		50					5	Δ				20				
40		H			55					10			✓		25	✓			
45	✓				60		EB			15		✓	✓		30				
50					5					20					35	✓			
55			✓		10					25					40	✓			
60					15		BD	✓		30			✓		45	N			
5		Ⓗ			20				✓	35	✓		✓		50				
10		ⒺⒷ			25		Ⓑⓞ			40	✓				55				

FIGURE 18. Sample five minute record of a nursery school child's activities during the free play period (from Arrington, 1939).

would also manifest friendliness through physical contact at another time, that is, that there would be a correlation between the two types of contact in the same individual (1939, p. 52).

As an explanatory commentary upon the protocols illustrated in Figure 18 Arrington states:

Interpreting the record of Child B for the 5-min period beginning at 9.42 am on February 25, 1930, we see first, by the encircled initials at the top of the record, that nineteen of the twenty children enrolled in the group were present on the roof playground when the record was begun. Form A indicates that Child B was physically inactive, though in contact with material, for brief periods at the beginning and end of the five minute record (1939, p. 53).

TABLE VII

KEY TO SYMBOLS USED IN RECORDING INTERACTIONS OF YOUNG CHILDREN
(FROM ARRINGTON, 1939)

Language		*Physical Contact*		
Social	Non-social	Subject-initiated by observed child	Object—initiated by another person with observed child	Subject-object—contact in which both observed child and other person are active participants
Δ =Teacher π =Group O =Observer V =Visitor 　Initials for 　children	talking to self vocalizing	Initial or symbol of person contacted Ex.—MB	Encircled initial or symbol of initiator of contact Ex.— MB	

Arrington's findings relating to both the social and nonsocial activities of young children cannot be done justice to within the space of the present chapter, but we may note a few illustrative results. Verbal interchange predominated the social contacts of children of all age groups (total age range 20-85 months). Speech was thus divided into three categories: (1) nonsocial, (2) child-directed, and (3) adult-directed. The amount of nonsocial speech exceeded that of social speech in the nursery school children but showed a considerable decrease in the kindergarten group (average age 66 months). Speech directed to adults decreased with age, whereas speech directed to peers showed a reciprocal increase. At all ages the children were found to converse primarily with members of their own sex! Physical contact was found to be surprisingly infrequent in all age groups, and was of relatively little discriminative value with reference to sex, age or individuals. There was a small correlation between frequency of verbal contacts and frequency of physical contacts.

From her measures of frequency and variability, Arrington delineated three patterns of social interaction: the *promiscuously social,* the *selectively social* and the *nonsocial.* For the promiscuously social child for instance "the mere presence of persons in his vicinity, regardless of who they are, appears to be an adequate stimulus for the initiation of social contacts" (1939).

The results relating to material-oriented activities were less satisfactory, particularly in the nursery school group. On Arrington's own admission this was probably due to the use of behavior categories which were overinclusive (e.g. manipulation of materials, irrespective of how). She demonstrated that the use of more restricted definitions with the older groups of children did indeed improve the sensitivity and discriminative value of the measures.

Arrington's studies are exemplary in their meticulous attention to all potential sources of bias, in their consideration and evaluation of methodological issues, and in their judicious exploitation of a situation's potential. Thirty-five years ago, the embryonic status of observational studies naturally demanded that Arrington's emphases were upon quantitative rather than qualitative data. Nevertheless, her work must be regarded as both a critical and classical contribution to the development of time-sampling studies. Her expositions and reviews (1937, 1939, 1943) should be mandatory bibliography for the behavioral scientist venturing into the human field.

Children's Reactions to Failure

In an attempt to find out how children behaved when confronted with a difficult or stressful situation, Zunich (1964) observed forty preschool children individually from behind a one-way screen. Each child was required to solve a puzzle-box test. This consisted of a small, colored wooden box which had a false bottom a little way beneath the lid. On the false bottom were ten small, colored and irregular-shaped figures which were almost the same thickness as the depth from the top of the box to the platform, so that the figures had to fit well and closely together before the lid would shut. After a preexposure session to familiarize the child with the situation, he was given the box with the pieces taken out and asked to put them back in the box so that the lid would be shut. During this ten-minute experimental session, an assistant remained with the child in the room.

The subject's responses were recorded every five seconds according to the following categories:

a. *Attempt to solve alone.* E.g., child tries to solve puzzle alone.

b. *Destructive behavior.* E.g., child intends to harm the object or persons connected with the difficulty.
   Ex.: Child throws the object or pushes it off the table.

c. *Directing.* E.g., child specifically states the course of action which he wants the adult to follow
   Ex.: "Put that part there." "Give me the red one."

d. *Emotional response.* E.g., child cries, yells, sulks, laughs, and whines.

e. *Facial expression.* E.g., child closes eyes, tightens mouth, becomes red in face, hangs out tongue, chews lips, and grinds teeth.

f. *Motor manifestation.* E.g., child stamps foot, moves body, clenches fist, sucks thumb, waves with hands, and pulls on ear.

g. *No attempt.* E.g., child makes no attempt to solve puzzle, and gives up almost at once or without exploring many of the possibilities of solution.

h. *Rationalizing.* E.g., child refuses to continue the solution.
   Ex.: "I don't want to do this," "This is a stupid puzzle."

i. *Seeking attention.* E.g., child calls attention to himself or his activity.
   Ex.: "Look what I did."

j. *Seeking contact.* E.g., child asks adult to come into physical contact with him.
   Ex.: "Come over and sit by me."

k. *Seeking help.* E.g., physical: Child asks adult to help him with some difficulty connected with the activity.
   Ex.: "I can't put this piece in—hold this for me."
   Mental: Child asks for ideas in trying to solve the problem.
   Ex.: "What can I do now?" or "How can I put this in?"

1. *Seeking information.* E.g., child questions in pursuit of factual knowledge. Ex.: "What kind of puzzle is this?" "What is this for?" (p. 20/21.)

The data were analyzed for all children together, as well as for three-year and four-year subgroups. By far the most frequent category was *attempt to solve alone.* In doing so, the children often manifested emotional and facial expressions and sought information. Incidence of destructive behavior was relatively rare. When separated into age groups, the older children showed a higher frequency of facial expressions and rationalizations, whereas the younger ones showed a greater tendency to make no attempt to solve the puzzle, and to seek information or help. All these age differences were statistically significant.

When separated by sex (there was an equal number of boys and girls) a higher frequency of destructive, emotional, and facial responses, rationalization and help-seeking was expressed by boys, whereas girls showed a greater incidence of information and contact-seeking as well as attempts to solve the puzzle alone. In other words boys showed more negative behaviors than girls.

This study, as many others, makes greater use of the content of verbal utterances in the delineation of behavior categories than we ourselves have hitherto done. This admixture of different response variables, each of which may be structured quite differently, raises new problems in the measurement of nonverbal behavior. Where a behavior category is defined primarily by motor patterns and only additionally elucidated by reference to verbal material, this recourse to extraneous data seems legitimate. It does not seem permissible however to attribute equal weight to both verbal and nonverbal features in the delineation of a response category. For example, in the present situation, had the child thrown down the puzzle saying, "I'm tired," would the response have been categorised as destruction, rationalisation, or both?

There is also an odd interpretation of the data in this study which may be misleading. Having calculated the total frequency and percentage of any response category, the author states that the "data indicates that the majority of children made an attempt to solve the test alone"; and again after obtaining the mean number of responses for boys and girls respectively, "a significantly greater number of boys showed. . . ." In the first instance the total frequency of solve alone was 1,728. Each subject could have a maximum score of 120 (5-second samples in ten minutes) on any category. Thus assuming some children concentrated exclusively on trying to solve the puzzle, fifteen subjects alone (out of 40) could in theory achieve the obtained total frequency score. But this would hardly count as a majority. Perhaps in fact the majority of children did solve alone, but the frequency data by themselves are not necessarily evidence of the fact. Similar objections apply to the second interpretation. Nevertheless, there has been an attempt to define the response categories unambiguously, if somewhat grossly. The interobserver agreement of 0.80 is reassuring, and it is admirable that the author was able to use a five-second sampling interval with the number of catego-ries under surveillance.

Exploration of Novelty in Children

A slightly more complex check list with ten-second intervals and a ten minute observation session was used in the study of exploratory behavior in young children (Hutt, 1966). The subjects of this study were three- to five-year-old nursery school children. Since the study was carried out in the school, and no specially designed experimental room was available, the ob-server had perforce to sit in the playroom with the subject, although she made every attempt to be as unobtrusive as possible.

The procedure for this study was as follows: Children were introduced in-dividually into a playroom with which they were already familiar and which contained five familiar toys as well as one completely novel toy, and they were allowed to play in the room for ten minutes. The identical procedure was repeated on six subsequent days.

The novel toy consisted of a red metal box (approximately 12″ by 8″ by 8″ mounted on four legs. On the top of the box was a lever which could be moved in four directions. Each of these movements was registered by a sep-arate counter (cf. Fig. 34). Different incentives (e.g. sounds or lights) were contingent upon specific manipulations, but here only the two simplest condi-tions will be described and discussed. One condition called *no sound or vi-sion* allowed only the tactile feedback from manipulations of the lever; the other, *vision only*, allowed the child to see the counters clocking up each movement as it was made. Any one child was only exposed to one incentive condition.

Detailed observations had already been made in a pilot investigation by the time the check list was constructed. Thus the behavior categories to be recorded could be clearly specified. Primarily we were interested in the re-sponses towards the novel object, as was Welker (1956); at the same time we did want to know what kinds of responses were made, so these were re-corded in detail. Figure 19 shows the first half of a completed check list of a subject in this study; the second five minutes were recorded on the back of this sheet. The first column indicates the time intervals and the next seven columns deal with responses directed towards the novel object. The follow-ing is a key to these and the subsequent columns:

Looking: Visual orientation towards the object, without any other ac-companying activity.

Holding: hands on lever but no manipulation; this and other object re-sponses assume synchronous visual orientation unless otherwise indi-cated.

Manipulating (conventional): manipulation of the lever with one or both

Direct Observation and Measurement of Behavior

NAME: John Eggleton WHERE SEEN: Nursery school (S)

DATE OF BIRTH: 28/3/1963 CONDITION: S , √

DATE: 29/9/1966 SESSION: III

67 91 25 06   0470   5742
68 94 25 67 ─ 0477 ─ 58 36

	Looking	Holding	Manipulating - conv	Manipulating - unconv	Other parts - visual	Other parts - manip	Counters	Gestures	Locomotion	Play with toys unconst	Play with toys const	Visual Exploration	Observer	Room	Notes
1	/														
2		/													
3		/													
4		/													
5		/													
6		/													
	1	5													
1		/													
2		/													
3								✓							
4													/		
5									/						pulls track
6									/					/	tapping window
		2							1	2			1	1	
1								✓							
2		/						/							scratches face
3												/			sofa
4				/											"buttons"
5				/											
6				/											
	1		3					1	1			1			
1		/			/										
2		/			/										watching , counting
3		/			/										
4		/			/										
5		/			/										
6					/										fingers
		5			6										
1					/										touching sides
2					/										
3								w✓							
4											/				pull dog in t -
5											/				pulls
6											/				track
		2						1			3				

FIGURE 19. Checklist used in the study of exploratory behavior in nursery school children. For explanation see text.

hands in the four directions while sitting or standing in front of the object.

Manipulating (unconventional): operation of the lever other than with the hands, e.g. a knee, elbow, head, etc. or while in an unconventional position, e.g. sitting astride it, or lying flat on the floor.

Other parts—visual: visual inspection of parts of the object other than the lever, e.g. underneath the box, screws, legs, etc.

Other parts—manipulation: manipulation of parts as above.

Counters: visual inspection of, or touching, fingering, rubbing of the counters.

Gestures: as defined in previous chapter; in addition, type of gesture was specified by initial letter, e.g. S for scratching, Y for yawn.

Locomotion: as defined in previous chapter; additionally method of locomotion could be indicated by a letter, e.g. R for running.

Play—unconstructive: activities involving other toys which consisted of banging, throwing, fingering, taking apart, chopping, etc., or those preparatory to another activity, e.g. picking up.

Play—constructive: activities which involved assembly of two or more toys, or which were inventive or entirely appropriate for the toy, e.g. pulling truck with dog in it, cuddling panda, etc. The toys involved were recorded in the Notes column.

Visual exploration: looking round the room or orienting towards specific objects like window.

Observer: all responses directed to the observer, most commonly visual orientation (indicated by V) but sometimes also touching, talking, etc.

Room: manipulation of any fixtures or furniture in the room.

Supplementary notes on other informative characteristics of the behavior or stimulus objects encountered were recorded as frequently as possible.

The arrows at the top of the categories in the check list refer to the four directional movements of the lever: the counters were read before and after each session, thus giving one measure of manipulatory responsiveness. The response categories could be summed at the end of any required interval, the totals at the end of each minute, and at the end of half the session (5 minutes) are shown in Figure 19. For each subject, the percent time attending to the novel object was calculated as follows:

$$\frac{\text{No. of object intervals}}{60} \times 100$$

If more than one object category was recorded in any one time interval, the latter nevertheless only obtained a score of 1. Since there were altogether sixty 10 second intervals in a ten minute session, the responses to the novel object were calculated as a proportion of this total.

One of the objects of this study was an assessment of the decrement in response to novelty upon repeated exposure to it. This responsiveness showed a fairly systematic decrease over the six sessions under the two incentive conditions (Fig. 20).

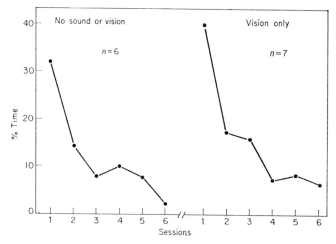

FIGURE 20. Proportion of time exploring a novel object on successive trials under (1) no sound or vision, (2) vision only, conditions (from Hutt, 1966).

When the counter readings were used as a measure of manipulatory exploration, remarkably similar results were obtained (see Fig. 1). (This agreement incidentally may be taken as a measure of internal consistency or validity of the method.) These decrements, whether in time or manipulatory activity, were exponential functions of time. When the manipulation score

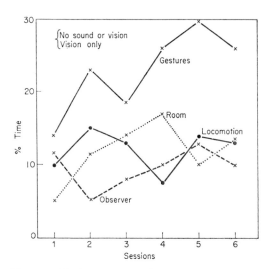

FIGURE 21. Proportion of time spent gesturing, exploring the room, looking at the observer, and in locomotion, from session to session, conditions (1) and (2) being combined (from Hutt, 1966).

was transformed by the use of Naperian logarithms, the regressions of manipulations upon time under both the no sound or vision and vision only
conditions were significant. Thus, under these two simple incentive conditions, young children fairly quickly learned about the novel object, and after
the fourth exposure showed very little interest in it.

As Figure 21 shows, it was also possible to obtain an overall distribution
of the different activities occurring in each of the six sessions. The decrease
in exploratory activity was complemented by an increase in gestures. This
was probably a reflection of the subjects' boredom, particularly as yawning
and stretching figured largely in the latter sessions. It was interesting too
that orienting responses towards the adult were most frequent in the first
and last experimental sessions, i.e. at the presentation of the novel object
when presumably the child wished for some reassurance and when the child
had become more or less tired of the situation and thus sought further stimulation from the adult.

In the next chapter it will be seen that the data derived from such check
lists could reliably be combined with the data obtained from film records.

It was possible to obtain much detailed data relating to a number of behavior categories in this study. However, although the categories pertaining
to the novel object were fairly clearly defined, the two play categories regrettably lacked this degree of precision. Consequently, in order to determine the nature and object of the responses in these latter categories, much
reliance had to be placed upon the notes entered. The two play categories
might profitably have been subdivided into four or more categories of
greater specificity. Although this would have considerably increased the
number of overall categories to be recorded, it would have systematized
much of the notes.

EVENT RECORDERS

Except for the present-day streamlined and sophisticated models, event
recorders are by no means a recent invention. All students of biology are familiar with the perennial smoked drum or kymograph used to record the
clonic and tetanic contractions of the gastronoemius muscle of the frog upon
electrical stimulation in one of the classical experiments of elementary physiology.

An event recorder is an automated device (however primitive) which registers the occurrence of a selected event. Most recorders are also able to
record the duration of the event. In the kymograph type, the drum revolves
at a constant and known speed while a metal arm, connected at one end via
an electric circuit, or mechanically, to the displacing agent, makes a mark on
the drum with the other. A mobile and somewhat primitive model may be
constructed by using a roll of paper whose central axis is made to rotate at a
constant speed; a slit or window in the enclosing box permits marks register-

ing the occurrence of an event to be made, as the paper passes the slit.

Although the activity of a crocodile seems an unlikely and even hazardous phenomenon to measure, Cloudsley-Thompson (1964) with some ingenuity succeeded. Using an extremely simple aktograph apparatus, he measured the diurnal rhythm of activity of the Nile crocodile. Since this animal's activity is infrequent and often slow, any rhythmic pattern would be manifest only after the averaging of several observations over a long period of time. To circumvent the uneconomical expenditure of time involved in making these observations by hand, some form of automatic recording device was essential. Cloudsley-Thompson's apparatus consisted of a corked tube, partly filled with water, and acting as a float; this was connected by thread to the lever writing on the clockwork drum. The drum revolved once per week. Movements of the crocodile registered as vertical strokes on the record. When several days' results were pooled, the author was able to demonstrate a clear periodicity in the crocodile's activity, a peak occurring in the early evening.

Since the observer is dispensable for this type of automated registration of an event, such studies do not strictly fall within the purview of this book. Nevertheless, as many of the currently available pen recorders can be used to record either physiological (autonomic, electromyographic, electroencephalographic) or behavioral (locomotory, manipulatory) activity, with or without an intermediary observer, reference will be made to the latter potential.

In the last decade and a half, event recorders have become increasingly sophisticated, and the machines currently available are able to record a great number of independent events simultaneously. Commercial companies in each country manufacture models which are naturally most suited to the needs of their own workers. Three such models are briefly described here.

The EMREC Event Recorder

This machine is constructed by Elliott Brothers (London) Ltd., and a twenty-four pen model is illustrated in Figure 22. Each pen traces a continuous line on the paper until an event is registered by the closing of an external switch (as when an event key is depressed) or the injection of an appropriate external voltage (as in completely automated recording). Such a registration energizes a relay type solenoid which results in the lateral displacement of the pen by about 3 mm. The pen continues in its displaced location until the end of the event is signalled by the opening of the switch (i.e. release of key). If the machine utilizes ink pens, these write directly on plain paper; if the pens are of the heated stylus type, they write on carbon backed paper, the stylus burning away part of the composite paper, thus leaving a black trace. The recorder incorporates a standard chart mechanism driven by a synchronous motor at speeds ranging from 1.3 cm (½ inch) per hour (for slow and infrequent events) to 102 cm (40 inches) per minute (for rapid events). Although this range of speeds is theoretically possible, any one model incorporates a more restricted range. The chart can also be driven by a handwound clock at speeds of 2.5 cm (1 inch) per hour to 7.6 cm (3 inches) per hour. The firm claims that a 19.8 m (65 foot) chart at a speed of 2.5 cm (1 inch) per hour will allow continuous recording for 1 month.

Recorders using ink pens appear to be more limited in that only one to five pens are available; of the heated stylus type, six-, twelve- and twenty-four-pen models are currently available, and thirty-six-, forty-eight-, sixty-, and seventy-two-pen models are projected.

FIGURE 22. The EMREC Event Recorder (Elliot Brothers, London Ltd.).

THE ESTERLINE-ANGUS EVENT RECORDER

This machine operates on very similar principles to the Elliot recorder already described. Esterline-Angus provides two models, a ten-pen and a twenty-pen one (Fig. 23). An additional advantage with this machine is that the pens are displaced by electromagnets; these can be calibrated to operate at various voltages and the wiring arranged so that each pen is electrically separate from the other. This method of operation permits cleaner stylus displacement than the close/open contact. The 15 cm (¾ inch) wide paper is driven by one of three mechanisms, synchronous motor, Selsyn, or

FIGURE 23. The Esterline Angus Event Recorder (pen model).

phantom, at speeds ranging from approximately 1 cm (⅜ inch) per hour to 7.8 cm (3 inches) per second. The phantom drive refers to the use of an external source as the motive power and when the paper motion is not proportional to time, but to an external motion. An additional advantage is a rheostat, which can adjust stylus heat, thus enabling narrowing or widening of the recorded trace. At the time of writing no details were available of the dimensions and weight of the machine. Apart from considerations of compactness, it is not possible to evaluate one of these two machines preferentially. Further operational details of the Esterline model are included in the study described below.

THE PEISSLER SIXTY-CHANNEL RECORDER

This machine (Fig. 24) is manufactured by the West German firm of Peissler. The prototype was designed primarily for use in studies of the social behavior of squirrel monkeys at the Max-Planck-Institut fur Psychiatrie in Munich (see, for example, Ploog, 1967). It is not therefore as flexible a recorder as one might wish, but it certainly is the most extensive machine of its kind currently available.

The keyboard is an integral part of this machine, whereas in the two previous examples the keyboards were separate and optional components. The keyboard push buttons in the Peissler machine activate crystal styli which record on paraffin-waxed paper. Channels 1, 2 and 3 are generally used for special markings. The large number of channels permits the specification of the *actor*, the *activity* and the *recipient*. Channels 4 to 15 (3 top rows at left on keyboard) are designed to enumerate twelve different individuals, namely, the actors; similarly channels 49 to 60 (at right of keyboard) can specify twelve passive recipients. Channels 16 to 48 (the midportion of the keyboard) are then able to register thirty-three different behavioral events.

With twelve or fewer animals in a group therefore, this machine is able to cover almost every behavioral contingency in ordinary circumstances. A severe limitation of this machine however lies in its mode of recording: depression of the appropriate *actor-activity-recipient* buttons merely programmes the machine, and recording only commences when the Begin button is depressed. Similarly, to terminate the recording of a particular behavioral event, the appropriate *actor-activity-recipient* buttons must again be depressed, followed by depression of the End button. This procedure clearly introduces a good deal of delay into the recording system, and hence this machine is contraindicated in those studies where temporal precision is essential.

Another disadvantage of this recorder lies in its very complexity: any one observer has a great deal of difficulty handling all the information generated by such a system. Although with practice this difficulty can be overcome, hitherto many of the studies where it has been in use have necessitated the presence of two observers, one to call out the event, the other to type it in (Castell, personal communication). If despite practice a single observer is unable to memorize much of the keyboard and record the events himself, the utility of the machine is vitiated.

This recorder can also punch its output directly on to tape for computer analysis.

FIGURE 24. The Peissler 60-channel Event Recorder.

Applications

Behavior of Fish

Clark, *et al.* (1954) used an earlier version of the Esterline-Angus recorder in studying the behavior of fishes, and although the results are not of immediate relevance, the authors' reasons for its use are generally applicable to all such recorders. Furthermore, the details of its operation are informative, hence are quoted here:

> The activities seen in the first several hundred 10 min. periods were recorded on paper, with the use of a tally system. The observer jotted down a specific mark each time a particular behavioural act occurred and kept a record of the minute in which it was enacted. This method was not entirely satisfactory because the observer was compelled to cease observing the fish too frequently while glancing at the clock or while recording a behavioural item on the tally sheet. This manual method of recording was replaced later by the use of an electrically operated polygraph assembled specifically for the purpose of recording behavioural observations rapidly without loss of some of them. This apparatus is composed

of two recorders and a keyboard which is somewhat similar to that of a type-writer. It may be held in the lap of the operator, who may use a technique similar to the touch system in typewriting. The keyboard contains 40 separate leaf-actuated microswitches, which may be pressed separately or simultaneously in recording every item of behaviour. Each recorder contains an unwinding roll of graph paper connected to a synchronous electric motor by gears of variable ratios. On each of the two recorders a series of 20 pens is hooked up inde-pendently of the 40 switches on the keyboard. Switches for controlling indepen-dent or simultaneous starting and stopping of these recorders are located on the keyboard. One machine, manipulated by the left hand, was operated at a slow speed. The recording during a 10 min. observation period produced notes cover-ing 15 inches of graph paper. The records indicated the exact duration, sequence, and time of occurrence for each behavioural item. A second, higher speed re-corder, in which 1.25 mins of observation ran to 15 inches of graph paper, was turned on just prior to copulations (or whenever copulations were expected) for the purpose of obtaining an accurate measurement of the duration of copulation (p. 153).

These authors have used two 20-pen recorders together and in conjunction with a forty-key keyboard and have described their manner of use fairly succinctly.

Oral Behavior of Neonates

In a study of newborn infants a very simple form of an Esterline-Angus event recorder was used. Since a special significance has been attributed to oral behavior, both by learning theorists and by psychoanalysts, Hendry and Kessen (1964) studied this behavior using systematic observation in an at-tempt to evaluate its drive-reducing properties.

Nineteen healthy newborn infants were observed at their first formula feed and again forty-eight hours later. Their mean age for the first observation was twenty-three hours and for the second, seventy-one hours. On each day subjects were seen between two successive feeds and observations were made during the first five minute of each half hour of the four hour period. The authors used an Esterline-Angus event recorder, with two manually op-erated telegraph keys. Two responses were recorded, one key being de-pressed for each behavior. The responses were defined as (1) hand-mouth contacting (HMC), any contact between hand and mouth, and (2) mouth-ing (M), any sucking-like movement. From the records several measures were obtained:

1. Total duration of HMC, i.e. total number of sampled seconds on one day.
2. Average length of HMC, i.e. duration divided by number of contacts.
3. Total duration of M.
4. Total duration of HMC accompanied by M, i.e. hand-sucking (HS).

Interobserver reliability for all the measures ranged from 0.96 to 0.99.

The eight scores obtained from the eight, half hour periods between feeds were combined in pairs to give four scores, one per hour. The results showed that both total duration and average length of HMC were greatest in the first hour after feeding but dropped appreciably in the second hour. Both measures increased again in the third and fourth hours, and total duration more than average length, the increase in the latter apparently being statistically insignificant. Similarly in mouthing, the longest duration was seen in the first hour after feeding, followed by a significant decrease in the second hour. This trend was seen in infants at both ages although the older infants showed an overall reduction in the duration of mouthing. Only individual differences appeared as significant variables in the hand-sucking measure.

The results certainly do not support a drive-reduction hypothesis, since oral behavior is most prominent when drive level is at its lowest (immediately after feeding). There is one aspect of the results of which the authors make surprisingly little: since average length and frequency of HMC are reciprocally related to total duration of HMC, it is possible to deduce from the graph provided that the average frequency of HMC was 10 ± 1 in each of the four hours between the feeds. This constancy seems remarkable, and since the authors comment that reliable individual differences were found in this measure, can we infer that each subject tended toward a characteristic frequency of HMC? In other words, were the individual differences also stable over time?

This study illustrates a very simple and straightforward use of an event recorder: only two independent categories were recorded, and where both keys were depressed simultaneously a third category was signified, so that degree or extent of overlap was not a point in question. For this type of study, where brief durations need to be recorded precisely, an event recorder seems the most appropriate recording instrument. It would have been helpful for potential users of such instruments if the authors had given some idea of the paper speed required to satisfactorily measure durations of one-fourth or one-half sec.

Behavior of Children in a New Situation

A study which used a pen-and-pencil event-sampling procedure may be briefly cited here, since it is not essential that the technique depends on the use of an automated device. Cox and Campbell (1968) wished to know how young children reacted to a novel situation in the presence and in the absence of their mothers. In the first instance they studied ten girls and ten boys between the ages of thirteen and fifteen months. Each child was accompanied to the observation room by its mother. The mother sat in one corner of the room, occupied with a questionnaire; a pile of four toys was available for the child in the opposite corner. Half the mothers remained with the children for the entire twelve-minute session; the other half were with the children for the first four minutes, left them by themsevles for four minutes, and returned to the room for the last four minutes.

Observations were made from behind a one-way screen, and the incidence of the following behaviors was recorded:

1. Child touching mother (child placed his hand, or some portion of it, on some part of his mother for less than 5 consecutive seconds).
2. Child holding the mother (S held some part of his mother for at least 5 consecutive seconds).
3. Child speech (each sound or word S uttered).
4. Child movement (the floor of the observation room was inconspicuously divided into a grid of nine, equal-sized shapes, and record was made of each square the S entered)
5. Child play (each toy the S handled).
6. Child touching other things (each other object touched, e.g. window, door, door knob, venetian blind).
7. Child places object in own mouth (each object so placed).
8. Child crying.

The observations were recorded on a time chart which was divided into 1-min periods; presumably the occurrence of categories in each of these periods was noted. The results showed that there was a decrease in speech, movement and play during the mother's absence, using the first four minutes as an index of base line performance. The control group, on the other hand, showed a slight but progressive increase in all these behaviors throughout the twelve minute period.

Since the method of recording did not permit duration of behaviors to be noted, the authors are unable to give any measure of the amount of a response category. This is particularly disappointing in the case of crying, since only two children of the experimental group did not cry; the others showed varying periods of continuous crying.

The purpose of this study would have been better served by the use of a time-sampling procedure or an event recorder which permitted the recording of activity durations. With the kinds of complex behavior categories used by these authors, frequency measures alone are inadequate to indicate how much of any particular activity was manifested. For example, a child who became distracted and moved desultorily from one toy to another would have obtained a higher score than one who concentrated its attention on one or two objects. Does one therefore interpret the decrease in movement during the mother's absence as resulting from absorption in a toy or from frozen terror? This study does help to illustrate the point that event sampling merely by incidence within a time period, without an index of overall frequency, is unsatisfactory for the recording of complex behaviors. The two exceptions to this generalization would be instances where the object of study was a brief and/or stereotyped behavior, (e.g. sneeze) or sequential ordering of acts (irrespective of their duration).

STENOGRAPH

Some workers have put to ingenious use a machine most commonly used in courtrooms for recording legal proceedings. Such a stenograph machine has a very limited number of keys but is quiet, compact and portable. Heimstra and Davis (1962) have described its use in recording simultaneously the behavior of each of a pair of rats.

> A Stenograph machine will print a number of letters of the alphabet as well as numbers from 0 to 9. Unlike a typewriter, one or any number of keys can be depressed together and will record on a paper tape which is 2.5 inches wide. The tape is automatically moved ahead one line after a key (or keys) is struck.
>
> A key, or combination of keys, is used to represent a given behaviour category for an animal in the pair being observed. When the animal is engaged in that particular category of behaviour, the proper key is depressed at regular intervals. A timing device such as an electric metronome, which will give audible signals at desired intervals can be used to maintain the proper intervals between depressions of the key. In an experimental situation which placed pairs of animals together in a relatively confined area, it was found that observations could be made and recorded at one second intervals on two animals simultaneously by means of this system. Obviously, working at this speed the observer must be thoroughly familiar with the behavioural categories utilized as well as the keyboard of the machine.
>
> As a key is repeatedly depressed, it prints the letter or number in a vertical column on the paper tape. Thus, if the key for the letter H on the machine was depressed 10 times, it would result in 10 Hs in a column on the tape. If another key, for the letter F, had also been depressed simultaneously, then the result would be two vertical columns on the tape—one of Hs and one of Fs. If each of these letters represented a category of behaviour for one of the animals in the pair, and if the keys had been depressed at one second intervals, the resulting columns of 10 Hs and 10 Fs could be translated as representing 10 seconds of a given category of behaviour for each animal (p. 209).

Other workers (Carter, *et al.*, 1951) have used it in recording human social interactions in a manner similar to that devised by Bales (1951).

This machine clearly has some advantages in certain situations, notably those where the observer must of necessity remain in the same room as his subject. Insofar as the stenograph prints out events, it may be regarded as a primitive form of event recorder, but strictly speaking it employs a time-sampling procedure in that observations are entered at regular intervals and no precise measure of event duration can be obtained. Nevertheless, it may be regarded as a happy compromise between the two procedures.

ATSL

A completely automated observer-to-computer data processing system has been devised and described by Tobach *et al.* (1962). This system is called ATSL, after the names of its originators. It consists of an Aronson keyboard containing twenty typewriter keys, each connected to a switch which in turn activates a Laupheimer converter (Fig. 25).

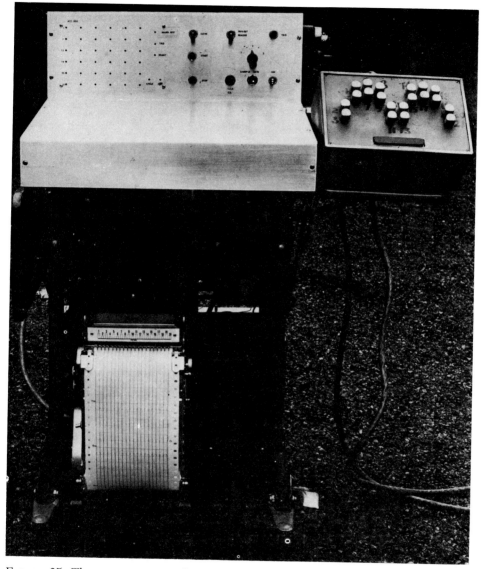

FIGURE 25. Three components of ATSL, of which the operations recorder is optional (from Tobach, *et al.*, 1960)

The Laupheimer converter registers, accumulates and transmits pulses from the keyboard, or from switches activated by an animal, to a tape-punch. The pulses produce a single input-item, called a 'bit.' Thirty-six bits equal one 'data-word.' The 36 bits of each word are accumulated in an appropriate binary register, transferred into a distribution (serialization) register, and transmitted to the punch at the rate of one, two or three words per second, thus producing a tape with serially punched words. 1-36 punches appear in any given word. A column of bits is called a 'character.' For compatibility with the IBM 1620 computer, the converter automatically inserts a 'parity' punch as needed so that each character contains an odd number of punches, and also automatically punches the thirty-sixth bit in each word to designate the end of that word (p. 258).

The paper tape is then processed by an IBM 1620 digital computer.

This system can provide all the types of data usually obtained from an event recorder—durations, frequencies, latencies, sequences and other inter-relations of various activities—by virtue of its automated analysis and is able to save much tedium and time.

Chapter 6

METHODS AND TECHNIQUES III:
MOTION PICTURE AND VIDEOTAPE

IT IS A popular misconception that films are the most desirable of techniques for behavior recording. Money permitting, it is many a behavioral scientist's dream to equip himself with the necessary apparatus for obtaining complete documentary records of his subjects. Film and video tape qua records are indeed ideal means of storing information. As Delgado (1964) has emphasized, cinematographic records are permanent and objective, and are not affected by problems of observer fatigue, though the latter advantage strictly applies only to fully automated procedures.

A critical factor that is often overlooked however is that in using such records the observer has merely transferred a two-dimensional replica of the behavior on to celluloid. In analysis, therefore, one starts from the same point as with the original behavior. The other methods of behavior recording already discussed incorporate some measure of first order analysis. In assigning activity terms to behaviors as in tape-recording, and in using preselected behavior categories as in check lists, one has already taken the initial step in categorization, and further data analysis consists of a regrouping or recombination of the categories. With film or video record however the process of analysis commences once recording is complete, and since the activity can be replayed at a more leisurely speed as in the case of motion pictures, or played over and over again as in the case of video tape, the temptation is great to make the analysis increasingly detailed. The synthetic procedures involved in the other methods of recording are considerably less arduous than the analytic procedure which confronts one with film.

It is imperative, therefore, that before launching upon the use of motion pictures or video tape, the aims of the study are specifically stated. We might consider for what kinds of investigation such records are most useful, since if the data required can be obtained equally well by some other means these should be the first choice. Considerable economy in time and effort would be effected if the observer has been able to carry out pilot studies so that he knows what he is looking for. The investigations for which motion picture and video tapes are particularly suitable fall broadly into five groups: (1) where the action proceeds so swiftly that it is not possible to record all the required elements by any other method (the prey-killing of the cat), (2) where the action is so complex that attention is focussed on certain components at the expense of others (responses of human newborns to sound), (3) where changes in the behavior are so subtle that satisfactory morphological delineation between one act and another is difficult (gaze behavior, Ch. 7), (4) where sequential changes in fairly complex behaviors are being considered (transition from investigation to play), and (5) where it is required to measure precisely specific parameters of certain brief or complex behavioral events (gait). These categories are by no means exclusive, and often an investigation may have more than one of these aims. It is assumed that, in general, film records are used only if a very detailed and systematic analysis of behavior is required. Films taken purely for the purposes of illustration of a point are not considered in any detail.

The kind of film or video tape used is obviously determined by the object of the study. In general, for detailed analysis requiring slow projection, motion pictures are preferable to video tapes, and if money is no obstacle, 16 mm film will be the medium of choice, since it will give better resolution and definition and provide more durable records than 8 mm film. Since in our own studies, we were financially limited, we generally used 8 mm film, particularly when the experimental or observational session was longer than two or three minutes. Video tape on the other hand, is probably more effective in recording social situations, where obtrusive cameras or operators are to be avoided. Judiciously positioned TV cameras, fitted with wide-angled lenses, can be remotely operated while the operator is able to check events on a monitor screen. This obviates the necessity of having the camera operator (or observer) intrude upon the scene of action. Telerecording is thus an excellent means of obtaining long, continuous records of behavior sequences where external manipulation of events is not required.

Animal Studies

Ontogeny of Behavior in the Jungle Fowl

In most ethological studies motion pictures are used for purposes of detailed description and qualitative rather than quantitative analysis. A neat example of this type of analysis against a classical ethological conceptual background is provided by Kruijt in his study of the Burmese jungle fowl (1964).

One pattern of movement shown from the very first day of the chick's life is head-shaking; it is evident in two feeding situations: when it has a piece of food too large to swallow in its bill, and (2) when anything sticks to the sides of its bill. The pattern consists of a rapid movement of the head from one side to the other and back again. When filmed at fast speed (64 frames per second) and subsequently analyzed frame-by-frame, each head shake was found to occupy five or six frames, i.e. about 0.08 seconds. Its function is to either remove the material from the bill or to pulverize it. This pattern also appears as an irrelevant movement during or at the end of fights. Kruijt says "they are called 'irrelevant' because they are similar to comfort and feeding patterns." Irrelevant movements seem to be the same as those Tinbergen terms displacement activities (1951), i.e. movements displaced from their original context.

Another irrelevant movement is intention ground pecking, where the food-pecking movement is performed, but the bill does not touch the ground. A more complex irrelevant movement, head zigzagging appears to be a combination of these two simpler movements, headshaking and intention ground pecking. This admixture is clearly seen in the film analysis from which a reconstruction is shown in Figure 26. Both vertical and horizontal components in this composite behavior tend to be slower and of smaller amplitude than when they are individually performed as intention ground pecking and head shaking respectively. Cinema analysis showed that one

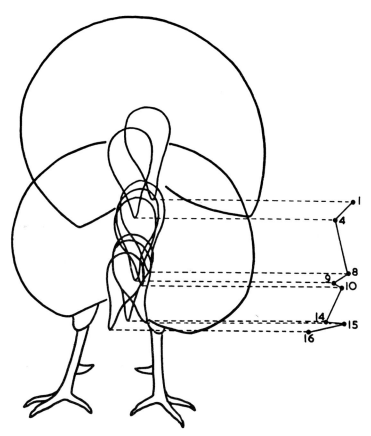

FIGURE 26. Extreme positions of the head to left and right during head zigzagging in an adult cock, drawn from motion picture (24 frames per second); first and last position of the erected ruff is also shown (from Kruijt, 1964).

sideways movement and return took nearly three times as long as a head-shake. Whereas the simpler feeding movements first appeared as irrelevant movements about the age of three weeks, the more complex combination of the two did not appear till about the age of six weeks.

By cogent deduction and collation of circumstantial evidence, Kruijt concluded that head zigzagging was associated with a very strong aggressive tendency (it always occurred during fights and never after) which was counterbalanced by an equivalently strong escape tendency (it was equally frequently manifested by winners and losers of fights). Since strong and simultaneous activation of two conflicting tendencies such as escape and aggression occurred late in the ontogeny of the bird, the behavior pattern that represented such a motivational condition appeared later than those representing different degrees of conflict or different motivational states.

Ontogeny of the Pecking Response in Gulls

In a study of an "instinctive," unambiguous, yet reasonably complex motor pattern of young gulls, the pecking response, Hailman (1967) made extensive use of Motion pictures. His film analysis moreover was of a more exacting and quantitative nature than Kruijt's. Hailman was concerned with various aspects of this response, chiefly its form, its development and the effects of several environmental factors. One of his first tasks was the description and quantification of the individual motor components of pecking. To elicit the response, the chick was presented with a stuffed head of an adult bird. The responses were filmed at 24 frames per second and subsequently viewed with a Perceptoscope (Perceptual Development Co., St. Louis) time-motion analyzer, a machine allowing variable speed or frame-by-frame and forward or backward projection.

Analysis revealed that pecking involved three primary motor components of the head. The approach phase of pecking could be differentiated into three stages: (1) at rest, (2) bill open, head moved slightly upward, and (3) head movement upward towards stimulus (model) bill and simultaneously rotating (Fig. 27A). Similarly the recovery phase was delineated into three stages: (1) bill closed, head lowered but not withdrawn toward body, with slight rotation back to the vertical; (2) rotation complete, head dropped below original position and body back to at-rest position; and (3) head raised and withdrawn to at-rest position (Fig. 27B).

The motor components of the head movement therefore are basically vertical, horizontal and rotatory ones, upon which the bill opening is super imposed.

These motor elements were quantified as follows: (1) The horizontal and vertical movements of the head were measured by successive positions of the tip of the lower mandible. Since only the upper mandible moves during bill-opening, and since the axis of head-rotation passes approximately through the tip of the

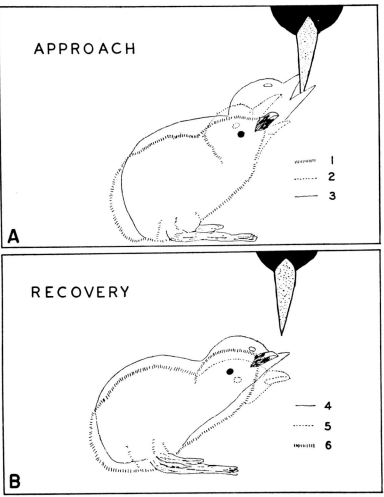

FIGURE 27 a & b. Drawing of a single pecking movement (from motion picture) showing approach and recovery phases (from Hailman, 1967). For full description see text.

lower mandible, the position of the lower mandible is affected relatively little by the other movements. (2) The opening of the bill was measured by the distance between the tips of the upper and lower mandibles. Because of head-rotation, the absolute distance measured on the projection screen is foreshortened (to zero when tthe head is rotated 90°). Thus it is necessary to convert the measured distance trigonometrically, utilizing information about the extent of rotation. (3) The rotation of the head is the most difficult component to quantify from lateral views of the chick. I measured the vertical extent of the eye, and observed the shortening of this distance upon rotation. The angle of rotation is then calculated triginometrically. Eye size is a convenient measurement, but is so small that a considerable reading error is introduced. This error is inherent in the calculated degree of rotation, which in turn introduces error in the calculated amount of bill-opening (p. 15).

Hailman was then able to demonstrate the relative degree of coordination of these components both from peck to peck within any one bird, and from bird to bird.

As one might expect, this type of analysis was an arduous task, requiring approximately two hours for the component measurement of each peck. Hailman then used an abbreviated form of analysis, which was still able to yield information essential to the demonstration of coordination and stereo-typy. Using the same film material, only the onset of each component, its peak, and recovery were recorded by frame number. These parameters for four successive pecks of a wild chick are illustrated in Figure 28.

Hailman says: "The peaks of the other motor components never differ from the peak of horizontal movement (i.e. intersection of model's bill) by

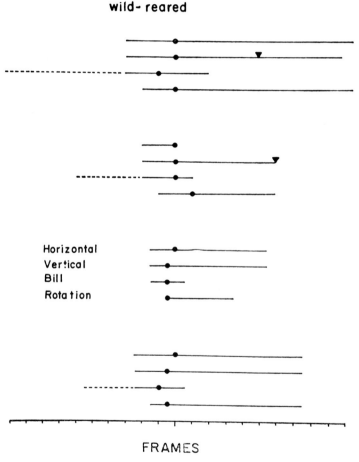

FRAMES

FIGURE 28. Duration and synchrony of the motor elements in four pecks of a single chick. (Length of line = duration; ● = peak of movement; ▼ = lowest points in downward movement of head. Note variation between pecks (from Hailman, 1967).

more than a single frame (about 0.04 sec.)." This indicates a remarkable degree of motor coordination. Although the durations of the individual components is more variable, there is still more consistency than one might expect, and in terms of actual time the whole response does achieve a high degree of invariance or stereotypy.

This study is a neat example of the use of motion pictures for both a qualitative and quantitative analysis of a superficially simple behavior pattern. Such an analysis of the ontogeny of motor patterns or skills in humans, e.g. reaching, walking, eating, is still awaited, despite the potential significance of such results.

Behavior During Brain Stimulation

Alonso de Florida and Delgado (1958) used time-lapse photography to record the behavior of cats during electrical stimulation of the amygdala. The animals were kept in a glass-fronted cage—one animal with implanted electrodes in a group of normal animals. A time-lapse camera took a picture every nine seconds for ten hours daily. After some preliminary study, they selected four categories of behavior: (1) walking or standing on all fours; (2) aggressiveness, "evidenced by threatening, snarling, flattening the ears, piloerection, fighting positions and striking;" (3) playful activity, i.e. pretending to fight and gentle pawing of objects; (4) contactual activity (sniffing, licking, nuzzling, and rubbing). The authors comment that though these categories were usually easily recognized, borderlines patterns were difficult to recognize, and in such cases more frequent filming or additional direct observation was necessary.

Most commonly it was found that ipsilateral movements of the facial muscles occurred synchronously with the stimulation. Closing the eye, lowering the ear, retraction of mouth, and rhythmic movements of upper lip and nostrils as in sniffing, licking the chops, and smelling floor and walls were more integrated patterns that were also observed. For each animal the total number of pictures in which each of the above four categories appeared was obtained, and their means were calculated for stimulation and control periods. Increments and decrements were obtained by subtracting the control period value from that for the stimulation period. The results showed that an increase in playfulness was associated with stimulation of the amygdala, as did contactual activity.

Although this form of recording is adequate and probably even appropriate for static aspects of postural or facial patterns, it seems somewhat doubtful whether it is really adequate for a complex category like playful activity. Is one picture per nine seconds sufficient for one to decide that pawing was gentle or that fighting was a pretense? The level of interpretative analysis achieved seems more refined than the recorded data would be expected to permit. Moreover, it is doubtful whether the two activity patterns mentioned really exhausted the category of playful behavior. Nevertheless, since identical procedures were adopted during stimulation and control periods, the differential results must reflect the effect of the experimental procedure.

Many other animal workers have used motion picture data in order to illustrate a critical point or substantiate a controversial argument. Tinbergen (1959) for example used motion picture analysis to illustrate the relative discontinuity between gull postures or displays which bear many similarities to one another: he showed that the transition between the oblique and forward displays occupied only about one-fifth seconds, whereas each posture was maintained for one to two seconds. Leyhausen (1965) has used illustrations from motion pictures in a comparative analysis and discussion of the pre-catching behavior of several species of cats: he is able to demonstrate interspecies similarities and differences in the morphology of the motor components and evaluate these with a phylogenetic emphasis. Wickler (1964) on the other hand, argues for a more extensive use of motion picture recordings, both for analytical purposes and as permanent documentations for the comparative behaviorist. Using his analysis of several movement patterns of species of *Labrides* and *Blenniides* (mouth-cleaner fish) he illustrates certain phylogenetic relationships, discusses the functions of the different movements, and demonstrates the survival value of imitating certain of these to a mimic. Detailed comparative analyses can nevertheless show that the similarities are relatively superficial, arising from convergent evolution. Wickler argues that fixed specimens of behavior are as essential for the behavioral scientist as preserved specimens are for the comparative anatomist: "naturwissenschaft setzt voraus, daB die Ergebnisse für möglichst viele nachprüfbar und wiederholbar sind, auch für den, der sie selbst zuerst fand." [Science demands that results must be replicable both by the original worker and by as many others as possible.]

A system for automatically interpreting film data has recently been developed by the National Biomedical Research Foundation, and has been described by Ledley (1965) and by Watt (1966), who has also discussed its application to an ecological problem. The system is known as FIDAC, Film Input to a Digital Automatic Computer.

> In essence, the system operates as follows. Each frame of the film is positioned in front of a cathode-ray tube spot generator which can produce an ordered array of rows and columns of spots of light very quickly. On the other side of the film from this tube is a photocell which measures the intensity of light transmitted by the cathode-ray tube through each small segment of the film. The intensity is measured as one of seven different gray levels, and this information is transmitted directly to the digital computer by means of a special register. (Various commercially available film scanners that can be attached to computers classify light intensity in up to 63 different grades.) What makes this system remarkable is that the computer itself not only analyzes the data, but controls the operation of the cathode-ray tube. Thus, as each frame of film is analyzed, the computer can

control the location of the array of spots of light, the density of spots in the array, and the area covered by the array of spots. Therefore, the system can operate so as to make an initial inspection of each frame of film to discover where the particularly noteworthy features occur on the frame, then a second inspection to examine the areas of special interest in more detail. This system operates with very high resolution (1000 lines along each of the X and Y axes) and with very high speed (input to the computer at 200,000 36-bit words per second).

Once a representation of each frame of film is stored in the central core memory of the computer, the next step is for the stored program to analyze the data in terms of some preconceived mathematical model (Watt, 1966, p. 256/257).

Watt has described in some detail how such a model might be developed in ecology. Many behavioral scientists are unlikely as yet to require this degree of mathematical sophistication and will be content with a much simpler model. Nevertheless, the analytical technique in itself is a valuable asset, even if its cost is likely to make FIDAC a somewhat illusory system for many of us.

Human Studies

Perhaps one of the earliest users of motion pictures for behavioral analysis was Arnold Gesell. In a paper discussing the technique of cinemanalysis (1935), he saw it as being particularly useful in behavior analysis at three different levels: (1) slow motion study, (2) selective pattern phase analysis, (3) minute pattern phase analysis. Although no definitions were given, selective pattern phase appeared to refer to a specific behavior episode or activity (e.g. separates hands, lifting right forearm vertically in lateral chest zone; opens right hand, dropping rattle between knees; semiextends left arm medially over abdomen, hand on left knee) whereas minute pattern phase referred to individual limb and facial movements. Since for both latter analyses, slow motion projection is necessary, it is difficult to see why slow motion analysis is regarded as analysis at a different level. Gesell went on to stress the analytic power of the technique by showing how behavior pattern phases could be further subdivided into three categories:

> (a) *a critical phase* in which the member is at rest or undergoes a complete shift or reversal of movement; (b) *a kinetic phase* when the movement is under way; (c) *a phase of resolution* or culmination when this particular movement is completed or resolved.

This he termed the minute pattern analysis. By this means of analysis he obtained 360 behavior data from a twenty-second sequence; he arranged this data in a matrix with the body segments (eyes, right arm, left toes, etc.) listed vertically and consecutive seconds horizontally. It is difficult to appreciate the rationale of this type of analysis in terms of behavior morphology or of economy of effort. If a second-by-second breakdown is all that is called for, then the minute frame-by-frame analysis is wasteful; furthermore, although this form of analysis may be of interest to those concerned with the dynamics of movement it is not really appropriate for the student of behavior, since the action is broken up not into functional segments but dynamic units which do not necessarily have a functional or morphological cohesion. To be fair to Gesell, however, he was merely presenting a method of behavior analysis, and it is only possible to evaluate such a method when it has been applied to a particular problem.

Maturation of Motor Activities in Infancy

Gesell's faith in the power of cinemanalysis was completely vindicated by a study he subsequently carried out with Halverson (1942). These authors made a painstaking film study of the motor development of an infant over the first seven months of its life. The daily film records amounted to 220 in number, taken from the 15th to the 235th day of age.

The records were made at 5:30 PM each day in a standard setting: the infant was undressed and placed supine on the floor of a cubicle 3 feet by 3 feet and 4 feet high, the roof of which had a hole to accommodate the lens or the movie camera. The pad on the floor was covered with a grey blotter marked off in 2-inch squares.

Three ten-second situations were filmed by the authors: (1) full length situation—mother held infant's head in midline position and ankles to obtain a full length posture; (2) moving ring situation—three interlocked red, white and blue plastic rings (4 cm in diameter) were moved horizontally across the field of vision to the child's left and then back to the right, each excursion taking five seconds, i.e. ten seconds in all; and (3) still ring situation—the same rings were suspended so that they hung just above the infant's chest.

The results were described under three categories: (1) head and eye behaviors, (2) arm behaviors, and (3) leg behaviors. Each category was subdivided into *postures* and *movements*. It is only possible to describe some of the results here, but the reader is urged to consult this fascinating and somewhat overlooked paper for himself. A frame-by-frame analysis was made of most of the behavior patterns, and in many cases it was necessary to run the film over and over again to observe consistent trends or tendencies. Categories A and B appeared to be the most important and are discussed below.

A. Initially the infant spontaneously adopted a *tonic neck reflex* position, i.e. head turned to side, extension of both ipsilateral limbs and flexion of contralateral limbs but in particular the upper limb. Most commonly the head is turned to the right, and in this study Gesell and Halverson observed a left tonic neck reflex only on one day for 1 percent of the time. In situation 1 the mother's constraint of the head in the midline position produced distress and crying which only ceased after two months. From day seventeen to day eighty-two the infant maintained a tonic neck reflex posture for an average of 44 percent of observation time (on some days this was 100%).

Even situation 2 had minimal effect:

> Even under the stress of the stimulus of rings moving across the field of vision
> the head posture remained consistently averted toward the right. There was no
> external stimulus which could bring about this orientation. The determining
> intrinsic stimulus factor was so strong that the head maintained its rightward
> orientation even after brief ocular pursuits of the ring momentarily diverted the
> head through a small arc toward the left.

The time spent in the tonic neck reflex posture only declined appreciably
after the seventieth day, and it is only after this time that the moving visual
stimulus is able to determine head position. The film records showed there
was increasing ability in rotating the head to and maintaining it in a midline
position, but the authors pointed out that this incremental ability was gradual and was attributable to maturation rather than to specific conditioning
or to incidental learning.

As a corollary to the predominance of the tonic neck reflex in early infancy were the spontaneous side-to-side head movements which were primarily elicited by situation 3, whereas attentive visual fixation would have
precluded such movements. In the authors' words:

> The trend is toward balanced bilateral facility of eye movements, but there is a
> strong rightward dominance correlated with the rightwardness of the underlying
> tonic-neck-reflex pattern.
>   This neuro-motor preference for the right sectors is a symptom of a deep-seated
> laterality which is also manifested in the *moving* ring situation. Here again there
> is a morphogenetic drag to the right, both head and eye movements favoring the
> right quadrant. But as the child matures (after the 112th day) there are widening
> excursions into the left quadrants. The eyes because of their more precocious
> emancipation surpass the head in these excursions. The head may move from
> extreme right through 120° toward the left but the eyes in their pursuit of the
> rings will make the full pursuit of 180°. The synchronization and coordination
> of eye movements and head movements change with the maturation of the con-
> trolling neuro-motor systems, but the eyes maintain an ontogenetic lead (p. 9).

B. Regarding arm postures, film analysis showed that the predominant
posture in the first seven or eight weeks was that of the tonic neck reflex. In
the next two weeks this asymmetry gave way to a symmetric bilateral extension of the arms at shoulder level, largely determined by the adoption of
the midline position of the head. In the next two weeks the arms were extended downward, moving obliquely towards the legs. At a later stage still
(23rd-26th week) there was bilateral flexion at the elbow which a few
weeks later was replaced by a combination of unilateral flexion and unilateral extension, ("In obedience to the rightwardness of the early tonic neck
reflex, the extension is most conspicuous in the right member"). After a stage
of bilateral extension the representative posture became flexion of the left
and extension of the right (33-39 weeks). Finally (43-52 weeks) there appeared a largely bilateral extensor posture interrupted by alternating pro-

pulsion movements, which resulted in a batting of the rings when supine, and which would be the precursors of crawling when prone.

A similar detailed analysis was also made for arm movements, as well as for leg behaviors. It is interesting however to note that this study did not utilize the method of analysis outlined by Gesell in his earlier paper (1935). He had instead been guided by the contours and dynamics inherent in the postures and activities themselves.

This study demonstrated with simplicity and some aesthetic gratification that there is a discernible and systematic trend in the ontogeny of motor behavior in the human infant, that there is an orderly patterning underlying behavioral phenomena which at first sight seem aimless, uncoordinated, and unpredictable. Film analysis enabled not only the elucidation of the molecular aspects, like visual fixation relative to head position, but also the molar ones, like trends in arm and leg postures and movements. Replaying the film over and over again, as well as the tracing of representative postures at weekly intervals, enabled the authors to discern the *Gestalten* of these trends which otherwise would have been submerged amidst the welter of adventitious details. Because of the minute analysis that is possible with film, these authors were able to delineate, with some precision, phases in infant neuromotor coordination.

This study also emphasizes the extent, often minimized by the empiricists, to which endogenous factors are prepotent in early infancy, even in the human species, and the limitations set by these factors upon the effects of exogenous stimulation. With the advent of the heyday of the learning theorists, it seems a great misfortune that the valuable information contained in such a paper should be relegated to the archives of behavior studies.

Motor Correlates of Crying

As a close colleague of Gesell, Ames (1941) held a similar orientation to the study of child behavior. While commending the detail and precision with which the facial expressions in crying are described in Darwin's *The Expression of the Emotions in Man and Animals*, she deplored the dearth of later detailed descriptions of emotional reactions. She herself attempted to supplement the Darwinian account by an analysis of the other motor activity involved in crying.

Her subjects were thirteen infants between the ages of eight and forty-eight weeks, filmed (at 16 frames per second) when lying supine on the floor and supine on the bath table. No stimuli were used to evoke distress reactions, and only spontaneous crying was studied. The relative incidence of the various motor patterns associated with states of crying and noncrying are shown in Figure 29. In general, crying seemed to be characterized by vigorous limb movements, more leg than arm activity, unilateral rather than bilateral limb activity, and strong flexor movements. Noncrying, on the

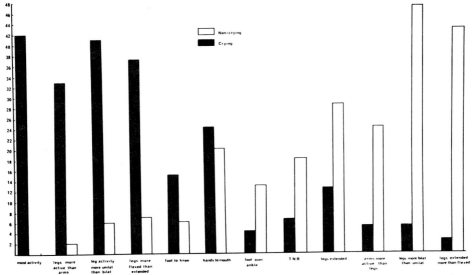

Figure 29. Frequency of occurrence of different behavior patterns in crying and in noncrying states (after Ames, 1941).

other hand, was characterized by bilateral rather than unilateral movements, greater arm than leg activity, and limb extension.

Ames found that once crying had started no particular temporal or spatial sequence of motor elements appeared to be characteristic of any age or even any individual. "Crying," she said, "seems more to disorganize the patterns prevailing at time of onset than to produce an invariable pattern." Table VIII gives one example of the development of crying. On the other hand, it was possible to see a characteristic pattern of onset of crying: "Forehead wrinkles just over inner corners of eyes, mouth opens, lines beside mough deepen, tongue flattens and then troughs, nose flattens and eyes squint shut, legs become unilaterally active." Ames saw the largely flexor movements in crying as having some protective significance.

It is rather sad that Ames did not make more of the analytical potential of her material. For example, if she were able to abstract a generalized pattern

TABLE VIII

AN EXAMPLE OF THE PATTERN OF ONSET OF CRYING (FROM AMES, 1941)

Time in frames*	Behavior
0:00	Supine, not crying, arms and legs extended, mouth closed, eyes open.
0:04	Vertical wrinkle appears in forehead between eyes; mouth opens, lines beside mouth deepen.
1:00	Mouth opens wider, tongue flattens, one leg flexes.
3:04	Legs extend, tongue troughs, nose flattens and eyes squint shut. Child is crying hard by now, but arms have not participated.

* There are 16 frames to a second. Thus 3:04 equals $3\frac{4}{16}$ seconds.

of onset, she should also have been able to obtain some measure of the sequential probabilities of the several components seen as dyads. It is regrettable too that she did not make a more detailed analysis of the patterns at different ages in order to see which components persisted and which dropped out or were modified, particularly since one of her assumptions was that ". . . such innate responses as exist in the organism at birth are soon altered by learning." We would very much doubt whether this is true of most of expressive behavior. The comparative analysis made by Andrew (1963) of expressive behavior in a number of primate species would justify these doubts.

Movement in the Newborn

Kessen *et al.* (1961) were concerned with obtaining a reliable and quantitative measure of the infant's movements in its first days of life. They wished to improve upon the existing stabilimetric devices in two ways:

> (a) in providing a fully comparable score, that is, a movement index that could be used in different research settings without introducing problems of mechanical comparability of instruments; and (b) in preserving a record of moment-to-moment changes in the behavior of the baby. For these purposes, motion-picture photography seemed appropriate (p. 96).

The infant was placed supine on a mattress; a Bell and Howell 16 mm (model DL-70) camera with a wide angle lens (10 mm) was fitted to a canopy three feet above the baby. The film was run at 16 frames per second and ten babies were filmed for five 30-second periods during each of their first five days. Behavioral events, such as crying, mouthing, hand-mouth contact, were recorded on an Esterline-Angus recorder via telegraph keys; depression of certain other keys operated signal lights which were subsequently used for synchronizing film and recorder data.

For analysis six frames from each thirty-second period were chosen, i.e. one frame per five seconds or per eighty frames (the 1st, 81st, 161st and so on). These frames were specially marked for identification. The film was fed past a projector lamp, the image being projected first on to a mirror placed at the front and slightly inclined backwards and from the mirror on to a plate glass surface approximately two feet above the mirror. The film take-up spool was driven via a variable speed control device operated by a foot switch. Each time a marked frame was projected, the film drive was stopped and a tracing made of specific details of the image projected on the plate glass. Only seven reference points (indicated by 7 dots) were used from the image for measurement of movement. These were: visible ear, right palm, left palm, right knee, left knee, right ankle, left ankle. Some other static reference point (e.g. light box) was also marked so that the tracings could be accurately superimposed. A calibration of the projected image was made by filming a 50 cm black paper strip. This yielded an image of 18.30 cm, so protocol data were multiplied by 50/18.3 to give a measure of actual displacement. A summary sheet of all the reference points from the six frames was finally made in colour code, and linear distances between successive representations of each reference point obtained. There was then available an *index of displacement* for several parts of the infant's body. The authors pointed out that "this is not a measure or total movement, but rather a measure of displacement over a predetermined interval."

The results indicated that there were stable individual differences in the movement index measure in the first five days and that this also showed systematic and significant increases during this period. There were no laterality effects evident in the limb movements, despite a frequent head preference for the right.

This study has made a major methodological contribution to the behavior literature since it is one of the very few which has provided a detailed description of the procedural and analytic steps in the use of a technique. Other workers should have no difficulty replicating such a study. It also provides a fairly precise method for measurement of movements which hitherto have been both recorded and measured, if at all, indirectly, as with a stabilimeter.

Since this technique is likely to be of value in other situations and with other subjects, certain questions of method might be raised here. If sampling is to be done once every five seconds, it seems somewhat prodigal in effort and cost to film at 16 feet per second; time-lapse photography (although probably involving some initial expenditure in equipment) would be more appropriate, and it is of interest to note that in a more recent study the authors have done just this, using a 35 mm Automax G-2 camera (Kessen, *et al.*, 1967). In this latter study they have improved upon the method of analysis too by using a Vanguard motion analyzer and an IBM 1620 programme which computes hypotenuses to determine the displacements. Equivalent measures however could be obtained, with less sophistication perhaps, from many of the currently available 16 mm editors.

It is difficult to see why these authors, in view of the precision in other respects, have been satisfied with individual points as reference indices for body parts. Although the selected points do probably prescribe a limb or part movement quite adequately, a limb outline may have provided more information at the cost of very little extra effort. These criticisms regarding matters of detail nevertheless detract little from the value of the techniques. A more serious criticism however relates to the authors' final evaluation in terms of movement index, which seems to completely vitiate the precision of the analytical procedures adopted. Such a gross measure might equally well be obtained using a stabilimeter, a technique upon which they were trying to improve.

Such a motion picture technique nevertheless could be used with great profit in the study of the development and acquisition of skills, even a simple one such as eating, and in investigation of motor performances in physically handicapped children, such as those with congenital agenesis of the limbs where prostheses are a substitute. In such analyses however the subject could be filmed against a gridded background or drape; this would facilitate measurement and circumvent the tedium of the arithmetical conversions necessitated by a calibration procedure.

This technique of motion picture recording and analysis has been used subsequently, with minor modifications of instrumentation or procedure, in other studies by Kessen and his colleagues (Williams, and Kessen, 1961; Kessen, and Leutzendorff, 1963).

Exploratory Behavior in Children

One of the major studies in which we decided to film the child's behavior was in that of exploratory behavior. We were concerned about what kinds of reaction the child showed when confronted with complete novelty, what kinds of motor patterns were manifest in the investigation of a novel object, how these patterns changed with the familiarity of the object and with the age of the subject. Considerations of continuity therefore determined that we did not use a camera with a mechanical motor since this would entail too many breaks in the recording. The Kodak Electric 8 Zoom camera was found to be a satisfactory instrument since it made use of preloaded cassettes, each taking standard twenty-five feet spools. With several cassettes at hand therefore only a few seconds need be lost in a ten minute session. Other features of some advantage in this camera were an Ektanar 10 to 30 mm f/1.6 zoom lens focussing to four feet, a fully automatic exposure meter and a reflex viewfinder. The zoom lens also enabled special attention to be given, when necessary, to subtle movements such as facial expressions. In general we used Kodachrome II films (25-40 ASA). In poor light conditions we found Adox U27 (400 ASA) to give adequate, though somewhat grainy records.

In many previous studies, observations had been made from behind a one-way screen. Such a screen may transmit only 10 percent of the available illumination, thus making filming impossible except with intense artificial illumination.

Since it was necessary that the camera was not in view of the subjects, we decided to simulate a one-way vision mirror. A large room measuring 24 feet by 12 feet was partitioned, to give a small waiting room, a 12 feet by 12 feet observation/playroom, and a filming cubicle (Fig. 30). A sheet of plate glass, measuring 10 feet by 2 feet, was inserted in the partition between cubicle and playroom, two feet above the floor. From this sheet of glass a tunnel of hardboard was built projecting into the filming cubicle, the sides subtending an angle of 90 degrees at one end of the glass, and an angle of 30 degrees at the other (Fig. 30); the roof of the tunnel was horizontal. The floor of the tunnel sloped upwards (at an angle of approximately 45° with the horizontal) to the rear aperture which measured 1 inch by 8 inches. The resulting shape of the tunnel therefore was that of an irregular pentahedron, lying on its side, the base being the glass screen and the apex the viewing aperture. The inside of the tunnel was painted matt black and then sprayed with black flock so that light in the tunnel was absorbed. The plate glass thus acted as a highly reflective surface (Fig. 31). This construction made it possible for the camera (fitted with a wide-angle lens) to be positioned at the aperture and have the whole room in view. Black drapes along the windows of the cubicle prevented light entering the tunnel from behind the camera, and also enabled the cubicle to be used as a darkroom for editing and analyzing film (Lee and Hutt, 1964).

The procedure for this study was the same as that described in Chapter 5, except that the observer was able to go into the cubicle rather than stay in the same room as the child. This was done with a reassuring comment to the child: "I am just going to finish off some work here for a few minutes. Would you like to play for a while with these toys?" The child's behavior for the next ten minutes was then filmed, and an almost continuous record was thus obtained. For the sake of economy one convention was employed: since primary interest was focussed on responses to the novel object, once ten or twenty-five seconds of an activity engaging another toy had been filmed, the rest of the activity sequence was recorded on a data sheet and its duration timed by a stopwatch.

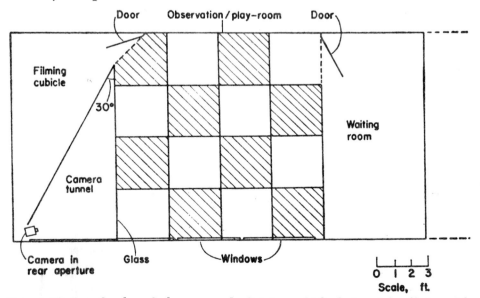

FIGURE 30. A scale plan of playroom and adjoining cubicle designed for filming children (from Lee, and Hutt, 1964).

FIGURE 31. View of the playroom taken from entrance to it.

The analysis of these data was unfortunately a somewhat tedious procedure. The film was played back on a viewer fitted with a frame counter, and
was analyzed in terms of activities, e.g. manipulates lever while looking at
window, or walks round kicking ball. For the purpose of this study, a very
detailed analysis was required only of behavior directed towards the novel
object. Thus different ways of manipulating the object were recorded separately. On the analysis sheet (Table IX) three columns on the left had in
turn the following: (1) frame-counter reading at the end of any activity,
(2) the number of frames occupied by that activity (obtained by subtracting the previous reading), and (3) conversion of number of frames to number of seconds (e.g. 240 frames filmed at 16 frames per second would occupy 15 seconds). For arithmetical convenience entries were made from
bottom to top of the paper.

When the experimental session had been completely recorded in this
manner and the duration of each activity obtained, the time spent in any
class of activities (e.g. locomotion, object investigation, etc.) could be calculated by summing the durations of the individual activities considered to be
in that class. The quantitative results obtained from the subjects who were
filmed were very similar to those obtained by the check list recordings. This
measure of reliability was reassuring.

For analysis of 16 mm film we have found the Acmade Miniviewer to be
extremely satisfactory (Fig. 32). This desk editor projects a sufficiently large

TABLE IX

ANALYSIS SHEET FOR MOTION PICTURE DATA

Frame No.	Frames	Secs	Activity
4226	114	7	screws it back on again
4112	75	5	puts light in mouth
4037	277	17	unscrews light
3760	59	$3\frac{1}{2}$	pushing object along
3701	179	11	getting off it—examining, feeling screws and sides
3522	88	$5\frac{1}{2}$	manipulating lever
3434	198	$12\frac{1}{2}$	climbing, sitting astride object
3236	70	$4\frac{1}{2}$	feeling counters, touching object
		30	pulling lorry apart—stands
3166	86	$5\frac{1}{2}$	pulling lorry apart
3080	117	7	pushing lorry
2963	127	8	sits—fixing lorry together
2836	163	10	walking round, holding lorry
2673	103	$6\frac{1}{2}$	stands touches window
		35	places barrels in lorry
2570	49	3	sits on floor with lorry and barrels
2521	177	11	walks to door and then to screen
		15	breaks lorry apart
2344	228	14	pulling lorry apart
		40	hugging golly
		20	untying golly's ribbon
2116	83	5	touches golly's buttons
2033	120	8	crawling around
1913	69	4	touching lever
1844	99	6	manipulating lever LH
1745	443	28	fingers lights while talking to herself
1302	7	$\frac{1}{2}$	putting light in mouth
1295	148	9	unscrews lights
1147			Begin

picture 6¼ inches by 4½ inches) to enable fairly detailed analysis, as well as the use of a superimposed grid, if necessary. Instant stop, start and reverse is by push button control. A manually controlled rotary transformer enables projection at variable speeds ranging from frame-by-frame to 75 frames per second. A time counter (for filming at a standard speed of 24 frames per second) can be substituted for the normally available footage counter. This machine is extremely easy to operate and is portable.

The results of a film analysis of the behavior of a group of children with gross brain damage are compared with those of normal children (Fig. 33). In terms of the time spent investigating the object, the brain-damaged children showed relatively little habituation over six sessions, in contrast to the normal children. In other words the brain-damaged subjects appeared to retain little information about the properties of the object from one session to the next.

Chronologically, studies using motion pictures antedated the same studies using check lists, and it was during the analysis of the films that the distinction between superficially similar behaviors, or at least between behaviors which had apparently similar effects became clear. Although the observer was naturally aware that qualitative changes were occurring from the beginning of the experiment to the end, even in the responses directed to the ob-

FIGURE 32. The Acmade Miniviewer: 16 mm motion picture editor.

ject, it was only possible to specify the nature of these changes after film analysis. Such an analysis showed that in the first two sessions visual fixation was synchronized with manipulation of the novel stimulus and the facial expression was one of concentration, brows slightly puckered, and mouth set in a firm line (Fig. 34 A, B). At a later stage, usually during the third or fourth sessions, manipulation became more brisk; it sometimes occurred with simultaneous visual exploration of other stimuli and the facial expression would become more relaxed (Fig. 34 C, D). Finally in the last two sessions the responses towards the object acquired almost a nonchalant air, vision and manipulation were no longer simultaneously directed towards the object and the facial expression became relaxed often with smiling (Fig. 34 E, F). Other objects might also be now incorporated in play activities. An older boy might use the lever in a most inventive manner, as a singer's microphone (Fig. 35).

This kind of qualitative analysis, leading to the distinction drawn between investigation and play (the latter responses described above), was made relatively easy by the ability to play the films repeatedly and slowly. It was also possible to specify which components of the total pattern were altered and the manner in which they were altered. Although an observer's attention is drawn to the gradual metamorphosis of exploratory activity over time, it would have been difficult to enumerate its characteristics using pencil and paper recordings or even tape recordings, since the observer is unaware of the transition until it is quite complete.

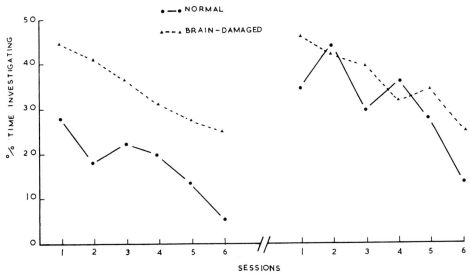

FIGURE 33. The proportions of time spent by normal and brain-damaged children of comparable ages in investigating a completely novel toy on the first and five subsequent exposures to it (from Hutt, 1968).

The Kinesics of Behavior

During the past decade and a half much has been heard of the study of *kinesics*. Birdwhistell in particular has reiterated its value for the analysis of behavior at the micro level (1963, 1965). Although the essentials of the method have been described and its implications for behavior study emphasized, little appears to have been published regarding its technical aspects: how recording is carried out, what form of analysis is made, or the form in which the results are finally presented. Recently however this deficiency has been partly rectified by a contribution which at least attempts to demonstrate how a kinesic analysis might proceed (Condon and Ogston, 1966). A motion picture (48 frames per second) was made, together with sound strip, of two subjects conversing. The film was then played through a time-motion analyzing projector. A segment of film (14 frames) occupying the time during subject B's utterance of the word "I" (subject A listening) is shown as illustrative material and is reproduced in full here (Fig. 36).

The authors' annotations read:

> Manually sweeping with the time motion projector from frame 11043 through 11045, Subject B's head, which had moved down and left slightly for one frame duration, symbolized by "(D,L) sli" in Figure 1, now turns right down and inclines right. Over the same three frames the mouth is closing with the upper lip moving back slightly while the lower lip moves back and up; the trunk is twist-

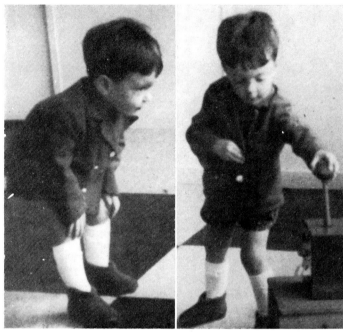

A Inspection.   B Tentative investigation.

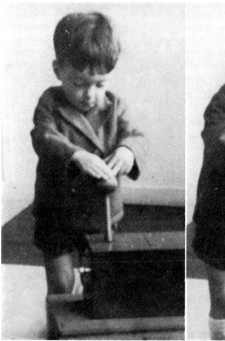

C Intent investigation.   D Brisk investigation (re-
                               laxed facial expression indi-
                               cating a transitional phase
                               from investigation to play).

E Unconventional
manipulation.

F Play, riding as horse, while
incorporating other objects.

FIGURE 34. Six frames taken in sequence from 16 mm motion
picture film illustrating the transition from investigation to play
in a three-year-old boy.

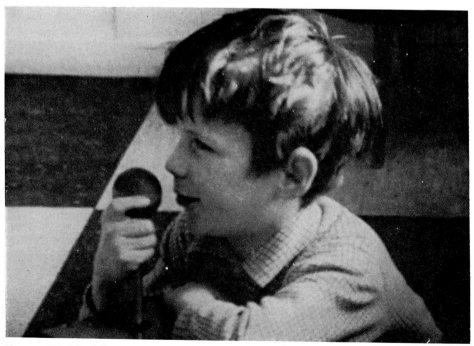

FIGURE 35. Playful response by a six-year-old boy using the lever as a crooner's microphone.

SUBJECT B

PHONETICS: a̯ a̯ a a a a e e e u̯ ə

FRAME NUMBERS (1/48 SECOND)	11040	41	42	43	44	45	46	47	48	49	50	51	52	53
HEAD	U		(D,L) sli	R,D,QR			D,R sli	D,R,QL sli		D,R			R,D	R,D V sli
EYES	1,2 D V sli							1,2 U V sli						
BROWS														
MOUTH UPPER LIP	F,D sli / C sli		B V sli / V sli / C	B sli / C			V sli / C	C		(F,U) sli / C			F,U sli / C	D,F sli / C
MOUTH LOWER LIP	U,B		B sli	B,U			B,U V sli	U		U,F sli			U,F sli	U,F
TRUNK	B,S sli		(B,L) sli	T_R sli			B sli	T_R		L,B sli			F,T_R sli	R
RIGHT SHOULDER	F			F,RO sli				RO					F,RO sli	F,RO
RIGHT ELBOW	F		F,S	F			F,S	F					F,S	(F,S) sli
RIGHT WRIST	LCK		E sli	LCK						F sli			LCK	
RIGHT FINGERS FIRST	(B,C) E		B,F / C,E	(B,C) E				(B,C) E sli		LCK			(B,C) E sli	
RIGHT FINGERS SECOND	C,F sli		(B,C) F	(B,C) F fst				(B,C) F		LCK			Æ sli	
RIGHT FINGERS THIRD	(B,C) F sli		(B,C) F	(B,C) F fst				(B,C) F		LCK				
RIGHT FINGERS FOURTH	(B,C) F sli		(B,C) F	(B,C) F fst				(B,C) F		LCK			LCK	
RIGHT THUMB	Æ		(B,C) F / AD	(B,C) F										

SUBJECT A

FRAME NUMBERS (1/48 SECOND)	11040	41	42	43	44	45	46	47	48	49	50	51	52	53
HEAD	R,D V sli		R,U V sli	L V sli			QL sli	R sli		R,U sli			R	
													R V sli	
EYES														
BROWS							U sli							
MOUTH	O V sli									O,W				
TRUNK	T_R sli		F,T_R sli				L V sli	R,T_R		R,S			T_R	
RIGHT SHOULDER	LCK		F sli				LCK	B sli		LCK				
RIGHT ELBOW	LCK		E V sli	E,P			LCK	S V sli		(S,E) sli			E sli	
RIGHT WRIST	X		E V sli	E,X sli			X sli	Y sli		Y,F sli			(Y,F) sli	
RIGHT FINGERS FIRST	(A,B) E sli / C,F sli		B,F V sli	(A,B) E / C,F			(B,C) F sli	LCK		(A,B,C) F			C,E sli / B,F sli	
RIGHT FINGERS SECOND	(A,B) E sli / C,F sli		B,F V sli	(A,B) E / C,F			(B,C) F sli	LCK		(A,B,C) F			C,E sli / B,F sli	
RIGHT FINGERS THIRD	C,F sli		B,F V sli	LCK			(B,C) F sli	LCK					C,E sli / B,F sli	
RIGHT FINGERS FOURTH	C,F sli		B,F V sli	LCK			(B,C) F sli	LCK						
RIGHT THUMB	(A,B) E sli / C,F sli		C,F sli	(B,C) F			C,F sli	LCK					C,E	
LEFT SHOULDER	LCK							F sli		LCK				
LEFT ELBOW	S sli		LCK					F sli		S, sli			LCK	
LEFT WRIST	LCK		E, sli	LCK				E sli		X			E	
LEFT FINGERS FIRST	LCK			C,E sli			LCK	C,E V sli		LCK				
LEFT FINGERS SECOND	LCK			C,E sli			LCK	C,E V sli		LCK				
LEFT FINGERS THIRD	LCK			C,E sli			LCK	C,E V sli		LCK				
LEFT FINGERS FOURTH	LCK													

FIGURE 36. The recording sequence of subject B saying *I* while subject A listens (from Condon, and Ogston, 1966).

ing right slightly, the right shoulder moves forward and rotates outward slightly; the right elbow flexes with the right wrist locked. Similarly, the fingers and thumb of the right hand move in specific directions during the same three frames. No movements were detected in other body parts.

The direction of change of the movements described above is thus sustained together during this period of time (3/48ths of a second).

Sweeping from frame 11043 through 11046 and detecting change of direction with frame 11046, the next "unit interval" is seen to begin and its terminal boundary must be detected. A sweep is thus begun from 11045 (the last frame prior to the commencement of the new interval) through 11046 and 11047 to see if change occurs in the head at 11047. In the present case, change does occur which indicates that this may be a one-frame unit. If no change had been detected, the next sweep would have gone through 11046, 11047 and 11048. This expansion of frame sweep continues until change is detected. The above procedure is carried out with respect to all body parts. The fact that almost all detectable changes of direction of the other body parts then moving were also found to occur at frame 11047 was considered to add to the decision to regard 11046 as a one-frame unit. (This redundancy factor in the change pattern is an important element in the decisional criteria for determining body motion "units.")

Thus through frame 11046, Subject B's head now moves primarily downward, but also continues to turn right slightly; the mouth continues to close but the upper lip is now relatively still and the lower lip moves back and up slightly; the trunk now moves back slightly; the elbow now supinates as well as flexes; while the right hand movements continue as before. The body parts have again sustained the direction of change together.

Using the same procedure, the next two frames, 11047 and 11048, reveal further changes in direction which are sustained by almost all body parts, until the next set of changes which are sustained through frames 11049, 11050 and 11051, terminating precisely with the end of the word "I" (p. 340).

It is remarkable how the patterns and constellations of behavioral changes reveal themselves: even the barest movement of a digit rarely occurs in isolation, the configurations of movement are clearly evident. These movements moreover bear a distinct relationship to the elements of speech. What is even more striking upon inspection of the figure are the synchronized and similarly configurational movements of the subject who is merely listening.

Such subtlety of detail would certainly not have been discernible by any other method than film analysis. However, what is disappointing is that no further progress appears to have been made towards a kinesic analysis of behavior. The procedure still awaits development to a degree which will permit some quantification and expression of movement in more systematic and general terms. Although Condon and Ogston emphasize its potential use in the analysis of pathological behavior, their illustrative material is again simply description at a specific and concrete level. To say that a characteristic differentiating a chronic schizophrenic's behavior from a normal's is "the 'semi-frozenness' of his body motion coupled with a monotonous quality in his speech" does not add much to a clinical description, and does not require the sophisticated cinematographic techniques used in this study. Furthermore, it remains to be proven that the degree of microanalysis involved in this type of procedure justifies, in terms of the data obtained, the enormous expenditure of time and effort. For instance, has filming at forty-eight frames per second really provided twice the information or even more information than filming at twenty-four or even sixteen frames per second? Any method or technique is only as good as the purpose to which it is put. In principle this technique appears a promising tool for students of behavior, but we still await its full application before any evaluation can be made.

Analysis of Human Gait

A most detailed microanalysis of a simple activity, namely walking, has been elegantly carried out by Murray and his colleagues (1964, 1966, 1967). Their results were based on an analysis of the movement patterns of sixty men ranging from twenty to seventy-five years of age. The method of recording enabled both the temporal and structural components of the pattern to be analyzed and hence the subtle interrelationships of the various components to be mapped out.

The recording technique consisted of interrupted light photography, carried out with a speed graphic camera. The subjects had reflective strips attached to them at a number of target points. They walked in semidarkness, and filming was done by an ASCOR Speedlight with a flash rate of twenty per second. Thus the target positions were serially registered on film at the moments of illumination. These workers used Royal X Pan Film.

According to Murray (1967) locomotion has three funtional properties: (1) support of the upright body, (2) maintenance of balance in the upright position, and (3) execution of the stepping movement. The manner in which these three functions are subserved is illustrated by a very detailed analysis of the walking cycle:

> A *walking cycle* is the time interval between successive instants of initial foot-to-floor contact for the same foot (right-to-right or left-to-left). For normal subjects, heel-strike marks the initial foot-floor contact.
> The *stance* phase is that period when the foot is in contact with the floor; and the *swing* phase, when the foot is off the floor moving forward to create the next step. Since the periods of stance and swing occur alternately for the two limbs, one limb must provide support and balance in order to free the opposite limb to swing forward to create the new step. Therefore, the prerequisite abilities to produce support, balance and the stepping mechanism are interdependent in function and must operate simultaneously and continuously for effective and independent locomotion. The futility of one prerequisite functioning effectively without the others is obvious (p. 292).

The analysis has clearly enabled definitions of a very precise nature to be made, and these in turn provided an operational definition of walking in terms of the linear and structural components rather than the temporal ones: "The definition of bipedal walking, compared to that of running, requires that the foot of the supportive extremity remains in contact with the floor until the opposite foot has made floor contact."

Analysis of the free walking movements of thirty normal men gave a mean speed of 151 cm per second with a standard deviation of 20. When the subjects were asked to walk fast, the mean speed increased to 218 cm per second (standard deviation 25). These figures indicate a fair degree of homo-

geneity in walking speeds, although in general, stride lengths of tall subjects were longer than those of short subjects. It was found that normal men
increased their speed of walking by taking longer strides in shorter periods
of time, a stride being measured as the linear distance "between successive
points of foot-to-floor contact of the same foot." Another finding of some rel-
vance was the relative independence of several stride dimensions and chro-
nological age from twenty to sixty years, but after sixty the men tended to
take shorter strides. Furthermore, for free or fast walking in normal gait, "the
duration of successive temporal components and the length of successive
steps are rhythmic. In contrast, these temporal and linear components are
arrythmic in many pathological gaits."

Murray also analyzed the rotation patterns of the upper and lower limbs,
the vertical pathways of the heel and toe, the transverse rotation of the pel-
vis and thorax, and the vertical, lateral and forward pathways of the head
and neck throughout the walking cycle. As an illustration of the kind of data
yielded by these analyses, Figure 37 shows the simultaneous rotation patterns of the hip, knee and ankle of a normal man. It is surprising how frequently a reversal in the direction of rotation occurs. As Murray comments:

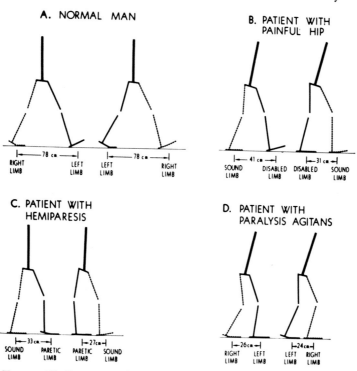

FIGURE 37. Patterns of hip, knee and ankle rotation for free speed
walking of one normal man (upward deflections in slide lines
= flexing excursions; downward deflections in dotted lines =
extending excursions) (from Murray, 1967).

The stance phase is never characterized by total extension of the three major joints, and only a brief instant at the beginning of the swing phase is characterized by total flexion. Careful scrutiny of all three patterns throughout the cycle reveals that although the directions of rotation are constantly shifting, the three major joints rarely rotate simultaneously in the same direction. Thus, the complex movement patterns of normal walking entail the ability to flex one joint as adjacent joints are extending, and *vice versa*. One cannot help being impressed with the sensory-motor control required to produce such coordinated movement.

It is also interesting and clinically significant for gait training to note the normal sequence of initial flexion preparatory to the swing phase for the hip, knee and angle. Again, although each of the three joints participates in some flexion which produces the relative shortening of the limb for foot-floor clearance, the initiation of the flexion movement is never simultaneous. Normal walking is characterized by a discrete sequence of flexion preparatory to the swing phase, with the knee flexing first, at the 0.40-sec. time in the cycle, the hip second, at 0.50 sec. and the angle last, at 0.65 sec. Indeed, by the time the ankle initiates flexion at the onset of the swing phase, the knee has almost completed its major flexion excursion (p. 302).

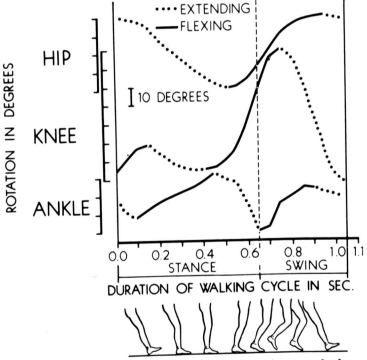

FIGURE 38. Line diagrams traced from photographic records showing positions of limbs and trunk at instant of initial foot-to-floor contact for both extremities for a normal man sixty-nine inches tall and three disabled patients (height B: 71 inch; C: 70.5 inch and D: 68 inch). Length of steps taken by each subject is shown beneath each figure (from Murray, 1967).

Murray also compared normal gait with patterns of abnormal gait in three patients, one with unilateral arthropathy causing hip pain, another with hemiparesis, and the third with bilateral resichials of paralysis agitans. As would be expected, the walking speeds of the three patients was much slower than that of normals, but the former also showed great irregularity in their forward displacement patterns as well as in the durations of the successive temporal components of the walking cycle. The limb positions at the instant of initial floor contact are more vertical and less oblique than those of normal subjects (Fig. 38). The technique of recording and method of analysis in this study are not only of theoretical and technical interest, but the data they have yielded are of clinical and practical importance. Such information is of particular relevance to those supervising rehabilitation and training programmes for the disabled. Although the recording technique uses photographic and not motion picture film, with certain modifications it may be useful in the analysis of other skills, for example in spastic children.

Chapter 7

SOCIAL BEHAVIOR

THE problems of accurately recording social interactions of several individuals taxes the ingenuity of the behavioral scientist most. Not only
are social behaviors inherently subtle and complex, but the fact that in any
natural social situation there are usually a number of individuals interacting
and moving about manifoldly magnifies the task of tracking a specific individual or reliably recording particular encounters. Attempts are made to cir-
cumscribe the problems as much as possible by reducing the number in the
group, by marking the animals and following them individually, or by recording only certain preselected activities. Despite these maneuvers human
behavior and social communication in particular appear so complex and sophisticated that its recording and analysis present a formidable task.

In this area perhaps more than in any other, we would have expected to
borrow extensively and benefit greatly from the pioneering work of the ethologists whose primary interest after all is in social behavior. Indeed we
have learned much from them concerning the identification of fairly stereotyped postures and displays, about the elucidation of causal and functional
mechanisms, and about biologically relevant interpretations. We have
learned little however of the essential techniques employed in obtaining
the data—of the mechanics of their discipline.

A surprising number of potentially valuable studies fail to give any details
of the recording techniques employed. Here we are concerned primarily with
the how-and-what aspects of methods and only secondarily with the why-
and-when aspects of the phenomena. Hence the number of studies we can
usefully refer to is strictly limited. However exciting the findings or original
the conceptualization, it is difficult to justify the inclusion of studies which
omit procedural details.

In this chapter the application to social behavior of the techniques already discussed will be considered by reference to animal and human studies which have utilized these methods.

TAPE RECORDING

Individual Distance in Monkeys

In an investigation of the characteristic spatial separation from conspecifics that gregarious animals maintain, Rosenblum *et al.* (1964) used ten pig-

tail and ten bonnet monkeys. The twenty animals were divided into four homospecific groups, each with one adult male and four adult females. One group at a time was observed in a daily randomized order between 09.30 and 13.30 hours at least three days a week for eight weeks. The observations were carried out as follows:

Using a random series, each S in the group was the focus of observation for a 90-sec period, the entire sequence of subjects being repeated once, for a total of 180 secs of focused observation for each S each day.

The E dictated the observed behaviours in the form of predefined highly codified behaviour patterns into a continuously running DeJur Stenorette tape dictation machine. The E recorded both the beginning and ending of each social behaviour in which the focus S engaged, including those it initiated and those of which it was the recipient, along with the partner(s) involved. In this manner a S's social behaviour could be tracked during its own focus period and also whenever it interacted with another animal during the latter's focus period. Thus the theoretical maximum score for each S's social behaviours, with five S's being observed was 900 seconds.

The continuously running dictation tape provided a record of the elapsed time of each observed behaviour. A standard electric timer was connected in parallel with the playback of the recorder thus allowing durations to be tabulated in one second intervals (p. 339).

Although a large number of behavior categories were recorded, the authors considered two to be particularly pertinent to the assessment of individual distance: (1) proximity (i.e. "passive standing or sitting within twelve inches of another animal without making contact or engaging the other in any additional social behaviour") and (2) passive contact (i.e. "remaining in physical contact with another without engaging the other in any additional social behaviour"). There was over 90 percent interobserver agreement on the durations of these behaviors, though this is to be expected with only two such clearly defined patterns.

The results showed that the bonnet monkeys spent significantly longer in passive contact than the pigtail monkeys. Although there was a similar trend in proximity behavior, the difference between the species was not significant. The authors concluded that "*proximity* and *passive contact* may be manifestations of different underlying systems and that the tendency to passive contact may well be a species-specific characteristic." Perhaps a few preliminary observations might have saved the authors time and effort in recording a substantial amount of data which was subsequently judged to be peripheral to the object of the study.

Social Behavior of Rodents

In studies of the social behaviors of rodents, Grant (1963) first made an analysis of these activities in the male laboratory rat, and subsequently, Grant and Mackintosh (1963) made a comparative analysis of the postures observed in the social interactions of several species of common rodents. In these studies one animal was introduced into the home cage of another and a commentary on their behavior was dictated onto a two-channel tape recorder by two observers, each describing one animal. Code words were used in recording the acts and postures.

Since one of the aspects these authors were interested in was the sequential patterning of these elements, a problem they had to face was how to decide when a sequence was not a sequence. In other words, which successive codes on one track of the taperecording belonged to one sequence, and which, to another? Grant adopted the convention that an interval of over three seconds separated an act from the preceding sequence.

Some of the postures described by these authors are shown in Figure 39. Grant's analysis of the behavior sequences exemplifies the traditional ethological analytical procedure.

Grant illustrates his treatment of the data by reference to four acts: threat, attack, aggressive posture and aggressive groom. He arranged these in a matrix as shown in Table X. Each cell denotes how frequently a particular preceding act was followed by every act. An analysis of which acts of one

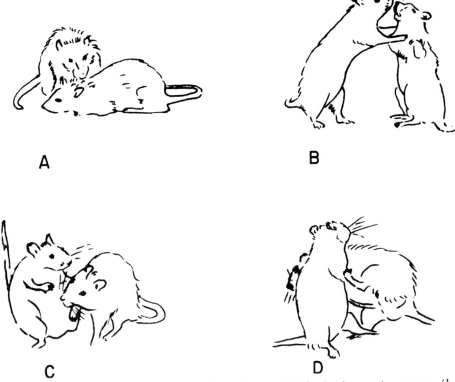

A   B

C   D

FIGURE 39. Social postures in the rat (from Grant, 1963). A: Aggressive groom (left animal), crouch (right animal). B: Offensive upright posture (left) and defensive upright posture (right). C: Upright posture (left), defensive sideways posture (right). D: Defensive upright posture (left), offensive sideways posture (right).

TABLE X

FREQUENCY WITH WHICH CERTAIN ACTS OF THE RATS ARE FOLLOWED
BY OTHERS; PRECEDING ACTS ARE ARRAYED VERTICALLY, SUCCEEDING
ACTS HORIZONTALLY (FROM GRANT, 1963)

	Threat	*Attack*	*Agg. Posture*	*Agg. Groom*	*Total*
Threat	—	12	44	75	131
Attack	0	—	52	14	66
Agg. Posture	0	0	—	19	19
Agg. Groom	14	1	15	—	30
Total	14	13	111	118	246

animal were followed by which acts of the other yielded a "cross-correlation sequence." By processes of both deductive and inductive reasoning, Grant then organizes the various postures and acts into motivational systems and these in turn into their component pathways. In other words he has constructed an ethogram of the social behavior of the rat.

To an uninitiated nonethologist however, much of the nomenclature and argument might appear to beg the question. Let us therefore consider how Grant arrives at one of his conclusions: "Aggressive Posture and Submissive Posture are expressions of aggression and flight occurring as end points of sequences." What evidence is there, for example, that submissive posture is on the flight pathway, or aggressive posture is aggressive?

Grant starts with a premise: "It is now recognised that agonistic social behavior is motivated by two main drives, Aggression and Flight."

In a previous paper, GRANT and CHANCE (1958), the Submissive Posture was taken as indicating that the rat showing this posture had submitted and had lost that particular encounter. This particular posture was used because it was easily recognised and there was a strong subjective feeling that the animals showing it had submitted. The following points indicate that this assumption was correct.

If the occurrence in sequences of Submissive Posture is compared with that of the more overt form of flight, Retreat, they are shown to occur in similar positions. Defensive Upright Posture and Defensive Sideways Posture lead to both Submissive Posture and Retreat at higher than the expected level.

Defensive Upright Submissive Posture 102 (expected 24)
Defensive Upright Retreat   96 (expected 43)
Defensive Sideways Submissive posture 105 (expected 19)
Defensive Sideways Retreat   41 (expected 33)
(P. 264).

Even on inspection, these Defensive postures clearly lead to Retreat much more frequently than would be expected by chance, but statistical tests would have strengthened Grant's argument. Other lines of evidence substantiate the flight nature of this posture: Grant states, "this posture is one of the few that occur as end-points of social behavior, the ratio of acts preceding it to acts following it is 454: 195," and again:

The cross-correlation sequences show that Submissive Posture occurs much more frequently as a response than it is responded to; the other rat usually stops acting socially and moves away. Also from the cross-correlation it can be seen that it occurs in response to the overt form of aggression, Attack. Attack responded to by Submissive Posture 27 (expected 4).

The first of these arguments does not *necessarily* identify the motivation underlying the posture, but the second argument is much more convincing. Grant continues his argument:

These facts seem to show that the Submissive Posture is an expression of submission motivated by a flight drive. If this is accepted, the Aggressive Posture, the equivalent posture of the aggressive animal in which it positions itself at right angles over the body of an animal in the Submissive Posture, can then be thought of as an expression of dominance motivated by an Aggressive Drive. Other evidence for this is its positive relationship with the more overt forms of aggression, Attack and Bite.

Attack   Aggressive Posture 52 (expected 5)
Bite   Aggressive Posture 10 (expected 2)

There is also a marked lack of correlation with the flight postures. Defensive Upright Posture and Defensive Sideways Posture lead to Aggressive Posture only once each as compared with expected values of 23 and 17 (p. 265).

Again he adduces three lines of evidence for the aggressive nature of the aggressive posture, the second of which seems more convincing and pertinent than the other two.

Although not as rigorous as it could have been, we believe that this kind of analysis is important. Grant's originality in the elucidation of distinct motivational pathways is to be applauded. We would like to see the application of some tests of significance particularly where figures do not unequivocally bear out a point, since such a small refinement would considerably accelerate a rapprochement between psychological and ethological disciplines.

Play Activities in Nursery School Children

In this study carried out over forty years ago, Bott (1928) as many others, was limited to written observations. Since certain aspects of the analysis were extremely original and pertinent to the protrayal of certain relationships operating in interactional behavior, and remain so today, relevant parts of the study will be described here. Moreover, many points of the author's methodological rationale are equally pertinent to spoken commentaries.

Bott was primarily concerned with developing a method for the satisfactory recording and analysis of the play behavior of young children between the ages of two and five years. As a preliminary to a more systematic formulation, she made a number of undirected diary-type observations. During this phase the durations of each recorded incident were timed with a stopwatch. These preliminary records showed that there seemed to be three main categories of behavior directed to: (1) *materials* used in play, (2) *adults* in charge, and (3) *peers*. Accordingly, subsequent observations were entered in three columns, one assigned to each category and with durations of each activity noted alongside. Various abbreviations and symbols were used to facilitate the recording.

The children were observed in a free-play situation of approximately one hour duration, the observer sitting unobtrusively in a corner of the room, three observers, each recording the behavior of a different child.

Only one category, relations with other children, will be described here in detail since it employed a method of analysis which must have been extremely original when first used by Bott. In this category five activities were selected for investigation: talking (T), watching (W), interference (Int.), limitation (lm), cooperation (Co.) Although it is arguable whether these activities are appropriate or satisfactory, it is clear that the author had reservations about the selection herself.

> The selection of categories for the classification of behaviour is, of course, a fundamental part in method. . . . In making our choice we tried to avoid predetermined categories, and to derive our types pragmatically out of preliminary unprejudiced observations. . . . As far as possible the element of judgment on the part of the observer was minimized by making an overt act the ground of discrimination. Thus, when a child interferes he does some specific thing which can be recorded in the column for descriptive entries. The variety of such acts may (and indeed already does) indicate the need for a further study of types of interferences in order to define the meaning of this category, but such a refinement of definition presupposes the collection of material on some rough and ready basis as we have used. . . . The fact that a method will provide for the analysis to be pursued to any level of refinement that may be desired is, we feel, an advantage and a mark of strength, for then circumstances alone need delimit the number of new problems that may be formulated for special study. It is desirable, however, that at whatever level analysis is to be pursued in a given study the terms employed to characterize the observable phenomena should be as unambiguous as possible. The fact that our observers had comparatively little difficulty in recognizing and classifying the behaviour of these children according to the criteria laid down is perhaps evidence that the concepts used were to a degree adequate, but comparability of the records was only attained through close conference and criticism concerning the use of these descriptive terms (p. 51).

The frequency with which each of the five response categories was shown by each child to every other child is shown in Table XI. The children initiating the action were arrayed by age on the ordinate, and the children towards whom the action was directed on the abscissa. Thus the totals at the right indicate overall frequencies of response for each child towards all other children, and conversely, totals at the bottom indicate the frequency with which behavior was directed to each child. The squares in heavy outline in-

SOCIAL RESPONSES AMONG ELEVEN CHILDREN UNDER
FIVE CATEGORIES

Talking, Interference, Watching, Imitation, Cooperation

TABLE XI. (From Bott, 1928)

dicate the pairs which had most interaction in terms of response frequencies.

Talking was clearly the most common response category, increasing in frequency with age. The oldest child, 0 (54 months), had the highest score, most (80%) of his interactions being verbal. Age however was not the only determinant of verbal activity. N, only a month younger than 0, was considerably less vocal, and four children (A, E, F and M) who showed similar frequencies of verbal behavior differed widely in age, being twenty-six, thirty-one, thirty-six and fifty-two months respectively.

Despite his age E was extremely active. Over half his interactions however were disruptive (interference, 157); not surprisingly all the other children responded to him in some manner but most verbally (36). Clearly M and O had a reciprocal relationship, O adopting a dominant role and M one of acquiescence (imitation, 18). From inspection of the matrix M could be seen to occupy a peculiar position in the social hierarchy. Much behavior was directed to him, primarily of a verbal kind, but he himself initiated very little positive interaction, much of it being of an imitative kind and largely directed at O.

It is not entirely clear whether all social encounters among the children were noted under one or other of these five categories or whether certain types of activities were omitted. In either case the resultant loss of a significant category, like fighting or quarrelling, seems surprising and regrettable.

In this age group generally aggression and destructiveness are often manifested both physically and verbally, occasionally with unpredictable effects. It would have been of some interest to the general reader to know whether this was a group of particularly well-behaved children, whether unruly behavior was preempted by the intervention of the staff, or whether it was included in a more general category such as 'interference.'

The categories used in this study are unsatisfactory in many respects. First, there is much disparity in the definitive power of the categories. Certain categories like 'watching' and 'imitation' are defined by the term itself; others, like 'talking' are far more general and perhaps less meaningful—an appeal and an expletive would both qualify for inclusion.

Despite the many reservations one may have about the particulars of this study, in general it was an exemplary attempt to record and analyze some aspects of the free-field behavior of young children. The author herself was well aware of the problems of systematic and representative sampling and of the hazards of behavior categorization and selection. Nevertheless she made every attempt to define specifically the response to be included in each category, and even if some classification appears to have been done retrospectively, an effort was made to achieve homogeneity and agreement in the process.

Colleagues of Bott also made use of this method of recording (with some minor modifications) and analysis in studying the sleeping and eating habits of children (Chant, and Blatz, 1928, Blatz, 1928) and their investigation of the effects of day sleep upon night sleep and the criteria operating in the development of eating habits for instance, are prototypical of later, and perhaps more sophisticated, studies. It is sad that the results of these studies as well as the methodological issues raised by these authors have been so undervalued by contemporary students of behavior.

Finally, Bott's method of analyzing and representing the children's interactional data is highly effective. Presented in this manner, relationships which may be subtle and submerged at a different level are revealed with some clarity. Trends and tendencies too become more evident, e.g. from Bott's data it is clear that children did not interact exclusively, or even primarily, with children of their own age, a fact which many may find surprising. Considering that this contribution was made forty years ago, it seems to be a particularly original one in its field.

CHECK LISTS AND EVENT RECORDERS

Behavior of Monkeys in Groups

In a study to determine the response patterns of juvenile rhesus monkeys in the absence of adult animals, Bernstein and Draper (1964) used both individual and group activity check lists. Since their list of categories and definitions is comprehensive and explicit, it is reproduced here in Table XII. These categories were those included in the individual check list, the group list containing only twelve of the major categories. For the group check list only the total number of animals participating in any of the activities was entered.

The three male and eight female animals were housed in an outdoor compound. Individual observations were made five times daily for twenty days for five minutes at a time. The check list was divided into ten 30-second in-

TABLE XII

DEFINITIONS OF BEHAVIOR CATEGORIES OF JUVENILE RHESUS
MONKEYS. (FROM BERNSTEIN, AND DRAPER, 1964)

Term	Definition
Drink	Licking or sucking of liquid.
Eat	Any object or portion disappearing entirely into the mouth.
Rest	No movement for the entire time unit with eyes closed or partially closed.
Auto	Self-directed activity including scratching, self-grooming etc.
Manipulate	Carrying, pushing or pulling of objects with the hands, mouth or feet.
Vocal	Any vocalization.
Groom	
Groom	Examination of the hair and skin of another animal using the hands with some mouth movements.
Social investigate	Examination of the body orifices or wounds of another using the mouth primarily.
Aggression	
Fight	Biting, slapping or vigorous pulling of another.
Threat	Mouth open, intent stare at another—at times with head weaving and lowered with lunging and barking.
Charge	Rapid approach to another usually following threat.
Chase	Rapid pursuit of another.
Flee	Rapid withdrawal from another.
Fear grimace	Teeth clenched, lips drawn back—with squealing at times.
Cringe-crouch	Lying prone with arms and legs drawn up to the body and maintaining this posture passively—sometimes with fear grimace and squealing.
Sex	
Sex present	Turns elevated hindquarters towards another, averts the tail and may look back.
Mount	Hands on hips of another, feet hold ankles of other.
Play	Includes play fighting and chasing and is characterized by frequent interruptions, deliberate positionings, incomplete behavior and silence.
Huddle	Extensive body contact with the weight of one partially supported by another. One or both may hold the other and one animal's head may rest on the back of the neck of the other animal.
Travel	Any change in body location of a full body length or more.
Proximity	Within 3 feet of another.
Contact	Any contact not otherwise indicated.
Passive	Remaining in one location throughout a time unit without engaging in any other activity and with the eyes open.
Lipsmack	Rapid lip and tongue movements producing a non-vocal sound, and directed at another at a time other than grooming.
High location	Located in the upper one-fourth of the compound.

tervals; "a check mark indicated the occurrence of an activity at least one time during the 30-second time unit." Both individual and group check lists were completed for one-hundred observation sessions.

The quantitative results were computed in terms of the percentage of intervals in which a particular activity occurred. The authors state:

> The outstanding characteristic of the juvenile group was the fact that group members averaged almost 85% of their time in proximity with one another. While in proximity individuals were in non-specific contact with one another about one-fourth of the time, huddled together an additional one-fourth of the time and groomed about one-fifth of the time. . . . Drinking, aggression, sex and play each occurred during 5% or less of scored time units and Ss were passive for approximately 8% of the time.

With behavior sampled every thirty seconds for only five minutes at a time, it may appear misleading to talk of percent time spent in activity A or B. But the authors have compensated for their relatively long time-intervals and short sessions by the number of observations carried out. Nevertheless, the problem posed by the fact that an event of brief duration (e.g. a grunt) and one of considerably longer duration (i.e. grooming) both obtain the same score becomes accentuated. Although this is an inherent limitation of any check list, its significance diminishes in inverse proportion to the length of the time interval. Moreover, the authors of this study omit to mention whether they recorded all animals simultaneously—with eleven animals this would be a formidable task for one observer—or whether specific animals were followed in any one session. From the details given, the former seems more likely, in which case it is difficult to see how all animals could be scored for twenty-five categories.

Maternal and Infant Behavior in the Monkey

One of the best studies utilizing a rather unusual form of check list was that used by Hansen (1966) in his investigation of the development of maternal and infant behavior in the rhesus monkey. There were two primary groups of subjects in this study: (1) the mother playpen group, which consisted of four infant males which had been with their mothers from birth to fifteen months of age, and (2) the surrogate playpen group, which consisted of two male and two female infants who were separated from their mothers at birth and reared with surrogate mothers (Harlow, and Zimmerman, 1959). The two groups were housed separately. Within each group, an infant and its mother occupied one of the four living cages which surrounded a central play area (Fig. 40). This area was in turn divided into four play cell units. The entrance from a living cage into the play area was such that only the infant, by virtue of its size, could pass through it. Observations were made of two-animal (mother-infant and infant-infant) and four-animal interactions, but only the former will be referred to here.

Hansen's check list is slightly unusual in that although he time sampled

PLAYPEN UNITS

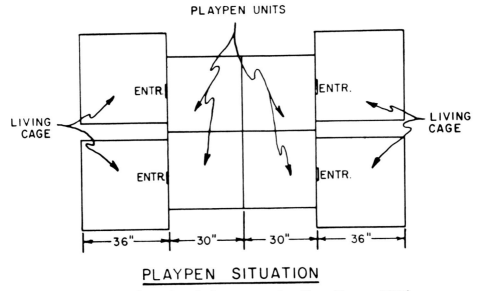

PLAYPEN SITUATION

FIGURE 40. Floor plan of playpen situation (from Hansen, 1966).

behavior every fifteen seconds, categories were denoted by symbols and were not entered at the heads of columns. In other words, his check list was extremely simple: two columns of ten rows each. Every fifteen seconds a signal light indicated a new time period and consecutive observations were entered in successive rows.

The subdivision of each row into two allowed the behaviors of the mother and infant to be recorded separately (upper and lower respectively). The units of behavior were defined in terms of motor patterns. A general symbol was used for a gross behavior category (e.g. a circle for play), and variations of this denoted subcategories. Some of the definitions of Hansen's major categories and their subdivisions are given below:

    I Mother-infant behaviours.
        A. *Cradling.* Providing active contactual support for the infant via use of the arms and/or the legs.
        B. *Grooming.* Spreading and picking through the fur with or without hand to mouth movements.
        C. *Punishing.* Mouthing, cuffing or slapping, clasp-pulling with fur or rejecting the infant, the latter defined as prevention of the infant's attempts to attain, maintain or regain contact.
        D. *Restrain-retrieve.* Restraining or retrieving the infant, the former referring to active interference with the infant's attempts to leave the presence of the mother; the latter, to maternal restoration of contact.

        E. *Signals to return.*
            (1) "Silly grin." A facial expression exhibited by the mother consisting of a simultaneous retraction of the corners of the mouth and lip-smacking with or without accompanying vocalization.

(2) "Affectional presenting." Assumption of the female sexual position involving a rigid posture, exposure of the genitalia, and visual orientation toward the infant, the latter usually evidenced by looking over the shoulder or through the legs.

III Infant-infant behaviours

A. *Threatening.*

(1) Threat face. A facial pattern involving a flattening of the fur on the head and retraction of the ears.

(2) Frown. A facial pattern similar to the human face, involving a wrinkling of the brow and a facial scowl.

B. *Play patterns*

(1) Rough and tumble play. Contact play consisting of mounting, tumbling and wrestling. Frequent shifts in the locus of mouthing, or nipping or head-shaking accompanying the mouthing, qualified for the scoring of this category. This category was further subdivided into mutual and unilateral participation. In unilateral participation, the non-participating animal was usually passive or submissive.

(2) Approach-withdrawal play. Visually oriented charges and attack-like manoeuvres which involved at least two or more canons or rebounds. The latter provision was superceded if the orientation component and the vigor of the activity involved indicated definite attack-like components in the behaviours exhibited. This category was further subdivided into mutual and unilateral participation; in the case of the latter, the non-participating animal was usually passive.

(3) Mixed play. Rapid oscillation between contact and non-contact play patterns with the non-contact patterns predominating.

C. *Nonspecific contact.* Diffuse body contacts such as are involved in brushing against, falling on, or bumping into an animal. This category was also scored for brief but definite contacts, which, because of their brevity defied analysis (p. 113).

Twenty reliability sessions yielded interobserver reliability coefficients ranging from 0.83 to 0.99, except for the infants' visual exploration of its mother where the correlation was as low as 0.64. No explanation has been offered for the relatively low reliability of this category, but it may be that the infant's close physical contact with its mother initially, makes evaluation of its visual inspection alone of the mother rather difficult.

In the two-animal interactions, two observers working simultaneously recorded behavior of infant and mother or other infant respectively for thirty minutes.

Perhaps the most striking results of this study relate to the decline in general of positive protective behavior of mother to infant, and the increase in negative rejecting behavior with increasing age of the infant. The amount of infant cradling done by the mother for example dropped sharply from the first to the third month, whereas mother's punishing behavior toward the infant increased from the first to the fifth month and then decreased as the

MOTHER–INFANT CRADLING

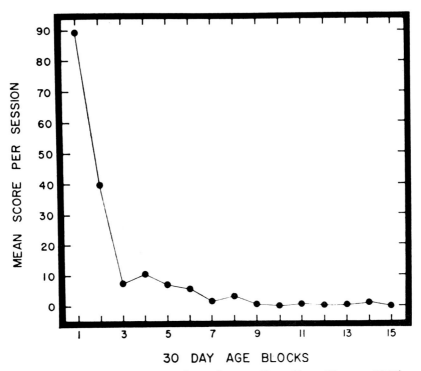

FIGURE 41. Time spent in mother-infant cradling (from Hansen, 1966).

infant grew older (Figs. 41 and 42). Intimate physical contact between mother and infant was initially very high and decreased as the positive phase progressed, rapidly in the first, second, and third months, and then more slowly. The increase in punishing and negative responses on the part of the mother coincided with greater peer interaction and exploration on the part of the infant. As Hansen comments, "One of the primary functions that the mother monkey served was seen in her contribution to the gradual, but definite emancipation of her infant."

One of the categories that distinguished the mother playpen group from the surrogate playpen group was the greater incidence of nonspecific contact in peer interactions in the latter group (Fig. 43). This category included "diffuse nondescript body contacts which resulted from clumsy and socially inept behaviors and reflected inadequate organisation and orientation between monkey infants." In other words, the surrogate group was gauche in its social behavior. The disparity between the two groups was greatest initially but was reduced with increasing age as the surrogate group benefitted from its experience.

These data illustrate the kinds of information yielded by such a study. This study is exemplary to the extent that attempts have been made to give

MATERNAL PUNISHMENT

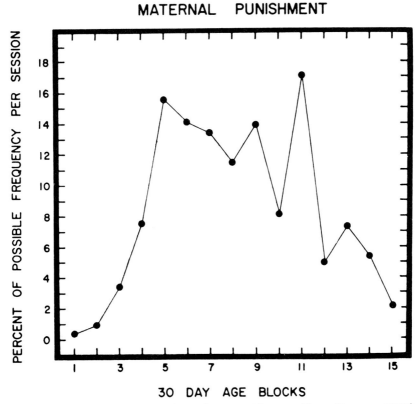

FIGURE 42. Time spent in mother-infant punishment (from Hansen, 1966).

clear and explicit definitions of the response categories. Some of these categories are perhaps not as adequately defined as others, and it might be argued, for instance, that physical contacts which are specific cannot legitimately be included in a category pertaining to nonspecific contact, but in general, the delineation and definitions are meaningful and satisfactory.

The definitions or descriptions classify social behavior on the basis of motor complexes supplemented by contextual elements. Thus, interpretation was a necessary part of the observational technique of this investigation as it is in most studies of social behaviour.

The great limitation of the recording method used in this study is the fact that a considerable period of experience is necessary before any observer can hope to be able to record reliably the great number of categories, particularly as the individual symbols of the code pose a feat of memory for any individual. However, the fact that these difficulties are eventually overcome with practice is demonstrated by the high interobserver reliability coefficients.

NONSPECIFIC CONTACT

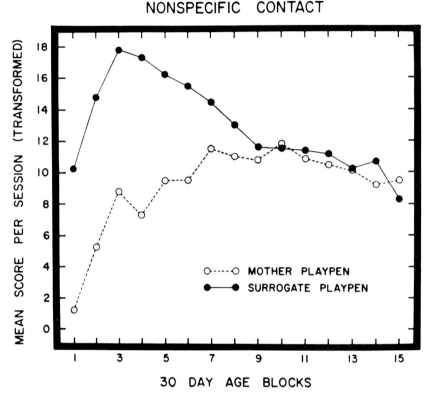

FIGURE 43. Time spent in nonspecific contacts (from Hansen, 1966).

Effect of Early Restriction on the Social Behavior of Monkeys

Monkeys separated from their mothers in early infancy and reared in socially restricted conditions show many features of aberrant or inappropriate responses in their subsequent social behavior. To investigate some of these effects, Mason (1960) compared six rhesus monkeys born in captivity and separated from their mothers in their first month and subsequently housed individually in cages where they were able to hear and see but not have physical contact with other young monkeys, with six monkeys caught in the field and kept with twenty monkeys of the same age. At the time of the study the former group was twenty-eight to twenty-nine months and the latter group twenty months old.

Each monkey was observed with another monkey of the same group for sixteen 3 minute sessions. Observations were recorded on a "multiple-category keyboard which operated the pens of an Esterline-Angus recorder, giving a continuous record of the frequency, duration and temporal patterning of social interactions." Mason used eleven response categories, and his definitions are given below with the percentage reliability he obtained given in brackets:

1. Approach: moves to within six inches of other monkey (75%).
2. Aggression: includes intense vocalisation (barks, growls), biting, pulling.
3. Groom: systematically picks through another's fur with hands (95%).
4. Mount: characteristically grasps the partners hips with hands and feet clasp her legs (96%).
5. Play: tumbling, mauling, wrestling and nipping. Less vigorous and intense than aggression, is not accompanied by intense vocalisation and rarely elicits squealing or other evidence of pain in partner (79%).
6. Sexual presentation: assumption of female mating posture. Hindquarters are elevated and turned toward the partner (60%).
7. Social facilitation of exploration: activity of one animal with respect to some inanimate feature of the room elicits approach, observation, or display of similar behaviour from another. (59%).
8. Social investigation: close visual, manual and/or oral investigation of the partner. Particular interest towards apertures.
9. Thrusting: piston-like movements usually accompanying mounting (95%).
10. Visual orientation: passive observation of other (66%).
11. Withdrawal: abrupt movement away from other. Not scored during play or aggression unless it terminated interaction (65%) (p. 583).

The behavior of each animal was separately recorded, the appropriate response key being depressed for the duration of a particular behavior.

Play was found to occur more frequently in the restricted than in the feral group, with mean total incidences of 342.0 and 179.8 respectively. It is not clear whether these scores refer to the frequency of occurrence of play bouts, or whether they refer to total duration of play activities; and since these measures are usually inversely rather than directly related to each other, interpretation of the behavior is critically dependent upon which score is used. It seems probable that the figures quoted above refer to a frequency measure. In both restricted and feral groups male animals were found to engage in much more play than females; in fact, no play occurred if a female pair were left together. Grooming occurred for longer periods of time in feral pairs than in restricted pairs, mean durations being 25.3 and 1.6 seconds respectively. The frequency of aggressive episodes was significantly higher and their duration, longer in the restricted animals. On the other hand, episodes of sexual behavior were more frequent in the feral group. There were no significant differences between the groups in the frequency of approaches, withdrawals or social investigation, which is reassuring for those interested in early environmental influences upon social development.

The poor interobserver agreement achieved in some of the categories in this study is very probably a reflection of imprecision in definition. Some of the descriptive terms used in the specification of certain categories appear to need further definition. For example, category 7 as defined would include many other behaviors than those which are truly exploratory. Again, the first part of the description of category 6 says little about the kind of behavior pattern displayed, and clearly the second part is insufficiently precise to enable reliable categorization. Sexual presentation and indeed many other acts and postures in infrahuman primates has been commonly and implicitly regarded as very stereotyped behaviors. More recently it has even been stated explicitly: "Only 3 observers were involved and the categories were so clear-cut that it was not necessary to test for observer agreement." (Hinde, *et al.*, 1964). The poor reliability achieved by Mason and his colleagues is thus a very salutary warning against the complacency which can all too easily beset workers in the behavioral field. Too often researchers are unduly confident that all other workers are as familiar with their species of study as they themselves are.

Finally, in terms of ease of scoring and facility in analysis, the event recorder has an advantage over other more detailed but time-consuming methods, and many of its limitations can be overcome by the use of adequately defined categories. Moreover, fairly precise measures of duration are available and assessments of temporal interrelations, such as synchrony, can be extremely accurate.

MOTION PICTURES AND VIDEO TAPE

Display of the Goldeneye Duck

Studying the behavior of individual animals who are interacting members of a large group is an extremely difficult task. Not only are the individuals *actors* but also *reactors* to the other members, and identification of stimulus-response behaviors on the one hand and spontaneous or endogenously triggered behaviors on the other require sensitive observational techniques or instruments.

The study of the courtship behavior of the goldeneye duck by Dane and van der Kloot (1964) is pertinent for several reasons but largely because in the author's words: "(it) may be a step in understanding . . . other complex behavioral sequences performed by free, living animals." The main aim of the study was to see if courtship behavior in this species formed " a predictable sequence" under natural conditions. In making this detailed study, Dane and van der Kloot used motion pictures, as they were of the opinion that "the only device which is able to record complex behavioral interactions in the field is the motion picture camera." They exposed 22,000 feet of film, using an Arriflex 16 mm camera with a 400 mm or 600 mm lens, and carrying a 400-foot magazine. This latter feature meant that interruptions for reloading film were considerably reduced (since the camera was electrically driven), four hundred feet being able to record almost fifteen minutes of behavior continuously. Filming was done at twenty-four frames per second. The birds were filmed on their breeding grounds as well as their wintering grounds.

The analysis of the film records was detailed and rigorous. Using a Bell and Howell Time and Motion Study Projector, the film was projected on to a gridded screen; each bird's grid number was noted every five feet of the film. As the film was projected, the data were transferred to sheets of paper, ruled with vertical lines spaced at regular intervals (each space = 1.6 seconds) along a horizontal time axis. Different birds were plotted on separate horizontal lines. It was thus possible to record all of the actions of a displaying group as a function of time. From these sheets too the exact sequence of events could be determined. The authors used the convention that, if within five seconds of the action of one bird there was no action from another, then the first action was not serving as a stimulus to elicit behavior from other individuals. (This convention is similar to that used by Grant and described earlier.) Although analysis was restricted to records of groups less than fifteen birds, it seems questionable whether all acts of other birds occurring within five seconds of act A by bird B are in fact responses to A. The descriptions and analyses of the various display postures and patterns are extremely detailed, and an earlier paper (Dane, *et al.*, 1959) descriptively defines each of these. These definitions followed a minute analysis of "an edge-numbered print with a Bell and Howell Filmotion Viewer." The original film was taken on negative film. The number of frames occupied in any display were counted. Despite the rapidity of these displays—many of them lasted just over a second—the authors were able to differentiate slow and fast or short and long versions of them by reference to the means and standard deviations of their durations, since there was no overlap. In other words, just as in Tinbergen's example of the gull (quoted in Ch. 6), there was temporal discontinuity between one display and another. The clarity of this discontinuity is impressive, as shown by an example from Dane *et al.*:

> The Bowsprit movement lasts for 0.78 ± 0.16 seconds with the shorter Head-Throw and 1.25 ± 0.12 with the longer. This is an example of two movements whose form is apparently identical, but which can be easily separated on the basis of their duration. This is also true of the Head-throw-kick. In both cases no intermediate forms have been seen (p. 270).

In their paper Dane and van der Kloot were concerned, *inter alia*, with the question of the intra- and inter-individual variability in the durations of certain stereotyped displays, four of which are illustrated in Figure 44. A simple movement pattern, like the head-throw, clearly has little intraindividual variability but more interindividual variability; in a more complex pattern, like the head-throw-bowsprit, the converse is true. In general, a bird was found to be consistently slow or fast in performing the several patterns, but what is so striking is the degree of homogeneity as indicated by the very small deviations about the mean. It is astonishing that "in the Head-Throw, for example, some birds do not vary the timing by more than 0.04 secs from instance to instance." The deviation was used as a measure of stereotypy or rigidity, the smaller the deviation, the more stereotyped the

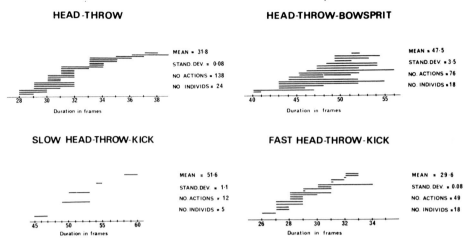

FIGURE 44. Durations of four display actions. Each heavy horizontal line represents the range in duration of one individual's actions; the abscissa gives the duration in frames of film. The total spread of individual ranges is equal to the group range. A reference is provided to the mean duration of each action, the standard deviation of the individual ranges, the number of actions analyzed, and the number of individuals performing the actions (from Dane, and van der Kloot, 1964).

bird. Such a degree of precision would not have been possible with any other method of recording.

The authors also used their grid plots to estimate distances between individual birds, and showed that different patterns were performed at different distances from other birds. Such findings are clearly of importance in evaluating the motivational significance of the various patterns.

Although 22,000 feet of film were exposed in the course of this study, only about 8,300 feet were analyzed in the manner described. The rest was rejected on grounds of undue size or complexity of the groups. It does seem wasteful to discard nearly two thirds of laboriously collected film data. It seems that such an expenditure was unwarranted, and could have been avoided since the authors seemed well aware of their requirements. On the other hand, the details of the systematic recording and analysis carried out are to be much appreciated.

Behavior in a Monkey Colony

In a chapter on "Free Behavior and Brain Stimulation," Delgado (1964) discussed different methods of behavior recording, the problems of definition of categories of activities, and how the data might be evaluated. Delgado's own unequivocal preference was for motion pictures, but since he was primarily interested in recording the behavior of his monkeys over several days and nights, this was not only the most appropriate technique but the only practicable one.

The animals were housed in a 7 feet by 3 feet by 3 feet cage in an air-conditioned, soundproof room. The cage was illuminated with neon tubes; a contant twelve hour light-dark cycle was used. Records were made on black and white Tri-X film (adequate for moderate illumination) using a 16 mm solenoid-activated Bell and Howell camera. Delgado found that night filming could be done using a high-speed infrared film and photofloods with infrared filters. For analysis he used a time and motion study projector, projecting the film in blocks of ten frames. Strictly speaking, the method was time-lapse photography at one frame per second rather than motion picture filming using the conventional motor speeds.

Behavior categories were identified by letter symbols (e.g. G = grooming, 0 = groomed, Y = playing, X = attacking, E = eating, etc.) and the animals by numbers (Fig. 45). Thus an entry under number 1 of 05 would mean monkey number one being groomed by monkey number 5; or DPJ under 2 would be monkey number 2 drinking, picking, and moving body. After viewing each block of ten frames, the appropriate behavior symbols were "typed with an electric IBM output typewriter connected to a bank of electric counters," the counters totalled the entries for each category every one thousand frames, i.e. thirty three minutes. Subsequently, many measures could be extracted from these protocols and a few of these, with examples of Delgado's results where available, will be listed here:

1. *Spatial distribution.* The boss monkey often occupied over 50 percent of the cage, crowding the other monkeys into a relatively small space; or specific physical locations were preferred for enacting certain behaviors.

2. *Motor patterns subserving the same activity.* The same end result can be achieved in many different ways, e.g. "drinking may be accomplished by taking water with the hand, with the tongue, by lapping or by sucking."

3. *Distribution through time.* Some behavior categories occurred predominantly at specific times of day (e.g. nestling was concentrated at midmorning and midafternoon), whereas others, such as walking, occurred uniformly throughout the day.

4. *Social contact.* Amount of contact, or avoidance, apparently indicated likes and dislikes; certain combinations of pairs of animals were never observed, others very seldom observed; and yet others frequently seen.

Time-lapse photography using short time intervals as Delgado did is an excellent method of obtaining records over a long period of study. Purists may wish to regard time-lapse photography as a method of time sampling. Strictly speaking so it is, but the more frequent the exposure, the more continuous the record. To argue that filming at sixteen frames per second was

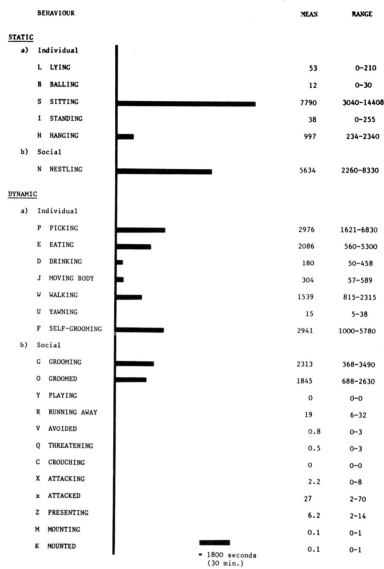

BEHAVIOUR		MEAN	RANGE
STATIC			
a) Individual			
L LYING		53	0-210
B BALLING		12	0-30
S SITTING		7790	3040-14408
I STANDING		38	0-255
H HANGING		997	234-2340
b) Social			
N NESTLING		5634	2260-8330
DYNAMIC			
a) Individual			
P PICKING		2976	1621-6830
E EATING		2086	560-5300
D DRINKING		180	50-458
J MOVING BODY		304	57-589
W WALKING		1539	815-2315
U YAWNING		15	5-38
F SELF-GROOMING		2941	1000-5780
b) Social			
G GROOMING		2313	368-3490
O GROOMED		1845	688-2630
Y PLAYING		0	0-0
R RUNNING AWAY		19	6-32
V AVOIDED		0.8	0-3
Q THREATENING		0.5	0-3
C CROUCHING		0	0-0
X ATTACKING		2.2	0-8
x ATTACKED		27	2-70
Z PRESENTING		6.2	2-14
M MOUNTING		0.1	0-1
K MOUNTED		0.1	0-1

= 1800 seconds
(30 min.)

FIGURE 45. Behavior categories with their code letters and their relative incidence (from Delgado, 1964)

no different in principle from filming at one frame per second would be an equally legitimate contention.

In terms of analysis time this procedure is relatively economical. Delgado reckoned that analysis of a single category like mounting, occurring in all six animals in the course of a whole day, would occupy at most one hour. Detailed analysis of all behavior categories occurring in one day took one month. As analyses go, this seems a remarkably quick procedure.

Since the analysis was carried out in blocks of ten frames (occupying 20 seconds each) one wonders what particular advantage accrued from filming at a speed of one frame per two seconds.

Social Encounters of Autists

Much of the literature on childhood autism, or the more generic schizophrenic syndrome of childhood, agrees with the main diagnostic feature of the disorder, described by Creak *et al.* (1961) as "sustained impairment of inter-personal relationships," and by Eisenberg and Kanner (1958) as an inability to relate to other people. Although the literature abounds with detailed clinical descriptions of such cases, little attempt seems to have been made to specify or to investigate systematically what particular aspects of social interaction are impaired.

By systematic observation of the nature of the social contacts made by these children in a fairly natural environment, we have attempted to delineate more clearly the components of such encounters. Analyses of film records were an invaluable complement to these observations.

Eight autistic children, all male and between the ages of three and six years, were observed in a hospital playroom and occasionally in the garden, with special reference to their social behavior. These children were nearly always solitary in their play. Occasionally, however, they would run to a nurse and climb onto her lap, or raise their arms as if to be picked up. When physically hurt, they would invariably run to an adult. These approach gestures were normal in form, that is, they were indistinguishable from those of normal children except for one feature—aversion from the face. Figure 46, a drawing from film, shows the typical response of an autistic child to the outstretched arms of an adult preparatory to being picked up. The child's arms are outstretched too, indicating a readiness to be picked up; but the face is held down so that the adult's face is not in foveal vision. Even when the child is in the adult's arms it keeps its face averted from the adult's face, and any attempt to make it fixate upon the adult provokes the child to shield its eyes with its hands (see Fig. 47). Similarly, in endeavors to make the adult perform certain actions, the child will appropriately move the adult's limbs, but will avoid looking at her face. Figure 48, for example, shows a child who wanted the nurse to accompany him in a particular direction; the child tugged at her while keeping his face turned away from her.

These observations and analyses of film records therefore indicate that, apart from aversion from the face, all other components of the social encounters of these autistic children are those shown by normal nonautistic children.

An experiment with autists, utilizing models of human and animal faces had already suggested that, despite the paucity of observable visual fixations upon the human faces, these children obtained sufficient information to be able to avoid these particular stimuli. Now this information can be acquired

FIGURE 46. Typical response of an autistic child to
outstretched arms of an adult (drawn from 8 mm motion picture film) (from Hutt, and Ounsted, 1966).

through peripheral vision, or fractional glances, or both. Fractional glances
would be fixations too brief to time or even observe reliably. Since clearly
this type of paranoid, darting glance occurs quite frequently in these subjects, film records seemed essential in their analysis. Moreover, it is not clear
how much information is obtained through peripheral vision; in this assessment too film analysis proved invaluable. Figure 49 shows three successive
stages in the gaze behavior of two children, both of whom wish to retain
occupancy of the chair. Child A is watching child B (Fig. 49A) but B is
looking down at his toy; B then looks at A out of the corner of his eye (Fig.
49B); A looks down at his toy, and B looks directly at him (Fig. 49C);
finally A looks up at B again, and B looks away. The number of frames and
equivalent time occupied by each part of the sequence is indicated. The fixations of the two children are so closely synchronized and change so rapidly
that each child must have been receiving more than minimal information
about the nature of the situation, albeit peripherally. It is striking that not
even for a fraction of a second did the two children make eye-to-eye contact. Such a sequence would have been too rapid to record or analyze by

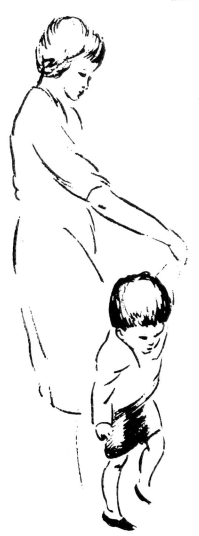

FIGURE 47. Response of an autistic child to repeated attempts of adult to make eye-to-eye contact (drawn from 8 mm motion picture film) (from Hutt, and Ounsted, 1966).

FIGURE 48. Autistic child attempting to lead adult, keeping face averted (drawn from 8 mm motion picture film) (from Hutt, and Ounsted, 1966).

any orthodox observational methods. This and other film sequences however supply documentary evidence of the persistent failure of these children to make eye-to-eye contact.

Substantial evidence of this kind enabled us to suggest that the loss of eye contact meant the absence of an appropriate releaser for true conspecific behavior: in adults it evokes a sense of rejection or detachment, in peers it inhibits aggression but also precludes normal interactions, and more specifically in the mother it fails to elicit true parental behavior other than caretaking responses (Wolff 1963).

COMPLEMENTARY USE OF ALL THESE TECHNIQUES

Group Size and the Social Behavior of Children

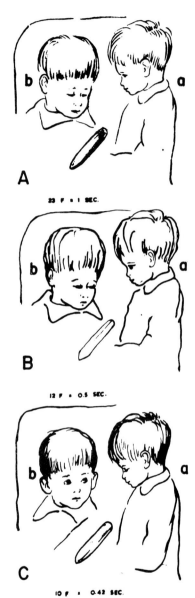

In a study investigating the effects of group density upon social behavior, all three techniques described in the previous chapters were used: (1) check lists, (2) tape recordings, and (3) 8 mm motion pictures (Hutt and Vaizey, 1966). Since these methods were used to obtain data relating to different aspects of the social interactions of children, a report of it may serve to illustrate the particular objectives that the several techniques are designed to achieve.

In the first instance it was hypothesized that, on the evidence from animal studies, increasing group density would adversely affect the social encounters of children. On account of the importance of individual differences in our species, the hypothesis contained an addendum which stated that the particular effects of group density would vary according to the individual. In view of our prior hypotheses regarding austic (Hutt, et al., 1964) and brain-damaged (Hutt, and Hutt, 1964) children, it seemed that these two groups of children might manifest, perhaps in exaggerated form, the reactions of introverted and extraverted individuals in the normal population. All subjects were between the ages of three and eight years, and the groups were matched for age.

The situation used for the observation was a 27 feet by 17.5 feet playroom where the children customarily assembled for free play. Three group sizes were used: (1) small (n < 6), (2) medium (n = 7 — 11), and (3) large (n > 12). Other children in the hospital formed the rest of the group (only two or three of the subjects were present at any one session). Groups and densities were arranged

23 F = 1 SEC.

12 F = 0.5 SEC.

10 F = 0.42 SEC.

FIGURE 49. A, B, C: Three successive states in the gaze behavior of two autistic children, indicating complete failure to make eye-to-eye contact. The number of frames and equivalent time occupied by each stage are indicated (drawn from 8 mm motion picture film) (from Hutt, and Ounsted, 1966).

in a 3 by 3 Latin-square design, four replicates of this design then being used.

Here we were primarily concerned about alterations in the incidence or frequency of different behavior categories. Thus check lists seemed an adequate and appropriate method of recording. The categories recorded were defined as follows:

1. Repetitive play = invariant pattern(s) of manipulation of toy or object, e.g. pushing a truck back and forth.
2. Constructive play = assembling, building or incorporation of more than one toy in activity.
3. Destructive play = throwing, banging, breaking, kicking toys.
4. Stereotypy = rocking, head shaking, shrugging, wincing, limb sucking, pill rolling, hand flicking.
5. Crying = any distress vocalization.
6. Locomotion.
7. Interaction with adult = approach, contact or converse; if encounter was initiated by the adult, a P was marked signifying the child's role was passive.
8. Interaction with child = similar to above.
*9. Cuddled = child rocked, patted or held in arms of adult, usually on adult's lap.
10. Alone = no other individual within a two feet radius.
11. Attack = hitting, pushing, pinching or kicking adult (A) or child.
12. Avoid = turn away from approach or contact of another.
13. Boundary = within three feet of periphery of room.
14. Looking = visual exploration or inspection unaccompanied by any other activity.

An observation period was of fifteen minutes duration for any one child. Each child was observed on three separate days under each and every condition. For each subject the mean of the three sessions under each condition was obtained. Effectively similar behaviors were then grouped together: (1) categories three, and eleven as aggressive/destructive behavior, and (2) categories seven, eight and nine as social interactions.

These two grouped categories and category thirteen showed the most marked effects of the different density conditions (Fig. 50). While the autists showed hardly any aggression in any condition, the brain-damaged children became increasingly aggressive with greater density. The normal children, on the other hand, showed a significant increase in aggression only when there was an appreciable increase in group size.

With respect to social encounters not involving any show of aggression,

* Preliminary observations had indicated that some children, in particular the autists, spent much of their time on the lap of an adult.

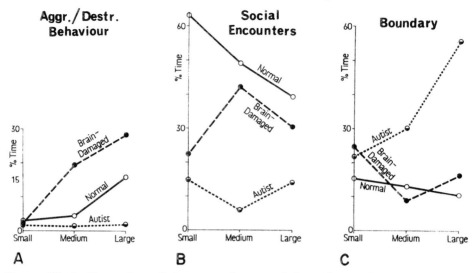

FIGURE 50. A: Proportions of time spent by normal, brain-damaged and autistic children in aggressive and destructive behavior. B: Proportions of time spent by normal, brain-damaged and autistic children in other types of social encounters. C: Proportions of time spent by normal, brain-damaged and autistic children on the boundary, i.e. within three feet of the periphery of the room, under three conditions of group density.

the most remarkable finding was that, despite the greater opportunity for interaction, the normal children reduced their encounters as group size increased. It appeared as if these children were endeavouring to regulate their sociability. In a similar but more extreme manner, the autists did this too. With increasing density they retreated more and more to the periphery of the room and were often found sitting facing the wall. Moreover, their social encounters, of which there was a slight increase in the large group, consisted almost entirely (in this latter instance) of approaches to the adults, to escape from the general melee it seemed, since the category "cuddled" was appreciably increased.

It is clear that the method of sampling was perfectly satisfactory for giving us some idea of the relative changes in the amounts of different behavior categories under specified conditions. Our initial expectation of individual differences in reactions to density conditions was substantiated. It is of particular interest that the extreme reactions of rats subjected to highly crowded conditions (Calhoun, 1962), phrenetic activity and pathological withdrawal, were similar to those shown by the brain-damaged and autistic children respectively.

The procedure was essentially the same in the tape-recorded part of the study. The observer now sat unobtrusively in a corner using a microphone which had a long cable leading out through a nearby window to the tape deck which was in an adjoining room. It was now possible to obtain much

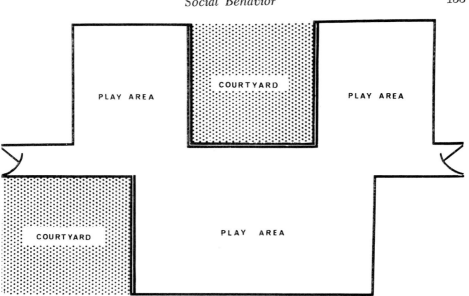

<small>Figure 51. New semistructured and partitioned playroom in which territorial behavior was manifested.</small>

fuller descriptions of the nature of the interactions. The transcript protocols were analyzed in much the same manner as described in Chapter 4.

The gross quantitative measures yielded the same results as the check lists did, and it would be repetitious to describe them again; hence only some additional and pertinent data will be described.

One of the most striking findings was one relating to the physical features of the environment. After this study had been launched, a new extension, including play, school, and occupational areas, became available. The children were thus moved into the new playroom which was the shape shown in Figure 51: three play areas, each approximately ten feet square extended from a central passage area of about six feet square. It will be appreciated that this was a marked contrast from the previous single large rectangular room.

Previously we had observed no behavior that could be called *territorial*, i.e. behavior serving to maintain possession of a physical area or space. We had however observed a good deal of *possessive* behavior, i.e. behavior consisting of attempts to gain or retain objects, mostly toys. In the new playroom the amount of possessive behavior remained about the same, but we suddenly noticed the appearance of territorial behavior. The normal children in particular now spent between 14 and 17 percent of their time in trying to prevent any encroachment or intrusion upon the area of which they were in possession. Only in the small group was there an absence of this behavior (Hutt, 1966). The brain-damaged children showed a negligible amount of territorial behavior but a good deal of possessive behavior. They were the ones most likely to fight over or snatch toys from the other children. It thus appeared that even the physical rudiments of territory (walls, and corners) were necessary before territory could be demarcated psychologically.

The recorded observations also suggested that the motor patterns involved in the expression of these two behaviors were different, the most notable distinction lying in the position of the elbow. In possessive behavior the arms tended to be adducted at the shoulder, with elbow flexion (i.e. elbows tucked into sides); in territorial behavior the arms, or more likely one arm, tended to be abducted, and the elbows, flexed. However, a definitive distinction between these patterns awaits a film analysis.

.The autists rarely, if ever, fought over possessions. If another child attempted to secure a toy an autist already had, the latter either relinquished it or would move away with it. Autists wanting toys other children were playing with were observed to keep looking at the toys and then pick them up as soon as they had been relinquished. Some forms of possessive behavior seemed symbolic rather than actual. For example, on several occasions children would take hold of a toy and sit beside it, have their legs across it or have it in their laps; if any other child attempted to take it he would be hit or pushed away, and the possessor would continue to sit guard over it, but not necessarily play with it.

Two young brain-damaged boys (K and P) were particularly aggressive in that they were very easily provoked to hit, push, kick or bite other children. They were nevertheless somewhat inhibited by an older and physically bigger boy (R). Their encounters were of particular interest. On one occasion R was playing with a new circus lorry; P tried unsuccessfully to obtain the lorry from R, whereupon he lay on the floor and wailed. Another boy then interposed himself between the two and immediately P reached out and hit R upon the head with a large wooden block. A very similar incident also occurred with K as the attacker. In ethological language this may be interpreted in the following way: P's motivation was ambivalent, since he was both aggressive towards K and fearful of R (or escape inhibited attack); the interposition of another conspecific (who released neither of these drives) reduced the escape tendency (by blocking access of P to R), and thereby disinhibited attack. Redirected aggression was also commonly observed. If an older or bigger child seized a toy from a less assertive child, the latter would kick the chair or hit another toy nearby; equally often they would appeal for the aid of an adult.

The personal space of an autist was clearly greater than that of other children. In the open rectangular room the autists tended to seek out corners or to place themselves under a climbing frame or inside a wooden hide where it was inconvenient to reach them (see Fig. 52). In the clover-shaped room

FIGURE 52. A characteristic posture and position adopted by an autistic child (right foreground) relative to other children playing in the same room (drawn from 8 mm motion picture film)

they were able to seclude themselves much more effectively. Upon the intrusion of other children they would move away or very occasionally push them away. One of the latter incidents will be described in detail later. -

It can be seen that in addition to providing the same kind of quantitative data, the tape recordings were also able to furnish a good deal of qualitative material. The nature of the interactive responses could be more fully described.

Motion pictures were used in those instances where an even more detailed analysis was required. Two such instances will be described here.

The two young brain-damaged boys, P and K, already mentioned, fought frequently with each other. We wished to analyze the motor patterns involved in these agonistic encounters in detail and hence filmed such encounters. A frame-by-frame analysis indicated the salient steps in such an encounter (Fig. 53), the most remarkable of which was the actual moment of attack. At the point when the attacker delivered his blow his eyes were seen

FIGURE 53. A: Agonistic encounter between two five-year-old brain-damaged boys. Approach to attack (twenty frames before contact). Note facial expression and threatening posture of attacker (left) and warding-off posture adopted by the other boy.

to be closed. This was observed to be characteristic of this child, but we are not able to say how general this is. This feature seems to be an excellent example of what Chance (1962) has called a "cut-off" act: a response which by altering the sensory input regulates specific arousal, thereby modifying the mood and enabling the animal to take decisive action. If we assume that initially the mood of the attacker is ambivalent, i.e. it comprises both aggressive and fearful components, we might expect the fear component to increase as he approaches the victim. By closing the eyes, and thereby reducing the fear evoking stimulation, his fear is prevented from rising to a level sufficient to inhibit his attack. Without slow projection and careful analysis of a motion picture recording such an observation would have been extremely difficult, if not impossible.

B: Moment of attack. Note closed eyes of attacker. (Both drawings from 8 mm motion picture film, sixteen frames per second.

It has already been mentioned that some autists would very occasionally push another child away. This happened most usually when the autist was the incumbent of the only comfortable chair in the old playroom, and another child wished to occupy it. We were able to film two such encounters. In both cases the autists characteristically engaged in stereotypies: one (A) rocking while twirling a small stick in his hand, and the other (M) performing wrist rotations. Frame-by-frame analysis gave the following results:

		Before encounter	*After encounter*
	Rocking speed	1/sec.	3.2/sec.
A	Amplitude	4.5 ins	11 ins
	Twirling speed	2.3/sec.	5.0/sec.
M	Rotation speed	2.0/sec.	5.0/sec.

We might say therefore that the intensity of the stereotypy was increased in these children following an encounter of a mildly agonistic kind. In all probability this indicates an increase in level of arousal or excitation.

These few examples may suffice to demonstrate how different techniques may be applied to slightly different problems in the same area. Their powers of resolution, so to speak, being of varying degrees, the information each is able to give differs in its degree of precision. By using all three techniques, we were able to obtain a comprehensive picture of the social interactions of these children integrating data from three different levels.

Chapter 8

DRUG ACTION UPON BEHAVIOR

I N GENERAL, clinical evaluations of drug effects in humans are based upon a global measure or rating of behavior. Most commonly a three-point rating of improved, unchanged, worse, is considered adequate. Such relatively crude and subjective behavioral assessments or the arbitrary quantification of symptoms contrast strangely with the sophisticated experimental design and statistical analysis often employed. The rationale of such a procedure appears to be that the use of a large number of subjects, however heterogeneous a group, and a complex experimental design obviates the necessity of adequate or meaningful behavioral measures. Such facile and unhelpful evaluations of behavioral changes also calls for invidious comparison with the refined and meticulous biochemical assays undertaken to estimate (say) blood levels of sodium, epinephrine, 17-hydroxycorticosterone or other metabolic substances.

The disregard for an adequate behavioral analysis is made alarmingly explicit in the comments of Pollard and Bakker (1960) when they take issue with Skinner over his criticism of psychoactive drug research (1958):

> He suggested that most of it did not go beyond the adjectival description of changes in behaviour and stressed the necessity of breaking up behaviour into convenient pieces, rigidly defining the variables operationally, and studying these pieces separately. This is a highly desirable goal. However, Dr. Skinner neglects to name the convenient pieces into which we may break up behaviour. One sometimes despairs of ever finding such convenient pieces of behaviour, except perhaps in Skinner's pigeons (p. 202).

Clearly the work of the ethologists was quite unknown to these authors. On the other hand, the experimentalists have attempted to demonstrate very specific drug effects both in animals and men: on operant conditioning (Cook, 1964), discrimination and delayed reaction (Gross, and Weiskrantz, 1961), exploratory activity in animals (Rushton, and Steinberg, 1964), and on eye-blink conditioning (Franks, and Trouton, 1958), rotary pursuit ability (Fleishman, 1956; Eysenck, *et al.*, 1957), and manual dexterity and reaction times (see Fleishman, 1960) in humans. The naive reader may wonder just how much the results of such atomized tests tell us about the organisms' unrestrained and natural behavior as well as those aspects we are seeking to modify. But the justification seems to be that:

psychomotor behaviour somehow seems a more "uncontaminated," less ambiguous, and more direct measure of performance than is, . . . verbal, conceptual or even perceptual behaviour. Most often the experimenter can observe clocks or counters or he can obtain continuous records on some kind of moving tape. All this inspires confidence in the experimenter that he knows what he is measuring (Fleishman, 1960).

The self-confidence of the experimenter seems a poor consideration for the collection of any data however spurious. But it is clear that the field of drug research has consolidated itself round these two somewhat intransigent and extremist positions.

It is a welcome relief therefore to find any workers in this field who are concerned with the assessment of drug effects upon *free* behavior, social or otherwise, in its natural context.

Attention to the biological context of the behaviour of an animal studied in a laboratory has not been a conspicuous feature of psychopharmacological studies up till now. This is not perhaps surprising in view of the way the methods of pharmacology are at present so largely modelled on those of physiology and biochemistry. Pharmacology, however, is the study of the action of chemicals in a living organism, in part or in whole, and hence it will have to take more notice of the relevant biological facts if in future it is to encompass its task adequately. (Chance, and Silverman, 1964 p. 66).

Because he has heeded his own warning so assiduously, Silverman's study is exemplary. Consequently, it will be described in some detail here. Other studies will deal with the assessment of drug effects upon relatively free-field behavior in humans.

DRUG ACTION AND SOCIAL BEHAVIOR

Silverman (1966) made a detailed analysis of the effect of drugs on the social behavior of rats, taking into account the postures, pathways and structure already worked out by Grant (1963) and Grant and Mackintosh (1963). He compared the behavior of drug- and saline-injected animals to the same partners (see Fig. 54).

The observers were conversant with the forty-odd elements or postures already identified; one observer watched the experimental rats and, another, the partners, uttering the code for each element as it occurred, recording on a two-channel tape recorder. Each session lasted ten minutes, in which time an average of approximately three-hundred elements were recorded.

Chlorpromazine Effects

Silverman found that doses of 4 mg per kilogram reduced those behaviors which involved approach of the animals, namely, aggression, investigation and mating; conversely, behavior involving withdrawal (escape) was increased. But behavior consisting of both approach and withdrawal elements,

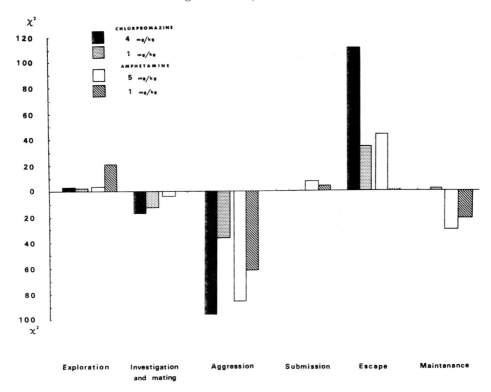

FIGURE 54. Effects of two doses of chlorpromazine and amphetamine upon various behaviors of the rat. Values of χ^2 are used for the ordinate scale, the blocks thus representing the extent of the differences in the category totals for six drugged rats from those for saline controls. Blocks above the zero line indicate increases and those below indicate decreases in the categories (after Silverman, 1966).

i.e. submission, was unchanged, as was behavior not directed to the partner, e.g. exploration. Examination of the *elements* within each category showed the drug effects to be even more selective. For instance, elements indicative of the most intense aggression (offensive sideways and attack) were reduced more than the less intense ones (e.g. aggressive groom). Similarly in the escape category most increase was found in the long-lasting postures, like defensive upright and crouch, and very little in the speedier retreat. Because of this differential action of the drug in reducing the swift activities and increasing static postures, it may appear that chlorpromazine primarily reduced locomotion and thereby produced the other effects incidentally. However, Silverman found that some slow elements (like aggressive groom) were also reduced and some fast ones increased. He comments:

> The locomotor effect does not, therefore, account for the motivational results, which must be independently controlled. It is, in any case, hard to see how a

reduction in locomotion would lead simultaneously to a reduction in Aggression, no change in Exploration (even its mobile element), and an increase in both Submission and Escape.

Partners of chlorpromazine-injected rats directed more aggressive and mating elements towards them, and showed less submission and escape; displacement activities also increased, suggesting that "chlorpromazine causes rats to present stimuli arousing the partner's aggression but not releasing it."

Amphetamine Effects

This drug was administered on the grounds that a central stimulant would be expected to increase all behavior equally. The specific results were as follows: an increase in escape and sometimes in submission and exploration, a reduction in aggression particularly in the more intense elements, and the partners of the experimental animals showed more exploration and less flight. "Aggression and Submission are truncated in that while low intensity postures may be increased, the higher intensity and consummatory postures are greatly reduced" (Chance, and Silverman, 1964). Silverman (1966) adds that "amphetamine-rats gave the impression of ceaseless exploring without reaching any consummatory situation."

Thus although chlorpromazine and amphetamine were seen to have contrary effects in that in general, the former depressed activity and the latter stimulated it; the drugs nevertheless did have qualitatively similar effects upon the specific categories of aggression and flight. This study has thus illustrated the importance of detailed behavioral measures and a knowledge of their significance and incidence in the normal repertoire of the animal before a valid and meaningful evaluation of drug effects can be made. Otherwise the results may at worst be spurious or misleading and at best be of doubtful relevance, as illustrated by Irwin's investigation (1964). Irwin's aim was to investigate whether or not there was a correlation between the locomotor drive state in rats (as measured in revolving treadwheel activity) and the tendency to engage in social interactional behavior. A negative correlation was found between "individual treadwheel counts and the time devoted to interactional behavior" in saline-injected animals. Methamphetamine was found to increase locomotor drive and depress social interaction, whereas a phenothiazine tranquilizer (perphenazine) decreased locomotion and increased time spent in social activity. To be fair to Irwin, these results were presented in a discussion; nevertheless, his concepts and measures of behavior are indicative of an arid orientation which has characterized the experimentalist for too long. Is treadwheel activity in a confined environment, for instance, really a measure of locomotor drive, if such a drive does indeed exist? And are investigatory sniffing, grooming, biting and mounting of the partner all equivalent indices of social interaction? Such oversimplification may yield speedy quantitative and respectable results, but their relevance to how the animal really behaves is tenuous, if not negligible.

DRUG TREATMENT OF HYPERACTIVE AND
AGGRESSIVE CHILDREN

Alderton and Hoddinott (1964) carried out a study to investigate the effects of thioridazine upon the day-to-day behavior of children who were clinically referred on account of their hyperactivity and aggression. In other words, these authors were concerned with a wider area of behavior than was prescribed by the symptoms. The subjects were nine boys between the ages of six and eleven years, three of whom had mild brain damage, the six others being primarily behavior disorders.

Three experimental conditions, each lasting three weeks, were used: no drug, placebo, and drug (25 mgm qid). Each subject served as his own control. Five main behavioral categories were investigated: aggressive, affectionate, constructive and destructive behavior, and activity level. The first two variables were further divided into verbal and physical, and adult- and peer-directed subgroups. The subjects were observed during seven 3-minute periods each day, five days a week for nine weks. Behavioral data were recorded on an observation sheet in terms of whether any of the categories (or subcategories) were present or absent during the three-minute period. Activity level was scored in terms of whether it was more than, same as, or less than usual. The analysis was made in terms of the number of three-minute periods (out of a total of 315) in which any of the behavior categories were recorded. The results showed that thioridazine significantly reduced aggressive and destructive behavior, as well as activity level. It had no appreciable effect however on affectionate or constructive behavior.

Despite the laudable attempt on the part of these authors to investigate drug effects outside the symptom area, so to speak, the study is less informative than it need have been. This is due to the fact that any behavioral category (although fairly objectively defined) was only recorded as present or absent; more subtle quantitative changes would thus have been missed. Since only one score for any category was possible, a subject who showed destructive behavior for only ten seconds and one who showed it for two minutes would both get equivalent scores. Similarly, it is not clear what particular parameters activity level was measuring: Was it locomotion, limb movements, or distractability? Furthermore, an interesting phenomenon evident from their graphs but not commented upon by the authors is that on both aggressive and destructive scores the subjects appeared to be better on no drug than on placebo! A more detailed analysis of the behavioral changes in this case would have been both of theoretical and practical interest.

ACTIVITY PATTERNS IN SCHIZOPHRENICS

Chapple *et al.* (1963) used the idiosyncratic activity patterns of schizophrenic patients as the dependent variable in assessing the effects of drugs. These patterns may more readily be recognized if they are referred to as

psychotic motor patterns: They consist of postures, of repetitive and ritualis-
tic locomotor patterns, stereotypies involving upper or lower limbs, and hal-
lucinations overtly manifesting themselves in mouth movements, inclina-
tions of head or trunk, etc. The authors attempted to specify rigorous criteria
for identification of these patterns:

> Kinds of behaviour patterns in which we are interested are those when the
> criteria for identification consist of the observable contraction of the mutually
> dependent idiosyncratic systems constituting them . . . persisting for measur-
> able periods of time without an immediate and "normal" shift to relaxation in
> a new posture.

These idiosyncratic patterns were established for each patient and the assumption made that duration and fequency were the most important and
possibly most sensitive measures that could be applied to them.

Observations were made from behind a one-way vision screen while patients carried on with their routine activities in their usual environment. Observations were made during at least four 5-minute sessions distributed during the day. Durations of activities were recorded by a simple pen recorder,
the particular type of the activity being entered in notational form on a log
sheet.

Two drugs, Thorazine® and GE-35 (an imipramine derivative) were
tested. Each drug, as well as placebo were administered for approximately
three months. This study was really in the nature of a pilot study, and
hence the results are not very comprehensive. But certainly the record
given shows that GE-35 increased percent activity relative to Thorazine.
It is regrettable that values for no-drug conditions were not given for a
more complete comparison. The effects of Nardil®, Tinlafon, Serpasil® and
Stelazine®, relative to placebo, are also given. The authors conclude that
"the results obtained by this method . . . suggest that useful indications of
changes in a patient's condition can be established."

True indeed, but this single measure severely restricts the conclusions
that can be drawn and may even make it difficult to specify, just what kind
of change has taken place. For example, if phenothiazine depressed all
motor behavior equally, whether idiosyncratic or not, (e.g. eating, locomotion, intentional movements, stereotypies, activity patterns) if would be far
less significant than if it selectively depressed the latter two.

BEHAVIORAL PARAMETERS AND DRUG EFFECTS

The hyperkinetic syndrome is characterized by overactivity and restless-
ness, distractibility, short attention span and outbursts of aggressive behavior (Ounsted, 1955; Ingram, 1956). In this study of an eight-year-old hyperkinetic epileptic girl, the subject was used as her own control (Hutt, *et al.*,
1966). She was admitted to hospital as an intractable social and domestic
problem. Soon after admission her fits were effectively controlled by a re-

gime of ethotoin 500 mg b.d. and primidone 250 mg t.d.s. Her hyperkinesis however was not ameliorated, and our task was to evaluate the behavioral effects of several chemotherapeutic agents.

This subject showed the paradoxical reaction to amphetamine described by Ounsted (1955): she was listless, tearful, lacked any initiative and disconsolately rolled on the floor. The phenothiazines on the other hand appeared to have a beneficial effect, and on admission she was receiving Stelazine. Several authors (Alderton, and Hoddinott, 1964; Badham, *et al.*, 1963; Oettinger, and Simonds, 1962) and found Mellaril to be effective in the mangement of hyperactive and aggressive children, and other workers had found Ospolot to satisfactorily control both fits (Fenton, *et al.*, 1964; Garland, and Sumner, 1964; Gordon, 1964) and hyperkinetic behavior (Ingram and Ratcliffe, 1963).

Thus the drug regimes investigated in this study, in their temporal order, were:

(1)	Stelazine	3 mg b.d. (on admission)
(2)	No drug	(except anticonvulsants)
(3)	Mellaril®	25 mg t.d.s.
(4)	Ospolot	50 mg t.d.s.
(5)	Ospolot	100 mg t.d.s.
(6)	No drug	(except anticonvulsants)

It was not considered ethically justifiable that anticonvulsant medication should be stopped, so this was continued throughout the period of the study, it being argued that attempts to control fits were kept constant while the dependent variable, namely, hyperactivity, was under investigation.

Behavioral observations were made in a standard situation at approximately the same hour each day. The situation was a familiar room where the child played by herself with five toys plus a novel object on each occasion. Each session was of twelve-minute duration: observations during the first ten minutes were recorded on time-ruled check lists, an entry being made every ten seconds, and the last two minutes were filmed. The important behavioral categories recorded included visual exploration, locomotion, toy-directed responses, room-directed responses, gestures, and investigatory responses. From each check list, therefore, it was possible to calculate what proportion of the ten minutes were spent on specific activities. Any additional detail was recorded in a separate column. On certain occasions the entire session was filmed. The filming was done in a specially constructed cubicle from behind a glass screen. The person making the observations was kept in ignorance of the drug schedule. The child was seen at least three times under each drug condition, and not before she had been on the drug for three days.

Measures of attention span (i.e. duration of serial encounters with the same stimulus irrespective of how these contacts were made) were obtained from a frame-by-frame analysis of the film records. By running the film through a frame counter during analysis the amounts of time spent on different activities were obtained. All filming was done at 16 frames per second. The film data and check list data were averaged for the other behavioral measures.

The child's mean attention spans and their standard deviations under the different drug conditions are shown in Figure 55. These results are also compared with measures obtained in the 1963 study. It can be seen that in general her attention spans were short and relatively invariable; she was also

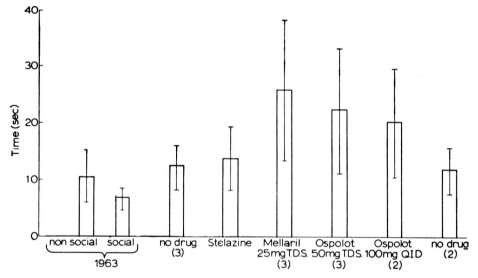

FIGURE 55. Means and standard deviations of attention spans under the different drug conditions. Numbers in brackets indicate the number of sessions upon which the readings are based (from Hutt, *et al.*, 1966)

more distractable in a social situation. Over a period of two years any maturational effect was slight and insignificant. Stelazine appeared to have little if any effect on this behavior measure. During administration of Mellaril however, her mean attention span was considerably increased, as was its variability. Both doses of Ospolot were less effective than Mellaril in this respect, but she was less distractable while receiving this drug than when taking no drugs. Mellaril differed significantly both from the no-drug and large Ospolot conditions; both Ospolot conditions were better than no drug but did not differ between each other.

Since the attention spans of these hyperkinetic children form a Poisson distribution, it is of interest to examine how the mode differs under the several drug conditions. The modes were as follows: (1) no drug, 10.2 seconds; (2) Stelazine, 10.5 seconds; (3) Mellaril, 12.6 seconds; and (4) Ospolot,

11.8 seconds. In other words, the mode was not appreciably modified by any drug condition.

The effects of the drugs on measures other than attention span are shown in Figure 56. Destructive activities were those that involved throwing or breaking toys, hitting the screen or fixtures; appropriate activities consisted of using toys or fixtures appropriately but not inventively or constructively, e.g. placing bricks, or tapping a top; constructive activities were those that involved assembling toys, building a design with bricks, making the top work, etc.

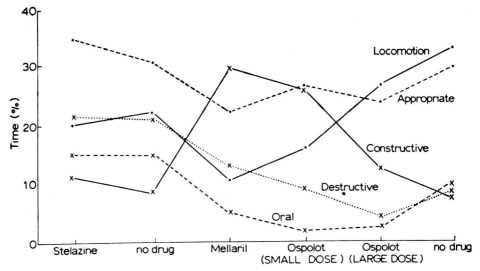

FIGURE 56. Proportions of time spent in different activities under the different drug conditions (from Hutt, *et al.*, 1966).

Locomotion which occupied about 25 percent of the child's time under no-drug conditions, was significantly reduced by Mellaril; this drug also increased the amount of the time spent on constructive or genuinely exploratory activities. The level of appropriate activities, generally rather desultorily performed, was not appreciably affected by any of the drug conditions. The amount of destructive activity and orality were both reduced, more by Ospolot than Mellaril. The relatively low levels of banging and throwing activities under the higher dose of Ospolot and the latter no-drug condition were in part a function of the greater amount of time spent in locomotion. Stelazine again had no appreciable effect on any of the measures, as compared with the no-drug condition.

Socially she was found to be most amenable while taking Mellaril: nurses and occupational therapists reported her to be quieter and more docile. Observational records indicated that the frequency of aggressive social encounters was only slightly reduced, whereas her locomotor activity and unconstructive play were considerably decreased. Ospolot appeared to evoke some unfavorable side effects: the child was often irritable, and on occasions bit herself. Since fit frequency was not appreciably altered by any of the drug conditions, it would appear that seizure threshold was not differentially affected by any of these drugs.

Many data were already available on the base line performance of this hyperkinetic child. An overall assessment, e.g. of improvement, in this case would depend on which behavioral parameter was chosen as the chief indicator, since the drugs selectively affected the different parameters. Ospolot, for instance, increased this child's attention span and its variability, and reduced her destructive and oral activities. Ingram and Ratcliffe (1963) reported that half their hyperkinetics were considered "much improved" or "cured" after treatment with Ospolot in doses comparable with our large dose, whereas we found locomotion to be considerably increased under this condition. The question is thus raised as to what particular parameters the assessment of improvement was based upon. Moreover, although no significant differences could be demonstrated between Ospolot (small dose) and Mellaril on any of the behavioral measures, the clinical assessment showed this child to be most improved while receiving the latter drug, thus suggesting that the total effects of thioridazine on the different behaviors were at least of practical, if not of statistical, significance. The social data however suggested that the reduction in aimless locomotor activity and desultory manipulatory activities contributed much towards this assessment, since the fact the amount of aggressive behavior was not reduced to such an appreciable extent. Some of the side effects, e.g. irritability, observed with the larger dose of Ospolot could be attributed to concurrent medication with primidone, as Garland and Sumner (1964) have pointed out.

Film records proved of great value in enabling a detailed analysis of the behaviors that were subtly modified by different pharmacological regimes. Even more important, the films provided a completely unbiased documentary record which could be retrospectively studied by any interested individual. The desirability of the latter advantage was particularly illustrated by the staff assessment of this child's general behavior: on two occasions complaints were made by different members of staff regarding the adverse effects of the drugs on the child's behavior in a social situation. On both occasions the child was receiving no drug but anticonvulsants. Reynolds *et al.* (1965) have demonstrated how the attitudes of the clinician can influence the drug responses of patients, and McDonald and Heimstra (1965) have shown how drugged rats can affect the behavior of non drugged animals. Recognition of the part played by such social influences makes motion pictures invaluable in the studies of drug effects, both as an objective record of the effects, and as an instrument in the analysis of their interactions with environmental factors.

The fact that no drug had a significant effect on the mode of attention span suggests that drugs in this kind of severely brain-damaged child can potentiate the influences of environmental factors, but are unable to appreciably modify the structural qualities of behavior. In other words the drugs enable a powerful environmental stimulus to hold the child's attention for a reasonable period of time, but the basic tendency to switch attention every ten to fifteen seconds remains relatively uninhibited. Perhaps with a child of this kind this is the most one can hope to do. Furthermore, since the normal structure of her behavior was such as to make her a social liability, any chemotherapeutic agent that made this less likely would be regarded as successful.

Chapter 9

SEQUENTIAL ANALYSIS

WE HAVE been concerned so far with the problems of identifying and recording elements of behavior and of their measurement in terms of frequency of occurrence, duration and intensity. Such an analysis, we have shown, is by no means unprofitable. The fact that behavior has a structure, that certain elements occur significantly more frequently than others relative to certain environmental changes, enables us to predict, with a considerable degree of confidence, what behavior will occur in a specified environment.

One problem with which hitherto we have not dealt is that of sequence. Elements of behavior are not randomly juxtaposed: some behaviors occur more frequently in temporal juxtaposition with each other than with others. Thus, on the basis of a few elements, we are often able to predict what will be the outcome of a particular sequence. Certain courses of action will end in laughter, in tears or in a temper tantrum. When we make such a judgment we are making use of our past experience of the statistical dependencies between events.

Any sequence of events between which conditional probabilities exist may be termed a stochastic process. Thus the statement that event A is followed by event B on 90 percent of occasions may be represented as a stochastic process. The most common stochastic processes are Markov chains. In such a chain, it is supposed that the occurrence of each event exercises some constraint upon the succeeding event; or conversely, that each event is contingent upon its predecessor. In this chapter we shall review four models developed to deal with statistical dependencies between behavioral events.

THE CHI-SQUARE MODEL

The majority of ethological studies which have attempted to analyze the contingencies between events have restricted themselves to analysis of dyads. The procedure adopted is described in the following paragraphs.

A table is first constructed on the model of a correlation matrix. All the separate behavioral elements of the animal's repertoire are listed vertically; these form the preceding acts. The same elements are again arrayed horizontally; these form the following acts. A diagonal line is drawn across the table from the top left hand cell to the bottom right hand cell.

A frequency count is made of the number of times each behavioral event in the left hand column *precedes* every item at the head of the table. These frequencies are entered in the lower segment of the matrix. A frequency count is then made of every occasion that an item at the head of the table *follows* an item on the left of the table. These figures are entered in the upper segment of the matrix. A simplified example is shown in Table X which is taken from a study by Grant (1963).

Only four behavior elements are considered: those designated as Threat, Attack, Aggressive Posture and Aggressive Groom. The kind of relationship which emerges from such a table is illustrated by the figures for Threat and Aggressive Posture. Whereas Aggressive Posture follows Threat forty-four times, Threat never follows Aggressive Posture. Again, Attack follows Threat on twelve occasions, but Threat never follows Attack. The row totals give the number of times a particular act *preceded* all other acts; the column totals give the number of times a particular act *follows* all other acts. Thus, Threat preceded Attack on twelve occasions, Aggressive Posture on forty-four occasions and Aggressive Groom on seventy-five occasions. Grant points out that acts which have a large number of following acts of all kinds, i.e. those whose row totals are largest, as Threat in the present example, are acts which mark the beginning of a sequence of behavior. Conversely, acts which have a large number of preceding acts but few following acts are generally end points of sequences of behavior.

The statistical treatment of data from matrices of this type varies from writer to writer. Grant himself employs the technique of calculating the expected frequency for each cell on the hypothesis that acts follow or precede each other in a proportion to their overall frequency of occurrence. The expected value for each cell is obtained from the ratio:

$$\frac{\text{row total} \times \text{column total}}{\text{grand total}}$$

By comparing the expected value with the observed value in each cell, we are able to see whether two sequential acts occur in association with each other more or less frequently than would be expected by chance. "Any major discrepancy between expected and observed will give indications of affinity or otherwise between the acts." (Grant, 1963) This, however, is at best a rough and ready technique. We are still left with the problem of deciding what constitutes a "major discrepancy" between observed and expected values. Grant applies no statistical tests to his data, giving only the observed and expected frequencies with which acts follow each other. Applying the simple χ^2 test to his data, we find that most of his published differences, but not all, give values significant at the 5 percent level of confidence or less. There are however forty-two acts or postures in Grant's matrix, giving $42^2 = 1764$ cells. By chance alone we would expect eighty-eight of the expected/observed frequency comparisons to produce values of χ^2 significant at the 5 percent confidence level and seventeen to eighteen at the 1 percent level. Thus, while this type of analysis forms a valuable initial step in studying the statistical dependencies amongst sequences of behavior, it requires careful statistical treatment. The statistical reliability of the χ^2 test could, for example, be enhanced by converting these into contingency coefficients.

THE FACTOR ANALYTIC MODEL

One manner in which the statistical treatment of this type of preceding-following matrix may be extended is illustrated by Wiepkema's (1961) study of the bitterling. Wiepkema first calculated Spearman's ρ and then factor-analyzed the correlations thus obtained. Factor analysis may be an especially powerful tool in ethological studies where a basic inquiry concerns the motivational systems underlying particular sequences of behavior. Factor analysis tells us whether the correlations among particular elements can be attributed to a single source of variance or whether two or more independent sources of variation (factors) have to be postulated. In self-generated behavior each independent source of variation (or factor) may be treated as evidence for a different motivational system.

The bitterling is a species of small fish. In the early spring, the males of the species defend a territory around a freshwater mussel, chasing away other males and unripe females, but admitting ripe females. Such females are led to the mussel within whose gills they deposit their eggs. While skimming over the siphons of the mussels, the male ejects sperm which may be drawn into the syphon and hence reach the eggs lying in the gills. Wiepkema recorded twelve clearly identifiable movements of territorial males towards other males and towards ripe and unripe females respectively.

The number of times each movement preceded or followed either itself or each other movement was then tabulated, as above. Ratios of the obtained frequency to the expected frequency (on the assumption of purely random sequence) were computed for each cell. These ratios were ranked in decreasing size by columns and by rows. Rank order correlations were then computed between pairs of columns (for correlations between items of behavior and preceding items) and between pairs of rows (for correlations between items and following items). The significance of the correlations was tested by means of t-tests. In this way it was possible to distinguish which items of behavior were significantly associated (positively or negatively) with other preceding or following items.

A table showing the significances of rank correlation coefficients is itself often informative. A more dramatic way of arranging correlational data has been devised by Dr. J.A.R.A.M. van Hooff (personal communication) of the

University of Utrecht. For any one item of behavior the magnitudes of its correlations with all other items may be represented graphically. In Figure 57 we have plotted two sets of Wiepkema's own correlation coefficients in the manner suggested by van Hooff. While visually compelling, it can readily be appreciated that the method does little to reduce the data, at least

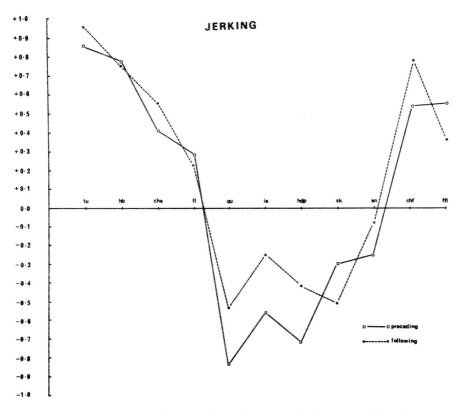

FIGURE 57. Distribution of correlations (Spearman's) between (1) jerking and preceding behaviors, and (2) jerking and following behaviors (after Wiepkema, 1961).

one graph being required for each behavioral item. In the case of the bitterling, with only twelve items to be considered, the method is feasible, but with larger behavioral repertoires to be considered—van Hooff has more than sixty categories for the chimpanzee, and McGrew 111 categories for nursery school children—a more drastic method of data reduction is required. Van Hooff himself proposes to use cluster analysis. In Wiepkema's own treatment, correlations of the preceding and following matrices were subjected to factor analyses, and factor loadings were computed for three factors using the principal axes method (Fruchter, 1954). After rotation, these factors were shown to account for 90 percent and 89 percent respectively of the total common variance of the preceding and following correlations. The relationships amongst the various behavioral elements could thus be specified in terms of a three-dimensional model in which each item was represented as a vector (Fig. 58).

In such a model the correlation coefficient between any two variables is represented as the cosine of the angle between two vectors. Therefore the

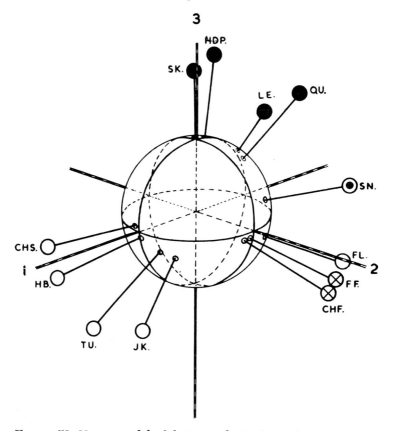

FIGURE 58. Vector model of factor analysis of correlations between successive behavior patterns (from Wiepkema, 1961).

higher the correlation between two items the smaller the angle between their vectors. The factor loadings of each item are represented by the projection of its vector upon each orthogonal axis. The length of each vector represents the amount of the common variance of that item accounted for by the proposed factors.

It is immediately apparent that the twelve vectors fall into three clusters, each consisting of four. The vectors of four movements having an aggressive function (head butting, chasing, turning beats and jerking) are closely grouped around factor one which Wiepkema called the aggressive factor. Vectors for four further movements (fin flicking, snapping, chafing and fleeing) are closely grouped around factor two, simply entitled the nonreproductive factor; and four movements used in courtship (skimming, head-down postures, quivering and leading) are grouped around factor three, therefore entitled the sexual factor. Chasing and head butting are almost pure measures of the aggressive factor since their loadings on the other factors are almost zero. Similarly fleeing is almost a pure measure of factor two, while skimming and head-down postures are almost pure factor three. Several vectors clearly have high loadings on two factors, for example jerking and snapping. The implication of this is that some social behaviors may be the result of simultaneous activation of two motivational systems.

Wiepkema's analysis commends itself in at least four different ways. First, it provides a rigorous method of testing the strength of association between contiguous behavioral events. Second, it is highly economical, enabling the intercorrelations between large numbers of events to be expressed as a function of a small number of variables. Third, the clustering of particular events about a single orthogonal axis may suggest a common motivational system for events which previously were not seen to be related. Fourth, the factor loadings of a particular vector may help resolve puzzling features of a behavior pattern by showing that it bears significant statistical relationships to two or more factors simultaneously: so-called ambivalent motivation will be of this kind.

THE INFORMATIONAL MODEL

The studies discussed so far have been concerned with dyadic sequences of behavior performed by one animal. We might however expect that a particular behavioral event is not wholly the effect of a single antecedent event but is determined by several previous events. Moreover, in both the cases considered above, and indeed, in most of the studies employing contingency tables, the behavior under consideration is social. It seems strange therefore to consider the stochastics of one animal's behavior in apparent isolation from that of its partner.

Altmann (1965) has developed a system for studying statistical dependencies between behavioral elements generated by each partner in turn and which extends to quadrads. His study of the behavior of rhesus monkeys deserves the status of a classic among ethological studies. All too often ethologists paint a vivid picture of the behavioral elements of an animal without giving a single figure as to its probability of occurrence or its duration; psychologists present meticulously quantified results subjected to analyses of variance while giving only the scantiest indications of how the animal behaves. Altmann both provides a detailed behavioral inventory of rhesus (1962) and also one of the most sophisticated mathematical treatments yet undertaken by an ethologist (1965).

He postulates a series of stochastic models which specify the probabilities of all behavioral events and sequences of events up to, and including, four

successive events. The aim of each model is to enable us to predict what behavior will occur at any particular time in relation to its antecedent events.
The model may thus be said to specify the stochastic structure of the interaction process. Altmann considers five such models. A zero order approximation to the stochastic structure assumes that all events are equiprobable and
independent of each other; under these circumstances prediction would be a
matter of chance. A first-order approximation is obtained by assuming that
successive behavior patterns are independent but have the same probabilities as in nature; thus the probability of any event can be empirically determined, given an adequate sample of the animal's repertoire. The analyses
used by Grant (1963) and Wiepkema (1961) are based upon second-order
approximations to the stochastic structure: that is, successive events are not
independent, but have a probability of occurrence which is determined by
the immediately preceding event. Altmann goes yet further: He considers
the possibility that any event is the outcome of the two, or of the three
immediately preceding events (third and fourth order approximations respectively). Moreover, as more and more preceding events are considered,
our uncertainty as to which behavior pattern comes next is correspondingly
decreased. Why, we may therefore ask, stop at a fourth-order approximation? Altmann provides an ingenious and quantitative answer.

Each model reduces by a certain amount our uncertainty of what behavior occurs next. Given the sequential dependencies between successive
events and a finite behavioral repertoire of 120 elements, the reduction in
our uncertainty on applying each model may be measured using the statis-
tics of information theory (Shannon, and Weaver, 1948; Miller, and Frick,
1949; and Quastler, 1955). If all behavioral events are independent of each
other, the uncertainty (U) associated with any behavioral event is given by
the expression:

$$U(y) = - \Sigma_k \, p(k) \, \log_2 p(k)$$

where k is the number of items in the behavioral repertoire and p(k) the
probabilities associated with each item. Similarly, if we consider two events
(dyads), the uncertainty associated with y, when x, its antecedent, is
known, is given by the expression:

$$U_x(y) = - \Sigma_{j,k} \, p(j, k) \, \log_2 p_j(k)$$

where $p_j(k)$ is the probability that $y = k$ when $x = j$. Similarly, for triads:

$$U_{wx}(y) = \Sigma_{i,j,k} \, p(i, j, k) \, \log_2 p_{i,j} \, (k)$$

and for quadrads:

$$U_{vwx}(y) = - \Sigma_{h,i,j,k} \, p(h, i, j, k) \, \log_2 p_{h,i,j} \, (k)$$

Now, if the behavior of an animal depends in part upon the immediately antecedent event, $U_x(y)$ will be less than $U(y)$ and $U_{wx}(y)$ less than $U_x(y)$ etc. Thus, the difference between the measures of uncertainty yielded by successive models will give a measure of the decrease in uncertainty (or conversely, the extra amount of information) yielded by that model. It is possible however that as we increase the number of elements considered in the sequence, we soon come into conflict with the law of diminishing returns, each new computation yielding only fractionally more than its predecessor. This problem may be dealt with by comparing each conditional uncertainty with its maximum possible value. The maximum possible uncertainty is simply $\log_2(k)$, on the assumption that at each event the animal has his total behavioral repertoire to choose from. We might expect that as more and more antecedent behaviors are considered, the behavior of the animal becomes more determined.

This indeed is the case. Using Shannon's measure of redundancy, Altmann computes an "index of stereotypy" for each order of approximation. This varies from 0 for the zero-order degree of approximation (all behavior patterns equiprobable) to over 0.9 for a fourth order of approximation. In other words, when our predictions are based upon three antecedent events, at least in the social behavior of the rhesus monkey, behavior is almost completely determined. Thus, the last stage of Altmann's analysis enables us to answer the question: Why stop at quadrads? We stop at a point, compatible with the amount of data available, where uncertainty is no longer being significantly reduced.

It is clear however, that the size of the population of sequences diminishes as an increasingly large number of elements is included in the sequence. Data might be preserved in such an analysis if it were possible to demonstrate that sequences such as ABCEDOFGIHJKLLLM and ACBEFGWHIJKLMLN belonged to the same population. Altmann himself points out that he found no evidence of the "single chain of events" often used to describe the behavior, particularly the sexual behavior, of animals. It would indeed be biologically unadaptive for animals to show such invariance, particularly in their social transactions with other animals. Nevertheless, granted that there will be considerable variability amongst animals (and most of all among humans) in the ordering of individual elements in a chain, in their timing and intensity, prima facie it might be expected that there will exist certain classes of behavioral chains most of whose elements will fall at similar temporal positions, and which will differ from other classes where quite different groups of elements will occur in temporal juxtaposition. Thus the sequences:

ZYXWWVTSRABUQPON

ZXYWVUTTSRBQPOON

although containing some elements common to the sequences above, almost certainly belong to a different class of behaviors. Certainly, there is much greater similarity between pairs than across pairs.

The simplest sequences are, of course, those containing only two items. Wiepkema (1961) has already shown that the correlations between pairs of items can be classified by means of factor analysis. We might expect that a system for classifying much longer sequences would also utilize factor analysis. A mathematical treatment (Multi-Scaler Analysis) by which sequences containing up to forty elements may be classified has recently been developed by Professor Louis Guttman of the Israel Institute of Applied Research, Jerusalem (personal communication). The method has recently been applied in a study of behavior genetics in the mouse (Guttman, and Liebig, 1968) but no detailed exposition of the mathematical treatment itself has so far appeared. For the reasons given above it should prove an important tool.

THE PHRASE STRUCTURE GRAMMAR MODEL

Several writers, Altmann (1965) among them, have questioned whether Markov processes are the most appropriate model for the comprehensive description of behavior and have proposed that models derived from psycholinguistics may be particularly worthy of study. This view has been iterated in a number of places. In his paper on The Problem of Serial Order in Behaviour, Lashley (1951) stated:

> I have devoted so much time to discussion of the problem of syntax not only because language is one of the most important products of human cerebral action, but also because the problems raised by the organisation of language seem to me to be characteristic of almost all other cerebral activity. . . . Not only speech, but all skilled acts seem to involve the same problems of serial ordering, even down to the temporal co-ordination of muscular contractions in such a movement as reaching and grasping (p. 221).

More recently, in a provocative and inspiring monograph, Miller *et al.* (1960) have laid stress upon the importance of plans in directing behavior. "*A plan is any hierarchical process in the organism that can control the order in which a sequence of operations is to be performed.*" The fact that in speaking, "people are able to construct and carry out very complicated Plans at a relatively rapid pace" suggests that the study of the rules of organization whereby humans generate their utterances might also throw light on how they control other sequential behaviors. As Miller *et al.* say: "This human ability [to construct plans] may be unique to human speech, but this seems unlikely." There is in principle, no reason why models derived from psycholinguistics should have applicability to any behavior other than language. Nevertheless, it is tempting to draw analogies between language and nonverbal behavior. Just as a language consists of a finite vocabulary of words, nonverbal behavior has a finite repertoire of elements. In speech the words, and in nonverbal behavior the elements are juxtaposed in strings with a definite start and end point; transition probabilities between adjacent words or behavioral elements may be empirically determined; and most important, both language and nonverbal behavior have a structure. By structure we mean that words and behavior elements appear to be organized hierarchically into groups of increasing or decreasing complexity. Within each group the words or elements bear close statistical relationships to each other, which they do not have to members of other groups.

It may be informative therefore to make a brief exploratory excursion into psycholinguistics in search of a descriptively adequate model of sequential behavior. In a highly readable introduction to the determination of syntactic structure, Miller (1962) gives the following illustration of constituent analysis of a sentence. Take the sentence. *Bill hit the ball.* It is intuitively obvious that *the ball* forms a more natural unit than *hit the*. One test of the organization of the sentence is to substitute a single word for subsequences and see whether this alters the whole structure of the sentence. We can, for example, substitute *it* for *the ball* or *acted* for *hit the ball* and maintain the structure of the sentence. We could not make a similar substitution for *hit the* or *Bill hit the* without radically altering the structure. We may represent the interrelationships between the various constituents by means of a generative grammar. It is not intended to give a detailed exposition of generative grammar. We shall restrict ourselves to those details which are necessary for following the ensuing discussion.*

The central idea is that "starting from a basic axiom, we apply rules of formation that permit us to rewrite the axiom in certain acceptable ways until we have finally derived the desired sentence" (Miller, 1962). The set of rewriting rules is referred to as the grammar. For example, we may illustrate a generative grammar by reference to our original sentence, *Bill hit the ball*, phrased in terms of rewriting rules (Fig. 59).

A representation of this kind is referred to as a tree diagram. Each branch of the tree ends in a terminal symbol, that is, symbols which cannot be rewritten. It can be seen that the terminal symbols, *the* and *ball* are related via a single node, NP; the same terminal symbols are related to *hit* via two nodes NP and VP; and to *Bill* via three nodes. We might anticipate that terminal symbols which share a common node bear a closer statistical relationship than symbols between which two or more nodes occur. This appears to be the case: the transitional probability associated with the subsequence *the ball* being higher than that associated with (say) *Bill the* or *Bill ball*.

Could a generative grammar, capable of representation by such a tree

---

* The article by Miller (1962) taken in conjunction with the short book, *Syntactic Structures*, by N. Chomsky (The Hague. Mouton, 1957) would provide an adequate introduction to the subject. A fuller introduction may be found in J. J. Katz and P. M. Postal: *An Integrated Theory of Linguistic Descriptions* (Cambridge, Mass., M.I.T. Press, 1964).

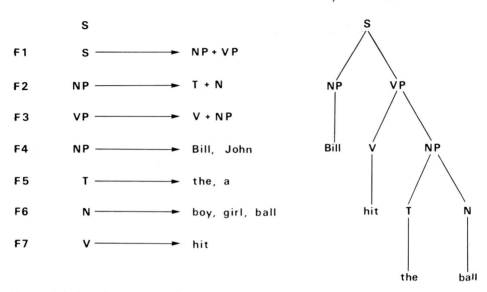

FIGURE 59. Set of rewriting rules applied to a simple sentence together with resulting tree diagram (from Miller, 1962)

graph, be applied to the formal analysis of structured nonverbal behavior sequences? To the best of our knowledge, only Marshall (1965) has attempted to do so. His paper, though little known, is highly provocative and contains at least the signposts for a syntactic structure of nonverbal behavior. Marshall takes as his data the observations by Fabricius and Jansson (1963) of the reproductive behavior of the male pigeon. The authors present their data in the form of a contingency table, showing the percentage of occasions upon which each behavior pattern is preceded or followed by every other. As terminal symbols, Marshall chooses seven of the sixteen behavior patterns. In Table XIII we reproduce the appropriate cells as a seven by seven matrix.

TABLE XIII
RELATIVE FREQUENCY WITH WHICH SEVEN BEHAVIOR PATTERNS OF
THE MALE PIGEON PRECEDE OR FOLLOW EACH OTHER.
(AFTER FABRICIUS, AND JANSSON, 1963)

	Bw	*Dr*	*A*	*D*	*Bi*	*M*	*Co*
Bw	—	40.4	7.5	23.5	0.3	0	0
Dr	92.4	—	4.4	1.0	0	0.3	0
A	73.0	11.5	—	4.9	0	0	0
D	5.9	0	0.3	—	43.6	7.5	0
Bi	2.7	0	0.9	66.2	—	9.8	0
M	0	0	0	1.9	0	—	98.1
Co	51.9	0	0	3.9	0	0	—

Three representative sequences of these behaviors are then considered:

1. Bowing *(Bw)* + Displacement Preening *(D)* + Mounting *(M)* + Copulation *(Co)*.
2. The same sequence as (1) with optional item Billing *(Bi)* interposed between *D* and *M*.
3. The same sequence as (2) with either or both of the optional items, Driving *(Dr)*, followed by Attacking *(A)* interposed between *Bw* and *D*.

A phrase structure grammar, capable both of generating the requisite behavior patterns and of representing the hierarchical organization of these patterns, is now constructed. The grammer, together with the conventions and abbreviations used, is shown in Figure 60.

1. SBSeq⟶Prep ⌢ Con

2. Prep⟶Int ⌢ Wa

3. Int⟶Bw ⌢ (Agg)

4. $Agg \rightarrow \begin{Bmatrix} (Dr) ⌢ A \\ Dr ⌢ (A) \end{Bmatrix}$

5. Wa⟶D ⌢ Bi

6. Con⟶M ⌢ Co

KEY

SBSeq:	Sexual behaviour sequence	Bw:	Bowing
Prep:	Preparatory behaviour	Dr:	Driving
Con:	Consummatory behaviour	A:	Attacking
Int:	Introduce	D:	Displacement preening
Wa:	Warm up	Bi:	Billing
Agg:	Aggressive behaviour	M:	Mounting
		Co:	Copulation

FIGURE 60. Generative grammar used by Marshall (1965) in his reanalysis of Fabricius and Jansson's (1963) data on the reproductive behavior of the male pigeon.

Taking each of the sequences, 1, 2, 3, in turn, the grammar asserts that their organization is in the form represented by the tree diagrams illustrated in Figure 61.

We have already seen that there is greater statistical dependency between terminal symbols which are separated by only one node, than between those

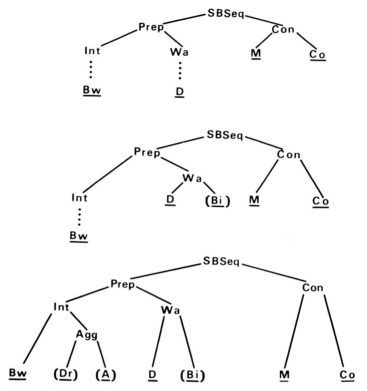

FIGURE 61. Tree diagrams showing successive stages in the application of generative grammar to reproductive behavior of the male pigeon (from Marshall, 1965).

separated by two or more. Thus, from tree diagram 1, we would predict that:

$$p^*(Bw/D) \quad \text{and} \quad p(M/Co) > p(D/M)$$

which, as can be seen from Table XIII is the case. Similarly, in tree diagram 2, we would predict that:

$$p(D/Bi) \quad \text{and} \quad p(M/Co) > p(Bw/D) > p(Bi/M)$$

since D, Bi and M, Co are each separated by one node, whereas Bw, D are separated by two nodes and Bi, M are separated by four nodes. These predictions also are verified.

By the same principle, in the tree diagram 3, we would predict:

$$p(Dr/A) \quad \text{and} \quad p(D/Bi) \quad \text{and} \quad p(M/Co) > p(Bw/Dr) > p(A/D) \quad \text{and} \quad p(Bi/M)$$

Referring again to the observed probabilities, the predictions are correct, except in one case, $p(Dr/A)$ being only 0.044. The reason for this is that the sequence defined by tree diagram 3 is not the only one to occur: referring to the probabilities of Table XIII it is clear that the animal may backtrack in the sequence before proceeding to the consummatory sequence, for in-

_____

* $p(A/B)$ is defined as the probability of B follows A.

1. SBSeq⟶Prep ⌢ Con

2. Prep⟶Int ⌢ Wa ⌢ (Prep)

3. Int ⟶Bw ⌢ (Agg) ⌢ (Int)

4. Agg⟶{Dr / A} ⌢ Agg

5. Wa ⟶D ⌢ Bi ⌢ (Wa)

6. Con ⟶M ⌢ Co

FIGURE 62. Recursive version of the generative grammar may look like this (Marshall, 1969, personal communication).

stance, p (Dr/Bw) is 0.924. Thus, the grammar requires rewriting to take account of backtracking. This is done by rewriting rules two to five to operate recursively (Fig. 62). This enables us to structure the tree diagram 3 in a new form (Fig. 63). This extension of the grammar now enables us to make the following predictions:

$p(Bi/D)$, $p(Bi/Bw)$, $p(D/Bw)$ and $p(A/Dr)$, $p(A/Bw)$, $p(Dr/Bw)$

$> p(Bi/Dr)$, $p(Bi/A)$, $p(D/Dr)$, $p(D/A)$

It is thus seen that the grammar in its recursive form provides an adequate model for describing recursive sequences of behavior leading to copulation.

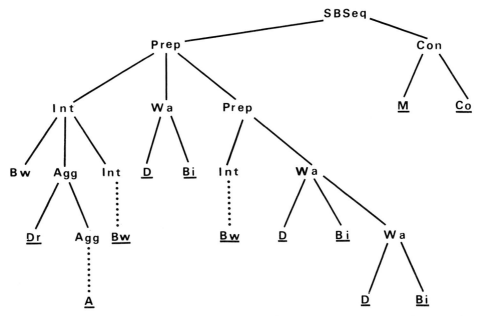

FIGURE 63. Tree diagram showing application of generative grammar in its recursive form to reproductive behavior of the male pigeon (Marshall, 1969, personal communication).

The chi-square model is the simplest and most widely used of those considered; it is also the least powerful. Certain regularities which are not apparent in the raw data may be manifested by measures of association or correlation, but demonstration of their mathematical coherence requires further treatment. Wiepkema's (1961) treatment by means of factor analysis is more powerful in that it attempts to account for all the correlations in terms of a limited number of sources of variance. Its limitation is that it takes into account only adjacent elements. On the other hand, Altmann (1965) has shown that the occurrence of any behavioral element may be treated as a function of at least three antecedent events. Altmann's own series of models for calculating the average reduction of uncertainty yielded by antecedent behavior sequences of increasing length is a particularly interesting venture in. linking ethology with the mathematical theory of communication. Unfortunately, the amount of uncertainty associated with the occurrence of a single item of behavior when considered alone is a function of the size of the behavioral repertoire. Thus, sequences of behavioral elements far in excess of quadrads may have to be considered in analyzing human behavior in order to achieve levels of uncertainty reduction comparable with those for rhesus.

Altmann himself has noted the suggestion that "nested constraints," such as occur in human communication and which cannot be generated by finite state Markov processes, may apply to nonverbal, nonhuman behavior. He is not hopeful however that extrapolation of phrase structure grammar to the analysis of nonverbal behavior is likely to prove fruitful.

> Whether such constraints occur in the communication processes of non-human primates remains to be seen. In any case, the extrapolation of Chomsky's analysis to sequences of communication in other animals will not be straightforward. Quite aside from the fact that the word units in Chomsky's linguistic analysis are not strictly comparable with the behavioural units in our study, there is the more difficult problem that Chomsky's analysis depends upon being able to distinguish that class of word chains which constitute the grammatically correct statements within the language. (What corresponds to this in the communication of non-human primates? Is it the set of sequences that do, in fact, occur?) Beyond that, Chomsky is dealing with the constraints of an individual's behaviour on his own behaviour, whereas we are dealing with the social constraints on behaviour within an intercommunicating group of individuals. That is, Chomsky is dealing with courses of action whereas we are dealing with courses of interaction (p. 518).

In view of the final objection, Marshall's (1965) analysis of Fabricius and Jansson's data (1963) is of particular interest; it provides a full description of behavior with great economy, taking into account only one animal of a pair. The strength of the model lies in its ability to deal with a considerably greater behavioral repertoire and much longer sequences that can be treated by Markovian processes alone. An evaluation of the various models presented in this chapter awaits a study in which all three types are applied to the same behavioral data.

Chapter 10

A FORWARD LOOK

TOWARDS AN ETHOLOGY OF MAN

*If there are historians of science a millenium hence, and if adequate docu-
ments remain, the middle years of the 20th Century will be looked on with
awe. The rate of biological understanding, which increased so slowly in the
years subsequent to the 16th Century, suddenly became exponential.*

THUS writes the editor of a recent symposium on *Ideas in Modern Biology* (Moore, 1965, p. vii). The past three decades have witnessed something approaching a revolution in our thinking about the structure and
growth of living things. Major advances have been made in cytogenetics,
molecular biology, cell physiology, experimental embryology and reproductive physiology to mention but a few. It is thus significant that in addition to
chapters on recent developments in these areas, Moore's collection contains
three chapters on ethology, the biological study of behavior. For, as Medawar (1967) has asserted, it required a "revolution of thought" to produce a
science of animal behavior in the style of its two pioneers, Lorenz and Tinbergen.

Whereas scientific investigation in its classical form meant isolating a phenomenon, subjecting it to single experimental interventions and recording
what changes took place, the ethologists showed that lawlike propositions
(Ryle, 1949) could be made about the naturally occurring behavior of animals in their own habitats. They showed that behavior could be analyzed
into natural units (see Ch. 3), that these units had a certain structural coherence among themselves, and that they occurred in regular, highly predictable sequences, locked in time with natural events in the animal world. Ethology was also characterized by a particular type of approach. Tinbergen
(1963) has described this approach as an endeavor to look at the phenomena of behavior through the eyes of the trained biologist; to ask the
questions, How did this behavior pattern develop? What are its causes?
What is its function? and What is its evolutionary significance? These may
be termed the problems of ontogeny, causation, survival value, and evolution, respectively. What the ethologists have done is both to remind scientists that the behavior of animals is as legitimately a subject of biological
study as their structure and that important biological questions may be

studied through the painstaking observation, description and recording of naturally occurring behavior. As Medawar (1967) too has reminded us, only when the basic cataloguing of the naturally occurring behavior patterns has been done is it:

> possible to start to obtain significant information from the study of the contrived behaviour—from the application or withholding of stimuli—for it is not informative to study variations of behaviour unless we know beforehand the norm from which the variants depart.

It is this return to nature approach of ethology which marks it off most clearly from the other discipline which purports to be the science of behavior, psychology:

> Experimental work in ethology is characterised by the fact that the problems selected for experimental analysis are, in general, those suggested by observation of the animal's natural behaviour pattern. . . . By contrast, most work in animal psychology in this country [America] is not based upon the researcher's interest in the animal as an object of investigation, but rather on the use of the animal, such as the laboratory rat, as a tool for the investigation of a problem which the investigator considers to be a problem of "general" psychology, rather than an aspect of the life of the rat. Indeed, there is an unspoken assumption in much of "rat psychology" that the justification for the work, and our conception of its significance, depend upon the extent to which we think the behaviour of the animal being used in the experiment is representative of the behaviour of animals in general, including human beings (Lehrman, 1962, p. 89).

Thus psychology and ethology, while complementary (Tinbergen, 1955) differ with respect to their methods of study, their emphases and in the way in which they frame their questions. Psychology has largely restricted itself to well-controlled laboratory experimentation, which at times may have only a tenuous connection with behavior in a naturally occurring situation. Ethology has started from behavior in its natural setting and only subsequently has learned to subject its data to laboratory experimentation. While psychology has been concerned with experimentation with human subjects as much as with animals, the ethologists have hitherto restricted their observations to subhuman species and in particular to subprimates.

It is interesting that those disciplines which are usually subsumed under the term biology, the study of living processes, are ones from which the study of human processes have largely been excluded. This pattern has been followed by ethology. There is still no discipline which may be called human ethology even though ethologists themselves have long recognized the value of their methods and of the biological approach for the study of human behavior. Tinbergen ends his classic work *The Study of Instinct* (1951) with a section entitled "The Ethological Study of Man:"

> Man is an animal. He is a remarkable and in many respects unique species, but he is an animal nevertheless. In structure and functions, of the heart, blood,

intestine, kidneys, and so on, man closely resembles other animals, especially other vertebrates. Paleontology as well as comparative anatomy and embryology do not leave the least doubt that this resemblance is based on true evolutionary relationships. Man and the present-day primates have only recently diverged from a common primate stock. . . . It is only natural, therefore, that the zoologist should be inclined to extend his ethological studies beyond the animals to man himself. However, the ethological study of man has not yet advanced very far. While animal neurophysiology and animal ethology are coming in touch with each other, there remains a wide gap between these two fields in the study of the behaviour of man (pp. 209-210).

Two decades later a perplexing situation exists. We have the beginnings of what purports to be an ethology of Man, based however, not upon an intensive analysis of human behavior, but upon extrapolation of findings and theoretical notions from the study of lower animals. Ethologists have not been eager to engage upon the detailed and systematic observational studies required by the construction of a human ethogram. Data more often have been collected in the armchair than in the field. This is especially surprising since ethologists have continually stressed that analysis of the causal mechanisms underlying behavior presupposes a detailed knowledge of the animal's behavior repertoire. Moreover, when Man has not been one of the species under consideration, they have shown commendable caution in inferring homology of mechanism from interspecific similarities of behavior. When one of the species is Man, interspecific leaps are considered quite legitimate, provided that they are always one-way. Extrapolations of behavioral mechanisms in animals from studies of Man would be smacked down as anthropomorphic.

Psychologists, on the other hand, have seldom placed their findings in the type of biological framework likely to excite the interest of ethologists and have not generally concerned themselves with the theoretical issues of concern to ethologists. In consequence, ethologists have tended to ignore findings from human studies relevant to their speculations about human behavior, often producing articles more notable for their epigrammatic headlines than for their perspicacity. For example, facism, criminality, delinquency and the battered-baby syndrome are some of the phenomena attributed to human crowding by writers such as Leyhausen (1965), Keywitz (1966), and Russell (1966). In practice it is known that battered babies come equally from professional and artisan families and equally from urban and rural dwellings (Helfer and Kempe, 1968; C. Ounsted, personal communication). Although Russell (1966) emphatically states that "animal studies, particularly with monkeys, suggest that crowding is a potent cause of aggression," we know of no study of infrahuman primates where density has been manipulated as an independent variable and other contributory factors have been controlled. No account is taken of individual differences nor of the fact that many humans choose to live in densely populated areas, actively seeking the advantages of urbanized living. These authors also assiduously ignore any published human studies which may report results contrary to their thesis. For example, the United States Navy Medical Neuropsychiatric Research Unit (Gunderson, 1963; Gunderson and Nelson, 1963) carried out a comprehensive study of the effect of group size on normal adults: they found that when different numbers of men were confined within a limited physical area, the size of the group (and the large group had between 80 and 100 men) had no effect on the incidence of emotional or somatic complaints (this being a sensitive index of disturbance). In the study already mentioned in Chapter 7 (Hutt and Vaizey, 1966), we found that not only were individual differences important in crowding effects, but so was the structure of the physical environment. In a room which was partially divided by half-walls, benches, hides, etc. increasing density provoked territorial behavior; this behavior was absent in an open rectangular room which had not even the rudiments of demarcation of physical territory. And yet in the exhaustive volume on the behavior of primates edited by de Vore (1965), there is scarcely a mention of territorial behavior as such occurring in any of the infrahuman primate species.

Now it may be said in defence of these animal behaviorists that they are engaging in stimulating speculation or in popularizing scientific findings for the interested layman. But there is a distinction between guarded speculation and considered analogies or homologies on the one hand, and melodramatic assertions, distortions and selective omissions on the other.

Having advocated an ethological approach throughout this book, it may be surprising that we should end on such a critical note. Our concern is that the very real case the ethologists have for the importance of their findings and for the applicability of their methodology to the study of Man should not be destroyed by an unseemly haste in inferring homologies, and by a reluctance either to uncover what is already known or to engage upon new fact-finding assays.

Neuroethology

In the last analysis, progress in the behavioral sciences most surely will be made when recordings of behavior are linked with simultaneous physiological recordings. It may be appropriate therefore in this final chapter to look at three pilot studies in which attempts have been made to effect such a linkage. Though concerned with cats, the first study, by van den Hoofdakker (1966), provides a methodological paradigm, particularly with regard to its behavioral analysis. This study will therefore be treated in greatest detail. The other two studies are considerably less thorough than that of van den Hoofdakker, but are of interest since their subjects were human.

Behavior and EEG in Cats

Domestic cats were observed in a square cage, the walls of which were made from plate glass. EEG recordings were made from electrodes implanted in the skull. The electrodes were connected to a light weight cable attached to a plug on the animal's collar and led to the ceiling of its cage, the cable length being sufficient to provide full freedom of movement. The EEG was recorded on magnetic tape concurrently with detailed behavioral observations. Observations were entered at ten-second intervals on a standardized form, an example of which is shown in Figure 64.

Three groups of behavior were recorded:

1. Body posture: sitting, crouching, sphynxing, or lying.
2. Head position: upright, lowered, or dropped.
3. Eyes: open, half open, quarter open, or closed.

TIME	10	20	30	40	50	60	10	20	30	40	50	60	10	20	30	40	50	60	10	20	30	40	50	60
HEAD	U	U	U	U	U	U	U	U	U	U	U	U	U	U	U	U	U	U	U	U	U	U	U	U
EYES	O	O	O	½	½	½	½	O	½	½	½	½	¼	¼	¼	¼	½	½	CL	CL	CL	CL	CL	CL
BODY	C	C	C	C	C	C	C	V/S	S	S	S	S	S	S	S	S	S/L	L	L	L	L	L	L	L

U = UP
C = CROUCHING
S = SPHYNXING
L = LYING
V = CHANGING POSTURE
CL = CLOSED

FIGURE 64. Example of completed protocol (from van den Hoofdakker, 1966).

Each behavioral element was clearly and fully defined. An entry was made under each of the three categories of behavior every ten seconds for a total period of five minutes. After a one-minute rest interval, behavior was again rated for five minutes and the process repeated up to a total recording period of one hour. It can be seen that with three behavior categories which can be in one of four, three or four states respectively, there are forty-eight theoretically possible combinations of behavior elements. In practice however only a limited number of combinations occurred, indicating that the behavior elements were intercorrelated in a specific way. For example, the upright and the lowered head positions could occur in association with the sitting, crouching, sphynxing and lying body postures, whereas the dropped

	Head			U	L	D	U	L	D	U	L	D
	Upr.	Low.	Drop.									
Sitting	1,1% n:12			0,2% n:4			0,1% n:2					
Crouching	2,2% n:13			2,5% n:15			0,7% n:4					
Sphynxing	2,2% n:12			3,2% n:17			9,5% n:33	0,4% n:2		14,7% n:29	7,8% n:8	
Lying	1,2% n:5		0,5% n:2	2,4% n:14	0,6% n:3	1,8% n:13	2,7% n:16	1,2% n:8	7,7% n:30	1,2% n:6	5% n:7	31,1% n:31
	Eyes-Open			Eyes-V2 Open			Eyes-¼ Open			Eyes-Closed		

FIGURE 65. Percentages of time of the various combinations of body posture, head position and width of the opening of the eyelids, *n* indicating number of periods (from van den Hoofdakker, 1966)

head position occurred only in association with the lying body posture. Similarly, while the combinations sitting/head upright and crouching/head upright occurred with the eyes open, they did not occur with the eyes closed. Figure 65 shows the width of the opening of the eyelids in each postural combination. Stable constellations of the three types of behavioral category were referred to as behavioral states.

The clock from which the observer recorded time, was used as a time marker on the EEG, thus enabling EEG and behavior to be retrospectively correlated. The EEG corresponding with each behavioral state was then automatically analyzed using an Ediswan frequency analyzer. The question posed by van den Hoofdakker was whether or not the different behavioral states were characterized by different relationships between EEG voltage and frequency spectrum.

For each behavioral state an analysis was made of the amplitudes of the components of the frequency spectrum. Two main types of EEG variability were discovered. In type A there was an inverse relationship between the frequency and amplitude of the EEG. In type B, the average voltage was variable, but the frequency spectrum always showed a predominance of low frequencies. In other words, in type B the frequency spectrum remained unaltered despite changes in the average voltage. Type C was a group of EEG's which showed a mixture of the characteristics of A and B. The latter was not, as might be thought, an indecisive category, but could be regarded as intermediate in a strictly mathematical sense. The mathematical relationships between the three states are clearly shown in van den Hoofdakker's monograph.

Consistent statistical relationships were demonstrated between the different behavioral states and the three types of EEG's. The data are summarized in Figure 66. EEG types B and C never occurred in the crouching position. The probability of type B occurring increased as the animal's posture moved from sitting to lying, his head position from upright to dropped, and his eyes from open to closed.

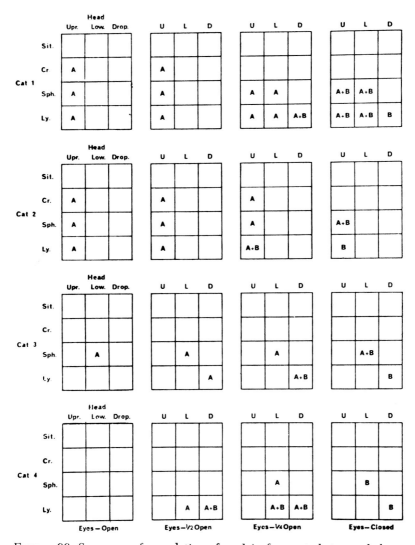

FIGURE 66. Summary of correlations found in four cats between behavioral state and different types of EEG activity (From van den Hoofdakker, 1966)

The behaviors with which van den Hoofdakker concerned himself were relatively circumscribed, comprising only the postural, head and eye changes between waking and sleeping in the cat. We might expect nevertheless that with forty-eight possible combinations of the behavioral elements and with three types of EEG category to consider, the data from even such a modest study as the present one would be totally unmanageable. The author shows that this is not the case. Only about half of the combinations which are theoretically possible actually occur, and within any one animal the correlations between each behavioral state and EEG activity are remarkably stable. By remaining undaunted at the apparent complexity of his problem, the author shows that the more meticulous the analysis, the greater the underlying regularity which emerges; and the greater the regularity, the greater the data reduction possible. The present study therefore serves as a valuable prototype for studies in which direct correlations are made between behavior and bioelectric activity.

In this study a ten-second observation interval was adequate as the behaviors were slowly changing ones; for more rapid changes of behavior, a greater degree of discrimination could be achieved using the tape recording, film or video-recording methods we have already discussed. Similarly, by utilizing other methods of automatic EEG analysis, it would be unnecessary to adhere to a ten-second EEG epoch, and more precise temporal correlations might thereby be achieved. Future developments in the correlation of behavior and physiological variables will be contingent upon technical advances. One further virtue of van den Hoofdakker's study is that the recording method is in principle quite simple and could be used in studies of humans with little more difficulty than in cats. In the following study (Lee, *et al.*, 1964) basically the same principle was used in studying the behavior of children while recording their EEG by means of long leads attached to a conventional EEG recording machine.

Exploration and EEG in Children

The children were observed in the same room as that used in the studies described earlier (Ch. 4). The room was empty except for a medical couch. They were told that they were to take part in a game of spacemen which entailed their wearing space helmets with wires attached to them. Four toys were brought into the room at a predetermined point in the recording. The children were quite familiar with the room and had previously had several resting EEGs. They were left free to wander around as they wished. Each child wore a conventional rubber headband, with scalp electrodes. The usual lead and headstand were dispensed with and a new lead was made. This consisted of a thirty-six feet length of miniature twelve-way screened multicable. The attachment to the patient was made by stripping the screen for approximately twelve inches, but leaving a 1-inch tag of screen protruding, on to which a strong safety pin was soldered. This pin was used to attach the cable to the patient's clothing. Orthodox crocodile clips were used at the wire extremities. A full eight-channel recording on any montage could be obtained. The lightweight lead was attached to the ceiling at the centre of the room, with sufficient wire trailing to allow the child free access to any part of the room. If the lead obstructed them in any way, the children just flicked it aside. From the ceiling the lead passed into the adjacent observation room. The EEG records were made on an Offner Type T eight-channel, portable machine with filters modified to attenuate frequencies in excess of 15 to 18 cycles per second. The children were observed through the one-way vision screen and a tape-recorded behavior commentary was made. Changes of activity were marked on the EEG pen write-out so that the behavior commentary and EEG record retrospectively could be synchronized.

The children remained in the room for approximately ten minutes each. For the first four minutes they were alone. An observer then took toys into the room and played with the child for two minutes. The child was next left alone with the toys for the remainder of the time. The records were remarkably free of muscle artefact, even when the child was moving about. Playing with the lead itself, such as swinging it round and round, had no effect on the record. Serious artefact was encountered only when the child made faces at himself in the one-way mirror or actually interfered with the electrodes.

The present pilot study of three small boys (two, age 4, and one, age 6 years) followed a series of preliminary recordings carried out on adults and children to establish the technical difficulties which were likely to be encountered and the modifications necessary. In practice only the attenuation of high frequencies and careful earthing procedures proved necessary.

The records obtained were technically of sufficient quality to make possible the following general associations between EEG and behavior:

1. Initial desynchronization of the EEG accompanied visual scanning of the room during the first two minutes. At approximately the third minute the dominant frequency of each EEG was established; this was 7 to 7½ cycles per second in two subjects (age 4 and 6) and 4½ cycles in the other (age 4).
2. Suppression of the EEG occurred when the observer entered with toys, and children visually fixated the various toys offered.
3. There was continued suppression of the EEG after the observer left the room while the children were engaged with the toy chosen. In each case this was a fort with soldiers. In one case suppression continued until the end of the session. This child (age 4 years) played with the fort continuously.
4. In the other two cases there was gradual recovery of the dominant rhythm. In the older child (age 6 years) this occurred more quickly than in the younger (age 4 years). (Presumably the fort was more novel for the younger child).
5. These two children then explored various parts of the room, returning on each occasion to the fort. The visual fixations on each stimulus (mirror, washbasin, door) were usually accompanied by suppression of the dominant rhythm followed by rapid recovery. Interestingly, the return to the fort was also accompanied by initial suppression in the case of the younger child.

The method was exploratory, but it clearly illustrates that usable EEG recordings can be made in rather less artificial circumstances than those which prevail during recording of the resting EEG. There was a fairly consistent pattern in the results obtained: initial desynchronization (inhibitory reaction); establishment of a dominant rhythm, which in turn blocked on the appearance of new stimuli; a gradual reemergence of the dominant rhythm in two subjects, possibly with increasing familiarity of the toy (this occurred more readily in the older child); and blocking as new stimuli were engaged.

Stereotypies and EEG in Autistic Children

Telemetry clearly offers many advantages over the method of recording just described. The movements of the subject are less hampered; he is likely to be less distracted by attachments; he is able to traverse a much larger area; and the recordings are less liable to interference and artefact. A large range of variables has been measured by telemetry in both man and animals (Slater, 1963), but here again the degree of precision with which behavior has been recorded has often been completely incompatible with that of the physiological recordings. An example of an attempt to record both EEG and behavior with precision is provided by a study of stereotyped behaviors in autistic children (Hutt, *et al.*, 1965). Bipolar recordings from the right and left occiput respectively were telemetered in two children by means of an Alvar Televar radio link. Each Televar unit enables one channel of EEG (or other physiological variable) to be recorded. A unit consists of a flat, cylindrical, plastic case 3 cm in diameter, containing a preamplifier, a transmitter and batteries. The units were placed in a small sachet which was pinned beneath the patient's collar leaving two short lengths of wire protruding, these being attached to suction cup electrodes. In the ceiling of the observation room was a circular aerial which enabled the signals to be relayed to an FM receiver in an adjacent observation room. The children were studied in the same room under three sets of conditions: A, the room empty; B, a box of colored blocks present; D, an observer present who attempted to engage the child in play with the blocks. The order of the situations was reversed for one child. Behavioral recordings were made using the tape recording technique: the tapes were subsequently transcribed, timed and matched against the appropriate EEG tracing.

The EEG record was then divided into epochs according to the length of the accompanying behavior. An epoch was defined as a section of the EEG tracing whose beginning and end points coincided with the initiation and cessation respectively of a category of motor behavior. Each epoch was assessed independently by two observers, without knowledge of the accompanying behavior. The duration of activity in the delta, theta, alpha and beta bands was measured, as well as the amount of low voltage irregular activity. It was thus possible to determine the bioelectric activity which accompanied each motor activity as well as the total amount of bioelectric activity of each type. Epochs which were technically dubious were timed, but not assessed.

No precise temporal association could be demonstrated between particular activities and specific patterns of EEG activity. In practice there were few instances where any one activity was accompanied by a single EEG rhythm. Especially during the more prolonged behaviors, the EEG would show first one rhythm and then another, or a rhythm would begin during one activity and continue into another.

If, however, the total duration of activity in each EEG category is considered, an interesting trend emerges. We shall consider in the present analysis one type of behavior pattern, stereotypies. Table XIV shows the frequency and duration of bouts of stereotypy in relation to the total duration of de-

TABLE XIV

FREQUENCY AND DURATION OF BOUTS OF STEREOTYPY IN RELATION TO
DESYNCHRONIZED ACTIVITY IN THE EEG. (FROM HUTT, ET AL., 1965)

| | | *Environments* | | |
	Case	*A*	*B*	*D*
Frequency of stereotypy bouts	S3	5	13	12
	S7	0	14	—
Percentage time stereotypy	S3	12.8	54.1	46.6
	S7	0	29.5	—
Desynchrony as percentage of assessable record	S3	26.5	38.0	70.9
	S7	56.7	74.6	—

synchronized activity in the EEG in each environment. We defined desynchronized as low voltage irregular activity or low voltage beta activity. Owing to an idiosyncracy of case 7, it was not possible to complete condition D: This whole session was spent in removing the adult's shoes.

Least stereotypy occurred in the relatively unstructured environment; there was a significant increase in the time spent in stereotypy in environment B. Both children showed a corresponding increase in the frequency with which stereotypies were initiated in environment B. The slight drop in the amount of stereotypy shown by case 3 in the environment D suggests that the adult is able to break up the pattern of stereotypy by engaging the child in play with the blocks, thus confirming an earlier finding (Hutt, and Hutt, 1965).

The amount of EEG desynchronization was also related to the complexity of the environment. Both children showed less EEG desynchronization in the empty room as compared with the more structured environments. Case 3 showed greatest EEG desynchronization in the social situation, D, and it is of interest that in this environment the telemetered EEG was similar to that obtained in the laboratory.

It seems, therefore, that stereotypy is more likely to occur in those situations where electrocortical activation is greatest. The present analysis, however, was based on visual inspection of the EEG; thus the association should be regarded only as suggestive. More precise formulation must await the use of automatic EEG analysis and suitable data handling techniques.

THE SCIENTIFIC STATUS OF OBSERVATIONAL STUDIES OF BEHAVIOR

Barker (1967) has depicted the naturalistic method as thus: "when a research psychologist does not intrude himself, his software, or his hardware into the data-generating circuits of his investigation, i.e. when he is not a source of inputs to, or constraints upon, the arrangements which produce the data." In contrast with experimental data, which are "problem centered and theory guided . . . naturalistic data are phenomena-centred and . . . atheoretical." If we add to these properties the three further facts (Willems, 1967) that naturalistic data are not replicable in the strict experimental sense, that they have a low yield for the time and effort spent on them and that they are not amenable to the tight control of an experiment, it is not perhaps surprising that such data are often dismissed as merely anecdotal. Indeed, as Siever (1968) has pointed out, observational is often used as a perjorative term of scientific diplomacy, when what is meant is inexact, soft or just plain bad. Because the experiment quite rightly is considered the most powerful tool in science—science here meaning physics and chemistry —we all too readily dismiss observational studies as nonscience. Thus, we may remember Mussen's chilling statement (Ch. 2) that reduction in the number of descriptive, normative studies is a sign of scientific maturing.

This however may be to take too narrow a conception both of the nature of science and of the nature of an experiment. Siever argues that there is but one science, its methods being experimental, observational or historical, depending upon the nature of the phenomena under study. Phenomena such as the formation of rock deposits which take place over millenia are amenable to neither direct observation nor experiment; the transits of stars are amenable to observation but not to experimental constraint; the expansion of gases with increasing temperature is properly a matter for experiment. The boundaries however between different methods of obtaining data are not clear-cut. The opposing theses that Newton's heat flow equation was derived from simple observation or from experimentation equally can be defended. The data of oceanography and meteorology (what Siever calls historical data) would be tedious, if not impossible, to obtain by direct observation but can be brought within the confines of direct observation by suitable recording techniques, e.g. timelapse photography. The observer thereby may, within the space of minutes, witness a sequence of events which originally occupied days, weeks or months.

To oppose therefore experiment and naturalistic observation as science and nonscience is conceptually unhelpful; what is important are the data for which one or the other method is the more appropriate. In the behavioral sciences we might postulate that observation is the more, perhaps the only, appropriate tool where the subjects under study cannot be programmed to take part in an experiment, for example, psychiatric patients and small children; or where there are social or ethical reasons for their not doing so. Furthermore, observation is the most appropriate tool when we wish to know what animals actually do in their natural habitat, physical and social. The choice of method may be simply a question of the scale of the phenomena under study rather than their nature. As Menzel (1967) has argued, we may 'zoom up' or 'zoom down' upon a phenomenon. The most precise analyses of perceptual constancy have been made in laboratory experiments, but it is only by zooming up to real-life situations that we can establish the generality of the constancy effects (Brunswik 1955). Again, we may observe that in the wild rhesus monkeys always move along natural boundaries rather than taking the shorter distances across open space (Menzel, 1967). By zooming down to a small baited observational area, we can analyze the determinants of our phenomenon by placing objects in various orientations and observing the changes effected in the animals' behavior by these artificially contrived boundaries. Menzel has shown that in this relatively simple experiment, the critical feature of objects in attracting the animals appeared to be verticality. Zooming out again, he was able to confirm that in the animals' free range the main objects which acted as paths for the animals were trees, rocks and other vertical structures. Menzel's paper is of particular interest both because it is written by an experimental psychologist who is also an unashamed naturalist and also because it shows very clearly the interplay of naturalistic observation and experiment.

Science, experimental or observational, demands three operations: first, rigorous measurement of the phenomenon under study; second the generation of lawlike propositions relating these measurements to other selected variables; third, the interrelationship of such lawlike propositions into theories.

This book has been concerned mainly with the first operation. It is hoped that the feasibility of such measurement, even in the case of free-ranging behavior, has been demonstrated. In Chapter 3 we endeavored to show that behavioral units can be identified, and in the subsequent three chapters we discussed a number of methods by which they might be measured.

By reference to findings as well as to methods, we attempted to demonstrate that in a wide range of species from the lower phyla to man, lawlike propositions about free-ranging behavior can be made. This theme was then developed at greater length in Chapter 7 with respect to largely environmentally triggered, social behavior and in Chapter 8 with respect to largely endogenously triggered, drug-induced behavior. A special case of the second operation was discussed in Chapter 9, where we considered statistical relationships among behavior elements rather than between behavior and environmental or physiological variables.

Since our concern has been methodological rather than theoretical, we have not specifically considered the third operation in detail. It should however be clear from many of the studies discussed that observational studies are as capable of raising theoretical issues as experiments. This was shown elegantly by Wiepkema's (1961) study of the bitterling. By demonstrating on mathematical grounds that all his observed intercorrelations could be accounted for by only three sources of variance, he was able to suggest the probable motivational determinants of all his observed behavior patterns. One of the impressive features of this study is that by exercising extreme rigor at an observational level a group of mechanisms was indicated which otherwise probably could only have been isolated by brain stimulation experiments. Indeed, the functional mechanisms proposed by ethologists from observational studies only have quite consistently been in accord with those derived from neurophysiological findings. At least one example exists in the human psychopathological literature where behavioral analysis made sense of an hitherto unexplained physiological phenomenon. In a study of autistic children (Hutt, and Hutt, 1965), it was found that stereotyped behaviors increased in relation to the structure of the environment; fewest stereotypies occurred in an empty room, more occurred when toys were introduced into the room, the greatest amount of stereotypy occurred in a social situation. By analogy with studies in primates, and other animals, the authors postulated that the occurrence of stereotypies was directly related to the arousal potential (Berlyne, 1960) of the environment, i.e. the degree to which the environment would be expected to increase level of physiological arousal. It was therefore hypothesized that these autistic children were in a state of chronically high cerebral arousal and that stereotypies subserved some mechanism for reducing arousal (see Hutt, and Hutt, 1968, for a treatment of the series of studies leading up to the hypothesis). The EEGs of the children were then examined and surprisingly were found to consist predominantly of low voltage, and irregular activity with no established rhythms. It seemed possible that this activity, which had previously puzzled the authors' electroencephalographer colleagues, represented a highly aroused electrocortical state. One other purely behavioral finding which also pointed to the possibility of autistic children being chronically hyperaroused, has already been referred to (Ch. 6): namely, the social interactions of autists being morphologically identical with those of normal children, except for their failure to make eye-to-eye contact. The arousal hypothesis has proved heuristically fruitful, enabling a large body of clinical, experimental and neurophysiological data to be integrated (Hutt and Hutt, in preparation). What is of interest in the present context, is the hypothesis itself, but the fact that it was derived entirely from behavioral observations in a free field. In short, the derivation of functional mechanisms is not the sole prerogative of the experimentalist.

It would be sad indeed, if in the infancy of the behavioral sciences, the spirit of two cultures often pervading the discourses of scientists of different disciplines, should be allowed to obtrude. We have stressed the observational approach in this book, not because we regard it as superior to the experimental but because for certain problems it is the more appropriate approach; for the study of certain organisms it is the only approach; and it is increasingly devalued by behavioral scientists. But, just as ethology and psychology are complementary, so observation and experiment are complementary. Their relation has been well expressed in Kelly's paraphrase (1967) of Schaller's paper (1965) on the mountain gorilla. While referring specifically to social behavior, its approach to enquiry is of wider generality; since it is also a statement with which the present authors are in agreement, it provides a fitting close to the book.

First he [Schaller] proposes a survey of as much of the primate's range as possible with emphasis on diversity of habitat, distribution and abundance of the species, and similarities or differences in group size, composition and food habits between populations of the species. To me, the significance of this principle is that by studying the diversity of settings it is possible to deduce basic functions of specific environments and to define the limits for adaptation. The second approach advocated by Schaller, is a series of detailed observations of the social life of selected groups of the total population, concentrating on the behavioral repertoire of each species. This orientation also has relevance for the study of human subjects in that it helps to document the social structure and the social organization of settings without increasing and confounding errors of measurement. With divergent methods it is possible to give a more representative account regarding what behaviors are normative for that setting. The third principle advocates an intensive study of specific aspects of behavior with joint field and laboratory experiments to clarify more complex relationships. These guidelines provide mutually complementary methods for either the development or confirmation of hypotheses. They also provide the basis for a research cycle which allows the investigator to begin with a natural setting and end with a series of new questions about the behavior in that same habitat (p. 214).

REFERENCES

AHRENS, R.: Beitrag zur Entwicklung des Physiognomie und Mimikerkennens. *Z Exp Ange Psychol, 2*(3):412-454. 2(4):599-633, 1954.

ALDERTON, H.R., and HODDINOTT, B.A.: A controlled study of the use of thioridazine in the treatment of hyperactive and aggressive children in a children's psychiatric hospital. *Canad Psychiat Assoc J 9*:239-247, 1964.

ALONSO DE FLORIDA, F., and DELGADO, J.M.R.: Lasting behavioural and EEG changes in cats induced by prolonged stimulation of amygdala. *Amer J Physiol, 193*:223-229, 1958.

ALTMANN, S.A.: A field study of the sociobiology of rhesus monkeys *macaca mulatta. Ann NY Acad Sci, 102*:338-435, 1962.

ALTMANN, S.A.: Sociobiology of Rhesus. II. Stochastics of social communication. *J Theor Biol, 8*:490-522, 1965.

AMES, L.B.: Motor correlates of infant crying. *J Genet Psychol, 59*:1941.

ANDREW, R.J.: The origin and evolution of the calls and facial expressions of the primates. *Behaviour, 10*:1-109, 1963.

ANTHONY, E.J.: On observing children. In Miller, E. (Ed.): *Foundations of Child Psychiatry*. Oxford, Pergamon, 1968.

ARRINGTON, R.E.: Interrelations in the behaviour of young children. *Child Develop Monogr, 8*, 1932.

ARRINGTON, R.E.: An important implication of time sampling in observational studies of behaviour. *Amer J Sociol, 43*:284-295, 1937.

ARRINGTON, R.E.: Time sampling studies of child behaviour. *Psychol Monogr, 51* (2), 1939.

ARRINGTON, R.E.: Time sampling in studies of social behaviours: a critical review of techniques and results with research suggestions. *Psychol Bull, 40*:81-124, 1943.

ASCHOFF, J.: Circadian rhythms in man. *Science, 148*:1427-1432, 1965.

ATTNEAVE, F.: Some informational aspects of visual perception. *Psychol Rev, 61*: 183-193, 1954.

AYLLON, T., and MICHAEL, J.: The psychiatric nurse as a behavioral engineer. *J Exp Anal Behav, 2*:323-334, 1959.

BADHAM, J.N.; BARDON, L.M.; REEVES, P.O., and YOUNG, A.M.: A trial of thioridazine in mental deficiency. *Brit J Psychiat, 109*:408-410, 1963.

BAENNINGER, L.P.: Comparison of behavioural development in socially isolated and grouped rats. *Anim Behav, 15*:312-323, 1967.

BALES, R.F., *Interaction Process Analysis*. Reading, Addison-Wesley, 1951.

BARKER, M.: *A Technique for Studying the Social Material Activities of Young Children*. Child Develop. Monogr. No. 3, New York, Columbia 1930.

BARKER, R.G. (Ed.): *The Stream of Behaviour. Explorations of Its Structure and Content*. New York, Appleton, 1963.

BARKER, R.G.: Naturalistic methods in psychological research. *Hum Develop, 10:* 223-229, 1967.

BARKER, R.G., and WRIGHT, H.F.: *One Boy's Day.* New York, Harper, 1951.

BARKER, R.G., and WRIGHT, H.F.: *Midwest and Its Children: The Psychological Ecology of an American Town.* New York, Harper, 1955.

BARKER, R.G.; WRIGHT, H.F.; BARKER, L.S., and SCHOGGEN, M.: *Specimen Records of American and English Children.* Lawrence, U of Kan P, 1961.

BARKER, R.G. and GUMP, P.V.: *Big School, Small School.* Stanford, Stanford P, 1964.

BARTOSHUK, A.K.: Response decrement with repeated elicitation of human neonatal cardiac acceleration to sound. *J Comp Physiol Psychol, 55:*9-13, 1962.

BERLYNE, D.E.: *Conflict, Arousal, and Curiosity.* New York, McGraw-Hill, 1960.

BERNSTEIN, I.S., and DRAPER, W.A.: The behaviour of juvenile Rhesus monkeys in groups. *Anim Behav, 12:*84-91, 1964.

BIRDWHISTELL, R.L.: Kinesic analysis of filmed behaviour of children. In Schaffner, B. (Ed.): *Group Processes.* Josiah Macy Jr. Foundation, 1955.

BIRDWHISTELL, R.L.: The kinesic level in the investigation of the emotions. In Knapp, P.H. (Ed.): *Expression of the Emotions in Man.* New York, Int. Univs. 1963.

BISHOP, B.M.: Mother-child interaction and the social behaviour of children. *Psychol Monogr, 65*(11), 1951.

BLATZ, W.E.: A study of eating habits in a nursery school. *Genet Psychol Monogr, 4*(1):89-115, 1928.

BOBBITT, R.A.; JENSEN, G.D. and KUEHN, R.E.: Development and application of an observational method: a pilot study of the mother-infant relationship in Pigtail monkeys. *J Genet Psychol, 105,* 1964.

BOTT, H: Observations of play activities in a nursery school. *Genet Psychol Monogr, 4:*44-88, 1928.

BRIDGES, K.M.B.: Measuring emotionality in infants. *Child Develop, 5:*36-40, 1934.

BROCKWAY, B.F.: Ethological studies of the budgerigar (*Melopsittacus unclulatus*): non-reproductive behavior. *Behaviour, 22:*193-222, 1964.

BROWN, R.G.B.: BURTON-JONES, N.G.: and HUSSELL, D.J.T.: The breeding behaviour of Sabine's Gull (*Xema sabini*). *Behaviour, 28* (1-2) 1967.

BRUNSWICK, E.F.: Representative design and probabilistic theory in a functional psychology. *Psychol Rev, 62:*193-217, 1955.

BUTLER, R.A., and HARLOW, H.F.: Persistence of visual exploration in monkeys. *J. Comp Physiol Psychol, 47:*258-263, 1954.

CALHOUN, J.B.: Population density and social pathology. *Sci Amer, 206:*139-148, 1962.

CARTER, L., HAYTHORN, W.; MEIROWITZ, B., and LANZETTA, J.: A noee on a new technique of interaction recording. *J. Abnorm Soc Psychol, 46:*258-260, 1951.

CARTHY, J.D., and EBLING, F.J. (Eds.): *The Natural History of Aggression.* New York, Academic P, 1964.

CARTHY, J.D.: *The Study of Behaviour.* London. Arnold, 1966.

CHANCE, M.R.A.: An interpretation of some agonistic postures; the role of "cut-off" acts and postures. *Symp Zool Soc Lond.,* 8, 71-89, 1962.

CHANCE, M.R.A., and RUSSELL, W.M.S.: Protean displays: a form of allaesthetic behaviour. *Proc Zool Soc London, 132:*65-70, 1959.

CHANCE, M.R.A., and SILVERMAN, A.P.: The structure of social behaviour and drug action. In Steinberg, H.; de Rueck, A.V.S., and Knight, J. (Eds.): *Animal Behaviour and Drug Action*. London, Churchill, 1964.

CHANT, N., and BLATZ, W.E.: A study of sleeping habits of children. *Genet Psychol Monogr*, 4 (1):13-43, 1928.

CHAPPLE, E.D.; CHAMBERLAIN, A.; ESSER, A.H., and KLINE, N.S.: The measurement of activity patterns of schizophrenic patients. *J Nerv Ment Dis, 137*:258-267, 1963.

CHOMSKY, N.: *Syntactic Structures.* S'-Gravenhage, Mouton, 1957.

CHOROVER, S.L., and SCHILLER, P.H.: Short term retrograde amnesia in rats. *J Comp Physiol Psychol*, 59:73-78, 1965.

CLARK, E.; ARONSON, L.R., and GORDON, M.: Mating behaviour patterns in two sympatric species of Xiphophorin fishes: their inheritance and significance in sexual isolation. *Bull Amer Nat Hist, 103*:135-225, 1954.

CLOUDSLEY-THOMPSON, J.L.: Diurnal rhythm of activity in the Nile crocodile. *Anim Behav 12*:98-100, 1964.

COCKRELL, D.L.: A study of the play of children of pre-school age by an unobserved observer. *Genet Psychol Monogr, 17*:377-469, 1935.

COHEN, J.; HANSEL, C.E.M., and SYLVESTER, J.D.: 'Mind Wandering.' *Brit J Psychol, 47*:61, 1956.

CONDON, W.S. and OGSTON, W.D.: Sound film analysis of normal and pathological behaviour patterns. *J Nerv Ment Dis, 143* (4):338-347, 1966.

COOK, L.: Effects of drugs on operant conditioning: In Steinberg, H.; de Reuck, A.V.S., and Knight, J. (Eds.): *Animal Behaviour and Drug Action*. London, Churchill, 1964.

COX, F.N., and CAMPBELL, D.: Young children in a new situation with and without their mothers. *Child Develop, 39*:123-131, 1968.

CREAK, M., *et al.,*: The schizophrenic syndrome in childhood. *Brit Med J*, 2:889, 1961.

DANE, B.; WALCOTT, C., and DRURY, W.H.: The form and duration of the display actions of the goldeneye (*Bucephala clangula* (L.)). *Behaviour*, 14:265-281, 1959.

DANE, B. and VAN DER KLOOT, W.G.: An analysis of the display of the goldeneye duck (*Bucephala clangula* (L.)). *Behaviour*, 22:282-328, 1964.

DARLING, F.F.: *A Herd of Red Deer*. New York, Oxford U. P, 1937.

DARWIN, C.: *Expression of the Emotions in Man and Animals.* London, Murray, 1872.

DELGADO, J.M.R.: Free behaviour and brain stimulation. In Pfeiffer, C.C., and Smythies, J.R. (Eds.): *International Review of Neurobiology*, 6. New York, Academic P, 1964.

DELIUS, J.D.: Displacement activities and arousal. *Nature, 214*:1259-1260, 1967.

DEMBER, W.N., and EARL, R.W.: Analysis of exploratory, manipulatory and curiosity behaviours. *Psychol Rev*, 64:91-96, 1957.

EIBL-EIBESFELDT, I.: The interactions of unlearned behaviour patterns and learning in mammals. In Delafresnaye, J.F. (Ed.): *Brain Mechanisms and Learning*. Oxford, Blackwell, 1961.

EISENBERG, L., and KANNER, L.: Early infantile autism. In Reed, C.F.; Alexander,

I.E., and Tompkins, S.S. (Eds.): *Psychopathology.* Cambridge, Harvard, 1958.

ESCALONA, S. *et al.:* Early phases of personality development: a non-normative study of infant behaviour. *Monogr Soc Res Child Develop, 17*(1), 1952.

EYSENCK, H.J.; CASEY, S., and TROUTON, D.S.: Drugs and personality. II. The effect of stimulant and depressant drugs on continuous work. *J Ment Sci, 103*:645-649, 1957.

FABRICIUS, E., and JANSSON, A.M.: Laboratory observations on the reproductive behaviour of the Pigeon *(Columbia livia)* during the pre-incubation phase of the breeding cycle. *Anim Behav, 11*:534-547, 1963.

FENTON, G.; SERAFETINIDES, E.A., and POND, D.A.: The effect of sulthiame, a new anticonvulsant drug in the treatment of temporal lobe epilepsy. *Epilepsia, 5*:59-67, 1964.

FLEISHMAN, E.A.: Psychomotor selection tests: research and application in the U.S. Air Force. *Personnel Psychol, 9*:449-467, 1956.

FLEISHMAN, E.A.: Psychomotor tests in drug research. In Uhr, L., and Miller, J.G. (Eds.): *Drugs and Behaviour.* New York, J. Wiley, 1960.

FRANKS, C.M., and TROUTON, D.: Effects of amobarbital sodium and dexamphetamine sulfate on the conditioning of the eyeblink response. *J Comp Physiol Psychol, 51*:220-222, 1958.

FRUCHTER, B.: *Introduction to factor analysis.* New York, van Nostrand, 1954.

GARLAND, H.G., and SUMNER, D.W.: Sulthiame treatment of epilepsy. *Brit Med J, 1*:1043, 1964.

GELLERT, E.: Systematic observation: a method in child study. *Harvard Educ Rev, 25*:179-195, 1955.

GESELL, A.: Cinemanalysis: a method of behavior study. *J Genet Psychol 47*:3-16, 1935.

GESELL, A., and HALVERSON, H.M.: The daily maturation of infant behaviour: a cinema study of postures, movements and laterality. *J Genet Psychol, 61*:3-32, 1942.

GOODENOUGH, F.L.: Inter-relationships in the behaviour of young children. *Child Develop, 1*:29-47, 1930.

GORDON, N.: The use of ospolot in the treatment of epilepsy. *Epilepsia, 5*:68-73, 1964.

GRANT, E.C.: Analysis of the social behavior of the male laboratory rat. *Behaviour, 21*:260-281, 1963.

GRANT, E.C., and MACKINTOSH, J.H.: A comparison of the social postures of some common laboratory rodents. *Behaviour, 21*:246-259, 1963.

GROSS, C.G., and WEISKRANTZ, L.: The effect of two "tranquillizers" on auditory discrimination and delayed response performance of monkeys. *Quart J Exp Psychol, 13*:34-39, 1961.

GUNDERSON, E.K.: Emotional symptoms in extremely isolated groups. *Arch Gen Psychiat, 9*:362-368, 1963.

GUNDERSON, E.K., and NELSON, P.D.: Adaptation of small groups to extreme environments. *Aerospace Med, 34*:1111-1115, 1963.

GUTTMAN, R., and LIEBIG, I.: A nonmetric multidimensional analysis of behaviour sequences in two inbred mouse strains, their hybrids, and backcrosses. Unpublished report, 1938.

HAILMAN, J.P.: The pecking response in chicks of the Laughing Gull (*Larus atricilla* L.) and related species. *Behaviour* (*Suppl. 15*), 1967.

HANSEN, E.W.: The development of maternal and infant behaviour in the rhesus monkey. *Behaviour, 27*:107-149, 1966.

HARLOW, H.F., and ZIMMERMAN, R.R.: Affectional responses in the infant monkey. *Science, 130*:421-432, 1959.

HARTSHORNE, H., and MAY, M.A.: *Studies in the Nature of Character-1. Studies in Deceit.* New York, Macmillan, 1928.

HARTSHORNE, H.; MAY, M.A., and MALLER, J.B.: *Studies in theNature of Character-II. Studies in Service and Self-control.* New York, Macmillan, 1929.

HEIMSTRA, N.W., and DAVIS, R.T.: A simple recording system for the direct observation technique. *Anim Behav, 10*:208-210, 1962.

HELFER, R.E., and KEMPE, C.H.. (Eds.): *The Battered Child.* Chicago, U. of Chicago, 1968.

HENDRY, L.S., and KESSEN, W.: Oral behaviour of newborn infants as a function of age and time since feeding. *Child Develop, 35*:201-208, 1964.

HINDE, R.A.: *Animal behaviour. A Synthesis of Ethology and Comparative Psychology.* New York, McGraw-Hill, 1966.

HINDE, R.A., ROWELL, T.E. and SPENCER-BOOTH, Y.: Behaviour of socially living rhesus monkeys in their first six months. *Proc Zool Soc Lond, 143*:609-649, 1964.

HINDE, R.A. and SPENCER-BOOTH, Y.: The behaviour of socially living rhesus monkeys in their first two and a half years. *Anim Behav, 15*:169-196, 1967.

HOFFMAN, K.: Versuche zur Analyse der Tagesperiodik. I. Der Einfluss der Lichtintensität. *Zeit vergl Physiol, 43*:544-566, 1960.

HOOFDAKKER, R.H. VAN DEN: *Behaviour and EEG of Drowsy and Sleeping cats.* Groningen, van Denderen, 1966.

HUBEL, D.H.: Transformation of information in the cat's visual system. In Gerard, R.W., and Dnyff, J.W. (Eds.): *Information Processing in the Nervous System.* Amsterdam, Excerpta Medica Foundation, 1962.

HUTT, C.: Exploration and play in children. *Symp Zool Soc London, 18*:61-81, 1966.

HUTT, C.: *Exploring Novelty.* London, British Film Institute, 1967a.

HUTT, C.: Temporal effects on response decrement and stimulus satiation in exploration. *Brit J Psychol, 58*:365-373, 1967b.

HUTT, C.: Exploration of novelty in children with and without upper C.N.S. lesions and some effects of auditory and visual incentives. *Acta Psychologia, 28*:150-160, 1968.

HUTT, C.: Effects of stimulus novelty on manipulatory exploration in an infant. *J Child Psychol Psychiat, 8*:247-251, 1967c.

HUTT, C., and COXON, M.: Systematic observation in clinical psychology. *Arch Gen Psychiat, 12*:374-378, 1965.

HUTT, C.; HUTT, S.J.; LEE, D., and OUNSTED, C.: Arousal and childhood autism. *Nature, 204*(4961): 908-909, 1964.

HUTT, C., and HUTT, S.J.: Effect of environmental complexity upon sterotyped behaviours in children. *Anim Behav, 13*:1-4, 1965.

HUTT, C.; HUTT, S.J., and OUNSTED, C.: The behaviour of children with and without upper CNS lesions. *Behaviour, 24*:246-248, 1965.

HUTT, C.; JACKSON, P., and LEVEL, M.: Behavioural parameters and drug effects. *Epilepsia, 7*:250-259, 1966.

HUTT, C., and OUNSTED, C.: The biological significance of gaze aversion with particular reference to the syndrome of infantile autism. *Behav Sci, 11*:346-356, 1966.

HUTT, C., and VAIZEY, M.J.: Differential effects of group density on social behaviour. *Nature, 209*:1371-1372, 1966.

HUTT, S.J.; CROOKES, T.G., and GLANCY, L.J.: The behavior of chronic psychotic patients during three types of occupation. *Brit J Psychiat, 110*:270-282, 1964.

HUTT, S.J.; HUTT, C.; OUNSTED, C., and LEE, D.: A behavioural and electroencephalographic study of autistic children. *J Psychiat Res, 3*:181-197, 1965.

HUTT, S.J., and HUTT, C.: Stereotypy, arousal and autism. *Hum Develop, 11*:277-286, 1968.

HUTT, S.J.; HUTT, C.; LENARD, H.G.; VON BERNUTH, H., and MUNTJEWERFF, W.J.: Auditory responsivity in the human neonate. *Nature, 218*:888-890, 1968.

HUTT, S.J., and HUTT, C.: *Behavior Studies in Psychiatry.* Oxford, Pergamon (in press).

HUTT, S.J., and HUTT, C.: *Autistic Children.* London, Allen and Unwin (in preparation).

INGRAM, T.T.S.: A characteristic form of overactive behaviour in brain-damaged children. *J Ment Sci, 102*:550-558, 1956.

INGRAM, T.T.S., and RATCLIFFE, S.G.: Clinical trial of ospolot in epilepsy. *Develop Med Child Neurol, 5*:313-316, 1963.

IRWIN, S.: In discussion for The structure of social behaviour and drug action. In Steinberg, H.; de Rueck, A.V.S., and Knight, J. (Eds.): *Animal Behaviour and Drug Action.* London, Churchill, 1964.

JERSILD, A.T., and MEIGS, M.F.: Direct observation as a research method. *Rev Educ Res, 9*:472-482, 1939.

KATZ, J.J., and POSTAL, P.M.: *An Integrated Theory of Linguistic Descriptions.* Cambridge, Mass., M.I.T. Press, 1964.

KAUFMAN, C., and ROSENBLUM, L.A.: A behavioral taxonomy for *Macaca nemestrina* and *Macaca radiata*: based on longitudinal observation of family groups in the laboratory. *Primates, 7(2)*:205-258, 1966.

KELLY, J.G.: Naturalistic observations and theory confirmation: an example. *Hum Develop, 10*:212-222, 1967.

KESSEN, W.; HENDRY, L.S., and LEUTZENDORFF, A-M.: Measurement of movement in the human newborn: a new technique. *Child Develop, 32*:95-105, 1961.

KESSEN, W., and LEUTZENDORFF, A-M.: The effect of nonnutritive sucking on movement in the human newborn. *J Comp Physiol Psychol, 56*:69-72, 1963.

KESSEN, W., and LEUTZENDORF, A-M., and STOUTSENBERGER, K.: Age, food deprivation, nonnutritive sucking, and movement in the human newborn. *J Comp Physiol Psychol, 63*:82-86, 1967.

KEYWITZ, N.: Population density and the style of social life. *Bioscience, 16*:868-873, 1966.

KNOBEL, M.; WOLMAN, M.B., and MASON, E.: Hyperkinesis and organicity in children. *Arch Gen Psychiat, 1*:310-321, 1959.

KRUIJT, J.P.: *Ontogeny of social behaviour in Burmese Red Junglefowl (Gallus gallus spadiceous).* Leiden, E.J. Brill, 1964.

LASHLEY, K.S.: The problem of serial order in behavior. In Jeffress, L.A. (Ed.): *Cerebral Mechanisms in Behaviour.* New York, Wiley, 1951.

LAUFER, M.W.; DENHOFF, E., and SOLOMON, S.G.: Hyperkinetic impulse disorder in children's behaviour problems. *Psychosom Med, 19*:38-49, 1957.

LEDLEY, R.S.: *Use of Computers in Biology and Medicine.* McGraw-Hill, New York, 1965.

LEE, D., and HUTT, C.: A playroom designed for filming children: a note. *J Child Psychol Psychiat., 5*:263-265, 1964.

LEE, D.; HUTT, S.J.; FORREST, S.J., and HUTT, C.: Concurrent EEG and behavioural observations on freely moving children. *Develop Med Child Neurol, 6*:362-365, 1964.

LEHRMAN, D.S.: Ethology and psychology. In Wortis, J. (Ed.): *Recent advances in biological psychiatry. Vol. IV.* New York, Plenum, 1962.

LEYHAUSEN, P.: The communal organization of solitary mammals. *Symp Zool Soc London, 14*:249-263, 1965.

LOOMIS, E.A.; HILGEMAN, L.M., and MEYER, L.R.: Childhood psychosis. 2. Play patterns as nonverbal indices of ego functions: a preliminary report. *Amer J Orthopsychiat, 27*(4), 691-700, 1957.

LORENZ, K.Z.: Methods of approach to the problem of behaviour. *Harvey Lect* (1958-1959), 60-103, 1960.

LORENZ, K.Z.: *On aggression.* London, Methuen, 1966.

MARLER, P., and HAMILTON, W.J.: *Mechanisms of Animal Behaviour.* New York, Wiley, 1966.

MARSHALL, J.C.: The Syntax of Reproductive Behaviour in the Male Pigeon. Medical Research Council Psycholinguistics Unit Report, Oxford, 1965.

MASON, W.A.: The effects of social restriction on the behaviour of rhesus monkeys. *J Comp Physiol Psychol, 53*:582-589, 1960.

McDONALD, A.L. and HEIMSTRA, N.W.: Social influences on the response to drugs. V. Modification of behaviour of non-drugged rats by drugged. *Psychopharmacologia,* (Berlin) *8*:174-180, 1965.

MEDAWAR, P.B.: *The Art of the Soluble.* London, Methuen, 1967.

MENZEL, E.W. JR.: Naturalistic and experimental research on primates. *Hum Develop, 10*:170-186, 1967.

MILLER, G.A. and FRICK, F.C.: Statistical behaviouristics and sequences of responses. *Psychol Rev, 56*:311-324, 1949.

MILLER, G.A.: Some psychological studies of grammar. *Amer Psychol, 17*:748-762, 1962.

MILLER, G.A.; PRIBRAM, K., and GALANTER, E.: *Plans and the Structure of Behaviour.* New York, Holt, 1960.

MOORE, J.A. (Ed.): *Ideas in Modern Biology.* Garden City, Natural History Press, 1965.

MORRIS, D.: *The Naked Ape.* Johnathon Cape, 1967.

MURRAY, M.P.; DROUGHT, A.B. and KORY, R.C.: Walking patterns of normal men. *J Bone Joint Surg, 46A*:335-360, 1964.

MURRAY, M.P.; KORY, R.C.; CLARKSON, B.H., and SEPIC, S.B.: A comparison of free and fast speed walking patterns of normal men. *Amer J Phys Med, 45*:8-24, 1966.

MURRAY, M.P.: Gait as a total pattern of movement. *Amer J Phys Med, 46*:290-333, 1967.

MUSSEN, P.H.: Developmental psychology. In Farnsworth, P.R., and Mc-Nemar, Q. (eds.): *Annual Review of Psychology*. Palo Alto, Annual Reviews, 1960.

NELSON, G.N.; MASADA, M., and HOLMES, T.H.: Correlation of behaviour and catecholamine metabolite extraction. *Psychosom Med, 28*:216-226, 1966.

NOWLIS, V.: Methods for the objective study of drug effects on group functioning. In Uhr, L., and Miller, J.G. (Eds.): *Drugs and Behaviour*. New York, Basic Books, 1960.

OETTINGER, L., and SIMONDS, R.: The use of thioridazine in the office management of children's behaviour disorders. *Med Times, 90*:596-604, 1962.

OLSON, W.C.: *The Measurement of Nervous Habits in normal Children*. Inst. Child Welfare Monogr. No. 3. Minneapolis, U. of Minn., 1929.

OLSON, W.C., and CUNNINGHAM, M.: Time sampling techniques. *Child Develop, 5*:41-58, 1934.

OUNSTED, C.: The hyperkinetic syndrome in epileptic children. *Lancet, ii*:303-311, 1955.

PARTEN, M.B.: Social participation among pre-school children. *J Abnorm Soc Psychol, 27*:243-269, 1932.

PIAGET, J.: *Origins of Intelligence in the Child*. New York, Routledge, Kegan and Paul, 1952.

PLOOG, D.; HOPF, S., and WINTER, P.: Ontogenese des Verhaltens von Totenkopf-Affen (*Saimiri sciureus*). *Psychol Fors, 31*:1-41, 1967.

POLLARD, J.C., and BAKKER, C.: What does the clinician know about psychoactive drugs? In Uhr, L. and Miller, J.G. (Eds.): *Drugs and Behaviour*. New York, Wiley, 1960.

PRECHTL, H.F.R., and BEINTEMA, J.D.: *Neurological Examination of the Newborn Infants*. London, Heinemann, 1964.

PRECHTL, H.F.R.: Problems of behavioural studies in the newborn infant. In Lehrman, D., Hinde, R., and Shaw, E. (Eds.): *Advances in the Study of Behaviour, Vol. 1*. New York, Academic, 1965.

PRECHTL, H.F.R.: Polygraphic studies of the full-term newborn infant. II. Computer analysis of recorded data. In Bax, M.C.O., and Mackeith, R.C. (Eds.): *Studies in Infancy*. London, Heinemann, James, 1968.

QUASTLER, H. (Ed.): *Information Theory in Psychology: Problems and Methods*. Proceedings of Conferences on Estimation of Information Flow, Monticello, Ill., July 5-9, 1954, and related papers. New York, Free Press of Glencoe, Inc., 1955.

REYNOLDS, E.; JOYCE, C.R.B.; SWIFT, J.L.; TOOLEY, P.H., and WEATHERALL, M.: Psychological and clinical investigation of the treatment of anxious out-patients with three barbiturates and placebo. *Brit J Psychiat, 111*:84-95, 1965.

RICHTER, C.P.: *Biological Clocks in Medicine and Psychiatry*. Springfield, Thomas, 1965.

RICKARD, H.C.; DIGNAM, P.J., and HORNER, R.F.: Verbal manipulations in a psychotherapeutic relationship. *J Clin Psychol, 16*:364-367, 1960.

RIESS, B.F.: The effect of altered environment and of age on the mother-young relationships among animals. *Ann NY Acad Sci, 57*:606-610, 1954.

ROSENBLUM, L.A.; KAUFMAN, I.C., and STYNES, A.J.: Individual distance in two species of macaque. *Anim Behav, 12*:338-342, 1964.

ROSENBLUM, L.A.; KAUFMAN, I.C., and STYNES, A.J.: Some characteristics of adult social and autogrooming patterns in two species of macaque. *Folia Primat,* 4:438-451, 1966.

ROSENSWEIG, S.: Investigating and appraising personality. In Andrews, T.G. (Ed.): *Methods of Psychology.* New York, Wiley, 1948.

ROWELL, T.E.: Female reproductive cycles and the behaviour of baboons and rhesus macaques. In Altmann, S.A. (Ed.): *Social Communication among Primates.* Chicago, U. of Chicago, 1967.

RUSHTON, R., and STEINBERG, H.: Modification of behavioural effects of drugs by past experience. In Steinberg, H.; de Reuck, A.V.S., and Knight, J. (Eds.): *Animal Behaviour and Drug Action.* London, Churchill, 1964.

RUSSELL, I.S., and OCHS, S.: Localization of a memory trace in one cortical hemisphere and transfer to the other hemisphere. *Brain, 86*:37-54, 1963.

RUSSELL, W.M.S.: Aggression: new light from animals. *New Society, 176*:12-14, 1966.

RUSSELL, W.M.S., and RUSSELL, C.: *Violence: Monkeys and Man.* New York, Macmillan, 1968.

RYLE, G.: *The concept of mind.* London, Hutchinson University Library, 1949.

SCHALOCK, H.D.: Observation of mother-child interaction in the laboratory and in the home. Unpublished doctoral dissertation. U. of Neb., 1956.

SCHALLER, G.B.: *The Mountain Gorilla.* Chicago, U. of Chicago, 1963.

SCHALLER, G.B.: The behavior of the mountain gorilla. In deVore, I. (Ed.): *Primate Behavior.* New York, Holt, 1965.

SHANNON, C.E., and WEAVER, W.: *The Mathematical Theory of Communication.* Urbana, U. of Ill., 1949.

SIEVER, R.: Science: observational, experimental, historical. *Amer Sci, 56*:70-77, 1968.

SILVERMAN, A.P.: The social behaviour of laboratory rats and the action of chlorpromazine and other drugs. *Behaviour, 27*:1-38, 1966.

SKINNER, B.F.: Drugs and behavior. Paper read at Annual Meeting American Association for the Advancement of Science, Washington, 1958.

SLATER, L.E. (Ed.): *Bio-Telemetry.* Oxford, Pergamon, 1963.

SOLOMON, P.; KUBZANSKY, P.E.; LEIDERMAN, P.H.; MENDELSON, J.H.; TRUMBULL, R., and WEXLER, D.: *Sensory Deprivation.* Cambridge, Harvard, 1961.

STONE, A.A.: Consciousness: altered levels in blind retarded children. *Psychosom Med.* 24:14-19, 1964.

STORR, A.: *Human Aggression.* London, Allen Lane, 1968.

STRAUSS, A.A., and KEPHART, N.C.: Psychopathology and Education of the Brain Injured Child. New York, Grune, 1955.

SYMMES, D.: Anxiety reduction and novelty as goals of visual exploration by monkeys. *J Genet Psychol, 94*:181-198, 1959.

THOMAE, H.: *Die Periodek in Kindlichen Verhalten.* Göttingen, Verlag für Psychologie, 1957.

THOMAS, D.S.: *Some new Techniques for Studying Social Behaviour.* Child Develop Monogr. No. 1. New York, Columbia, 1929.

TINBERGEN, N.: *The Study of Instinct.* Oxford, The University Press, 1951.

TINBERGEN, N.: Psychology and ethology as supplementary parts of a science of behaviour. In Schaffner, B. (Ed.): *Group Processes I.* New York, Josiah Macy Jr. Foundation, 1955.

TINBERGEN, N.: Comparative study of the behaviour of gulls. *Behaviour,* 15: 1-70, 1959.

TINBERGEN, N.: On aims and methods of ethology. *Z Tierpsychol,* 20:410-433, 1963.

TINBERGEN, N., and PERDECK, A.C.: On the stimulus situation releasing the begging response in the newly hatched herring gull chick *(Larus argentatus argentatus* Pont.). *Behaviour,* 3:1-39, 1950.

TOBACH, E.; SCHNEIRLA, T.C.; ARONSON, L.R., and LAUPHEIMER, R.: The ATSL: An observer-to-computer system for a multivariate approach to behavioural study. *Nature,* 194:257-258, 1962.

DE VORE, I. (Ed.): *Primate Behavior.* New York, Holt, 1965.

WATT, K.E.F.: Ecology in the future. In Watt, K.E.F. (Ed.): *Systems Analysis in Ecology.* New York, Academic, 1966.

WELKER, W.I.: Some determinants of play and exploration in chimpanzees. *J Comp Physiol Psychol,* 49:84-89, 1956a.

WELKER, W.I.: Variability of play and exploratory behaviour in chimpanzees. *J Comp Physiol Psychol,* 49:181-185, 1956b.

WELKER, W.I.: Effects of age and experience on play and exploration of young chimpanzees. *J Comp Physiol Psychol,* 49:223-226, 1956c.

WICKLER, W.: Phylogenetisch-vergleichende Verhaltensforschung mit Hilfe von Enzyklopädie-Einheiten. Research Film, 5, 1964.

WIEPKEMA, P.R.: An ethological analysis of the reproductive behaviour of the bitterling *(Rhodens amarus* Block). *Arch Neerl Zool,* 14:103-199, 1961.

WILLEMS, E.P.: Toward an explicit rationale for naturalistic research methods. *Hum Develop,* 10:138-154, 1967.

WILLIAMS, J.P., and KESSEN, W.: Effect of hand-mouth contacting on neonatal movement. *Child Develop,* 32:243-248, 1961.

WOLFF, P.H.: Observations on newborn infants. *Psychosom Med,* 21:110-118, 1959.

WOLFF, P.H.: Observations on the early development of smiling. In Foss, B.M. (Ed.): *Determinants of Infant Behaviour.* Vol. 2, London, Methuen, 1963.

WRIGHT, H.F.: Observational child study. In Mussen, P.H. (Ed.): *Handbook of Research Methods in Child Development,* New York, Wiley, 1960.

WRIGHT, H.F.: *Recording and Analysing Child Behaviour.* New York, Harper, 1967.

WRIGHT, H.F., and BARKER, R.G.: *Methods in Psychological Ecology: A Progress Report.* Lawrence, Kansas Field Study of Children's Behaviour. U. of Kan., 1950.

ZUNICH, M.: Relationship between maternal behaviour and attitudes toward children. *J Genet Psychol,* 100:155-165, 1962.

ZUNICH, M.: Children's reactions to failure. *J Genet Psychol,* 104:19-24, 1964.

Appendix

GLOSSARY OF MOTOR PATTERNS OF FOUR-YEAR-OLD NURSERY SCHOOL CHILDREN[1]

W. C. McGREW

The frequency of occurrence of each pattern is indicated next to its definition, the total number of patterns observed being 10,789. The figures in brackets indicate the average duration of each pattern.

I. HEAD

1) Bite
   To seize an object between the teeth.   5 (3.4)
2) Blow
   To force air through the mouth.   14 (3.5)
3) Blow nose
   To force air through the nostrils onto an object.   1 (2.0)
4) Cough
   To expel air suddenly and noisily through the Glottis.   3 (1.6)
5) Cry
   To secrete tears accompanied by loud vocalisations and reddening of the face.   3 (4.7)
6) Duck
   To move the head downward and forward at the atlanto-occipital joint, often repeatedly.   11 (1.6)
7) Look
   To rotate the head slightly with a short, quick movement at the atlanto-occipital and the atlanto-axial joints.   13 (1.7)
8) Mouth
   To move the lips over an object inside or against the mouth.   2 (2.6)
9) Shake Head
   To move the head from side-to-side at the atlanto-axial point rapidly and repeatedly.   8 (7.5)
10) Sneeze
   To exhale air from the nose and mouth with sudden involtary explosive action.   2 (1.6)
11) Spit
   To force an object (usually saliva) explosively from the partially closed mouth by blowing.   1 (1.6)

---

[1] The present glossary in prototypic. An up-to-date version of the glossary may be obtained from the author, Dr. W. C. McGrew, Department of Psychology, 60, The Pleasance, Edinburgh 8, Scotland.

12) Turn-Head
   To move the head from one side to the other at the atlanto-
   axial joint.   21 (1.7)

13) Yawn
   To move the jaw down while simultaneously opening the
   mouth wide, usually with a deep inhalation.   2 (1.9)

II. HAND

1) Drop-Hand
   To let an object fall freely by releasing it by finger extension
   but without imparting force into it.   53 (1.4)

2) Finger
   To manipulate with only the finger(s).   23 (3.8)

3) Grasp
   To take hold of an object by hand and finger flexion.   28 (2.0)

4) Manipulate
   To move the hands with continuous flexion and extension
   while in contact with an object.   1541 (5.2)

5) Pick
   To probe an object with the fingers or with a pointed instrument using alternate flexion and extension.   23 (2.4)

6) Roll-Hand
   To move an object between the opposed fingers by turning it
   over, often repeatedly and around its main axis.   18 (6.0)

7) Specialized Manipulation
   To manipulate an object in a manner appropriately unique
   to that object, i.e. as defined by that object's function, e.g.
   scissors, pliers.   129 (8.6)

8) Squeeze
   To apply force to an object by flexing the fingers around it.   8 (4.9)

III. LIMB (U.L. = upper limb; L.L. = lower limb)

1) Dip
   To lower an object into a fluid quickly and then raise it
   quickly by arm extension and flexion.   14 (2.0)

2) Hand-to-Head
   To move the arms quickly and continuously from a distal
   location to contact with or close proximity to the head,
   by elbow flexion.   62 (1.8)

3) Hit
   To move an object suddenly and forcefully into contact with
   another object by arm extension.   99 (2.9)

4) Hold out
   To extend the arm away from the body, usually horizontally,
   often toward another person.   44 (2.1)

5) Kick

To extend one leg suddenly, usually making forceful contact with an object and the toe while the other leg remains on the substrate.   15 (2.3)

6) Lift—L.L.

To raise one leg by knee flexion while the other remains motionless, usually on the substrate.   57 (2.3)

7) Lift—U.L.

To raise an object by elbow flexion only.   84 (2.0)

8) Lower L.L.

To lower the leg by hip and knee extension.   12 (1.5)

9) Lower U.L.

To lower an object by elbow extension only.   56 (1.6)

10) Move L.L.

To move the legs in an amorphous, unstructured manner.   86 (4.4)

11) Move U.L.

To move the arms in an amorphous, unstructured manner.   126 (2.5)

12) Pat

To hit quickly and usually lightly using the palmar side of the hand or the flat surface of an instrument.   49 (3.2)

13) Place L.L.

To move the leg to a particular location with a single continuous movement, usually an extensor movement.   70 (2.3)

14) Point

To move an object by extending the arm away from the body, usually horizontally.   92 (1.7)

15) Reach U.L.

To move the arm away from the body toward an object usually with arm abduction and extension, with the hand open and fingers spread.   169 (1.4)

16) Remove

To move the arm out of a container by elbow flexion.   116 (1.9)

17) Shake U.L.

To move the lower arm rapidly, violently, and usually repeatedly within a small space by wrist and elbow motion.   55 (3.4)

18) Shrug

To quickly move the shoulder(s) up and then immediately down to the original position.   3 (2.5)

19) Stamp

To extend the knee and bring the sole of the foot quickly and forcibly down onto the substrate.   1 (3.2)

20) Stick

To move the arm, thumb side of the hand first, by flexion of the elbow.   47 (2.4)

21) Tap

To move an object lightly and rapidly against another object by repeated elbow flexion and extension.   78 (4.1)

22) **Throw U.L.**
   To move an object through the air by releasing it from the hand at the end of an explosive overarm extension with simultaneous trunk movement.   6 (1.4)

23) **Touch**
   To move the arm lightly and momentarily into contact with an object by a rapid extension and flexion.   20 (1.6)

24) **Turn U.L.**
   To rotate the arm at the elbow.   25 (5.4)

25) **Turn over**
   To move the arm, thumb first, by wrist rotation and flexion.   45 (1.7)

IV. LIMB-OBJECT

1) **Adjust U.L.**
   To manipulate an object with slight, apparently restrained movements of the arms.   23 (2.0)

2) **Drop U.L.**
   To let an object fall freely by releasing it by moving the arms apart but without imparting force to it.   28 (1.9)

3) **Pick-up U.L.**
   To lift an object by arm extension alone immediately after grasping it, in a continuous motion.   981 (1.8)

4) **Place U.L.**
   To move an object to a particular location with a single continuous movement of the arm, usually in a horizontal direction, then downward.   893 (1.9)

5) **Pour U.L.**
   To tip an object with slight arm movements and usually with wrist rotation.   222 (3.2)

6) **Pull U.L.**
   To apply force to a resisting object by arm and trunk flexion, causing it to move toward the body.   130 (3.2)

7) **Push U.L.**
   To apply force to a resisting object by arm extension causing it to move away from the body, or from its original position.   115 (3.6)

8) **Put down U.L.**
   To move an object to a location below shoulder level usually with a single, continuous arm extension downward.   37 (2.5)

9) **Roll U.L.**
   To move an object by arm extension (usually) by turning it over, often repeatedly and around its main axis.   23 (9.3)

10) **Rub**
   To move the arm with pressure over an object, usually by rapid alternation of elbow extension and flexion, but often a single, flicking motion.   122 (4.5)

11) Scoop

    To move the arm (hand leading) down, horizontally, and up again in a smooth U-shaped motion; during the horizontal part the hand is immersed in a loose material.   210 (3.0)

12) Scratch

    To rub the finger tips over an object, fingers partially flexed.   29 (1.9)

13) Smooth

    To move an object, usually the palmar side of the hand, lightly and horizontally along the surface of a material, by elbow flexion or extension.   15 (3.2)

14) Transfer

    To move an object from one hand to another.   38 (2.0)

15) Twist

    To move an object by alternated abduction and adduction of the shoulder and wrist.   12 (7.4)

V. GROSS

1) Hop

    To move suddenly upward into the air by leg or foot extension, landing on one foot with horizontal motion.   5 (1.8)

2) Jump

    To move suddenly upward into the air by leg and foot extension, landing on two feet in the same location without horizontal motion.   36 (2.1)

3) Lean

    To apply force to an object by shifting the body weight against it and moving the limb and trunk joints in coordination.   107 (1.6)

4) Move

    To move the limbs and trunk in an amorphous, unstructured manner.   86 (4.4)

5) Rock

    To move the trunk at the hips rhythmically back and forth or from side to side.   24 (9.8)

6) Somersault

    To move the body one full revolution forward head first, with the knees and hips maximally flexed, heels over head, around an object.   1 (1.2)

7) Suspend

    To move the limbs and trunk irregularly while suspended from the hands.   62 (4.1)

8) Swing

    To move the body backward and forward with regular movement while freely suspended from the hands, by alternate hip flexion and extension.   19 (6.2)

9) Turn
 To rotate the trunk face-first around the longitudinal body
 axis. 480 (1.4)
10) Wrestle
 To move the body violently while grappled with another
 person; it appears to be an attempt to forcibly move the
 other's body, often by alternating between pushing and
 pulling it. 11 (2.1)

VI. GROSS—OBJECT

1) Adjust
 To manipulate an object with slight, apparently restrained
 movements of the arms and trunk. 10 (6.6)
2) Lift
 To raise an object by hip and leg extension. 29 (2.6)
3) Pick up
 To lift an object by arm and trunk extension immediately
 after grasping it, in a continuous motion. 181 (1.8)
4) Place
 To move an object to a particular location with a single
 continuous movement of the arms and trunk, usually in a
 horizontal direction, then downward. 51 (2.7)
5) Pour
 To tip an object with slight arm and trunk movements. 15 (2.9)
6) Pull
 To apply force to a resisting object by arm and trunk
 flexion, causing it to move toward the body. 130 (3.2)
7) Push
 To apply force to a resisting object by limb and trunk extension, causing it to move away from the body or from its
 original position. 130 (3.9)
8) Put down
 To move an object to a location below shoulder level, usually with a single continuous movement of the limbs and
 trunk downward. 37 (2.5)
9) Reach
 To move the arm away from the body toward an object,
 usually with arm abduction and extension, with the hand
 open and fingers spread, with simultaneous trunk flexion. 157 (1.3)
10) Roll
 To move an object by arm and trunk extension by turning
 it over, often repeatedly and around its main axis. 19 (2.4)
11) Throw
 To move an object through the air by releasing it from the
 hand at the end of an explosive overarm extension with
 simultaneous trunk movement. 6 (1.4)

VII. POSTURAL

1) Bend
   To flex the body at the hips from a leaning, standing, sitting, or kneeling posture.   236 (1.3)

2) Crouch
   To stoop low with extreme knee and hip flexion, the legs being drawn close to the body and only the feet in contact with the substrate.   41 (2.0)

   3) Crouch up
   To move into crouching position from a lower position (e.g. sitting) by knee and hip flexion.   7 (1.4)

4) Fall
   To move suddenly downward from an upright posture so that the weight no longer rests on the feet, either intentionally or unintentionally.   48 (1.7)

5) Kneel down
   To move into a posture in which the body rests primarily upon the knee(s) from a higher position by knee and hip flexion.   48 (1.9)

6) Kneel straight
   To kneel erect, i.e. the vertebral column becomes more straight and vertical, combined with upward trunk movement through hip extension.   11 (2.2)

7) Kneel up
   To move into a posture in which the body weight rests primarily upon the knee(s) from a lower position by gross trunk and limb movement.   32 (1.9)

8) Lie
   To move to a reclining posture by lowering the body from a higher position by trunk and limb movement.   26 (2.7)

9) Sit down
   To move the body by hip and knee flexion into a position in which it rests primarily upon the buttocks, by lowering it from a higher posture.   161 (2.1)

10) Sit straight
   To sit erect, i.e. to make the vertebral column more straight and vertical.   5 (1.3)

11) Sit up
   To move the body by hip and knee flexion into a position in which it rests primarily on the buttocks, by rising from a lower position.   11 (2.2)

12) Stand straight
   To move the body while standing from leaning to upright by making the vertebral column more vertical.   9 (2.6)

13) Stand up
   To move the body by extension of the knees, hips and intra-

vertebral joints into an upright position, with the feet approximately a shoulder's length apart. 377 (1.7)

14) Tiptoe down
To flex the feet while standing with the feet extended lowering the body into a standing posture. 3 (1.3)

15) Tiptoe up
To extend the feet while standing so that the body is raised and supported only on the toes. 12 (1.6)

VIII. LOCOMOTORY

1) Climb
To move upwards on an object usually by alternately raising the arm and leg of one side, then the arm and leg of the other side. Head usually faces upwards. 129 (4.2)

2) Climb down
To move downward on an object usually by alternately lowering the arm and leg of one side, then the arm and leg of the other side. Head usually faces down. 29 (4.4)

3) Crawl
To move forward on hands and knees propelled by the limbs. 24 (2.7)

4) Gallop
To move forward on foot at a rapid pace, alternating limbs, so that during each stride both feet are off the substrate instantaneously. Characterized by an irregularly rhythmic quality resulting from differential time intervals between foot-contacts with the substrate. 4 (3.9)

5) Hop-loco
To move suddenly upward into the air by leg or foot extension, landing on one foot in a different location with horizontal motion. 5 (1.8)

6) Jump-loco
To move suddenly upward into the air by leg and foot extension, landing on two feet in a different location with horizontal motion. 36 (2.1)

7) March
To walk in a brisk, stereotyped manner with exaggerated movements in an even stride. 2 (2.1)

8) Run
To move the body forward at a rapid pace, alternating legs during each stride with both feet off the ground instantaneously during each stride. 287 (3.7)

9) Scoot
To move an object over a flat surface by pushing against the substrate with the legs through knee flexion. 40 (3.8)

10) Skip
To move the body forward by alternating legs, placing one

foot on the substrate and hopping slightly on it before shifting the weight to the other foot to repeat the same movement.   65 (3.3)
11) Slide
    To move the body in constant, frictional contact down an
    inclined surface with the hips slightly flexed.   34 (3.1)
12) Step
    To move the leg forward once, placing it on to the sub-
    strate while shifting part of the body's weight on to it.   173 (1.6)
13) Stumble
    To suddenly miss one's step (break stride) while in lower
    limb locomotion.   6 (1.2)
14) Walk
    To move the body forward at a moderate pace, alternating
    legs and placing one foot firmly on the substrate before
    lifting the other.   1114 (3.2)

AUTHOR INDEX

SUBJECT INDEX

A

Acmade Miniviewer, 114, 116
Actions, units of behavior, 22
Activities,
　defined, 48, 49
　durations of, 71, 114
　frequency of change of, 71
　number of, 45, 71
　periodicity in, 4
　termination of, 49
Activity vocabulary, reliability checks of, 35
Actones, 22
Aggression, books on, 8
Ambivalent motivation, 175
Animals in captivity, interpreting experiments
　on, 7
ATSL, 94
Attention span, 49, 50, 58, 59, 165
Attention switching, 50
Autistic children, 25, 151, 154
　EEG in, 194, 195
　eye contact in, 149
　level of arousal in, 198
　social encounters of, 147
　stereotypies in, 194, 195, 198

B

Battered babies, 187
Behavior, structure of, 11
　ecological approach to, 15
　ethological approach to, 15, 16
　experimental psychological approach to, 17
　natural units of, 32
　observational approaches to the study of, 15
　profiles, 47
　protocols, 46, 77
　raw material of, 22
　the biological study of, 24
Behavior commentaries, 38, 40, 43
　conventions of, 48
Behavior disorders, 163
Behavioral elements, when is catalogue com-
　plete, 36, 37
　and ordinary language, 34
　correlation between, 172, 173, 174
　identification of, 29
　　by function, 31, 32
　　by morphology, 29, 30, 31
　quantification of, 33
Behavioral Gestalten, 30
Behavior patterns, rank order of occurrence of,
　36

Behavioral repertoire, 4, 5, 6, 7, 34
Behavioral and physiological measures, corre-
　lations of, 12

C

Cats, aggressiveness in, 103
　EEG and behavior in, 189, 190, 191
　play in, 103
Causation of behavior, 24, 185
Check lists, 67, 134, 150, 165, 189
Children, autistic, 25, 151, 154, 194, 195, 198
　brain-damaged, 53, 115, 117, 151, 153, 154,
　　155, 163
　EEG and behavior in, 192, 193
　ethical judgment and behavior in, 89
　exploration in, 18, 19, 20, 192, 193
　hyperkinetic, 57
　motor patterns in, 34
　observation of, 21, 22
　play activities in, 130
　reactions to failure in, 79
Chimpanzees, exploration in, 73
　play in, 73
Clinical adjustment, measurement of, 10
Cluster analysis, 173
Contingency tables, use of, 170, 171
Contour, perception of, 30, 31
Conventions adopted in using check-lists, 69
Crocodile, diurnal rhythm of, 86
Crowding, effects of in man, 187, 188
Cumulative frequency curves, 18

D

Descriptive labels, use of, 23
Diary type records, 45
Displacement activities, arousal reducing func-
　tion of, 7
Drugs, effects of, 159
　amphetamine, 162
　chlorpromazine, 160
　GE-35, 164
　Nardil, 164
　Serpasil, 164
　Stelazine, 164
　thioridazine, 163
　thorazine, 164
　Tinlafon, 164

E

Ecology, and ethology compared, 22-24
Ecological approach to direct observation, 15,
　21
EEG, and stereotypies, 194, 195